CANADIAN PUBLIC FINANCE

Explaining Budgetary Institutions and
the Budget Process in Canada

Canadian Public Finance

Explaining Budgetary Institutions and the Budget Process in Canada

GENEVIÈVE TELLIER
TRANSLATED BY KÄTHE ROTH

UNIVERSITY OF TORONTO PRESS
Toronto Buffalo London

French title: *Les finances publiques au Canada: Le fonctionnement de l'État à la lumière du processus budgétaire* (Bruxelles: Éditions Bruylant 2015)

© University of Toronto Press 2019
utorontopress.com
Printed and bound by CPI Group (UK) Ltd, Croydon, CR0 4YY

Library and Archives Canada Cataloguing in Publication
Tellier, Geneviève, 1962–
[Finances publiques au Canada. English]
Canadian public finance : explaining budgetary institutions and the budget process in Canada / Geneviève Tellier.

Translation of: Les finances publiques au Canada.
Includes bibliographical references and index.
ISBN 978-1-4875-9442-8 (hardcover). ISBN 978-1-4875-9441-1 (softcover)

1. Canada—Appropriations and expenditures. 2. Canada—Appropriations and expenditures, Provincial. 3. Municipal finance—Canada.
I. Title. II. Title: Finances publiques au Canada. English.

HJ7663.T4513 2019   336.71   C2018-905778-5

We welcome comments and suggestions regarding any aspect of our publications—please feel free to contact us at news@utorontopress.com or visit our internet site at utorontopress.com.

North America
5201 Dufferin Street
North York, Ontario, Canada, M3H 5T8

2250 Military Road
Tonawanda, New York, USA, 14150
ORDERS PHONE: 1–800–565–9523
ORDERS FAX: 1–800–221–9985
ORDERS E-MAIL: utpbooks@utpress.utoronto.ca
This book is printed on acid-free paper with vegetable-based inks.

UK, Ireland, and continental Europe
NBN International
Estover Road, Plymouth, PL6 7PY, UK
ORDERS PHONE: 44 (0) 1752 202301
ORDERS FAX: 44 (0) 1752 202333
ORDERS E-MAIL: enquiries@nbninternational.com

University of Toronto Press acknowledges the financial assistance to its publishing program of the Canada Council for the Arts and the Ontario Arts Council, an agency of the Government of Ontario.

 Canada Council **Conseil des Arts**
for the Arts **du Canada**

 ONTARIO ARTS COUNCIL
CONSEIL DES ARTS DE L'ONTARIO
an Ontario government agency
un organisme du gouvernement de l'Ontario

Secrétariat aux relations canadiennes
 Québec

 MIX
Paper | Supporting responsible forestry
FSC
www.fsc.org FSC® C013604

Contents

Part 2: Budget Preparation

Part 3: The Budget Vote

Part 4: Budget Implementation

Figures

Tables

Preface to the English Edition

This book is the English translation of one written in French at the request of a European publisher. Such a request from abroad gives a good indication of the curiosity that exists outside of Canada about how Canadian public institutions function and, in particular, the country's budgetary process. Indeed, Canada is often cited for its budgetary control mechanisms, which have been in place for quite a few years now to slow the growth of public expenditures, and its federal system, which emphasizes the sharing of jurisdiction (including fiscal responsibilities) among different levels of government.

It quickly became clear, as I was writing this book, that its content also had to target a Canadian readership. Very little has been written explaining how Canadian governments formulate and manage their budgets and addressing the role that budgets play in today's democracies. Moreover, many of the studies published on Canada are limited in scope, analysing either the federal government or a single province. Although the budgetary systems of the federal and provincial governments are similar, they are not identical, and some provincial and territorial governments have recently undertaken important innovations. Therefore, I wrote this book for both Canadian and foreign readers, and I have tried to present an overall view of budgetary policies and issues across Canada, rather than focusing on the federal scene or on a single province or territory.

This edition is not significantly different from the original French one. However, I have made some changes. First, I updated most of the statistical and budgetary data presented in the tables and figures in order to present the most recent information available. Second, I added new English-language references, especially in the reading suggestions at the end of each chapter. I did not remove all the sources in French, since it seemed important to supply the broadest possible range of research on public finance in Canada. Finally, I included certain changes adopted recently that modify the budgetary procedure (for example, the Parliamentary Budget Officer of the Canadian Parliament is now an independent parliamentary agent), although they do not substantially transform the budgetary process. However, some proposed reforms that could have important repercussions, including presentation of gender-sensitive budgets, Senate reforms (notably with regard to adoption of bills), and changes to the information contained in the reports to be submitted to Parliament, have a serious chance of being adopted. At time of writing, these reforms were still on the drawing board, and we will no doubt have to wait several years to evaluate their effects if adopted.

In closing, I would like to acknowledge the following people and organizations for their support for this project: Mat Buntin, of the University of Toronto Press, for the valuable support he provided since the early stages of this project; Käthe Roth, who translated the book, and whose judicious suggestions helped me focus my thoughts; the external evaluators for their enthusiasm and relevant comments (and I will ask their forgiveness if certain expectations were not fully met); and the Secrétariat du Québec aux relations canadiennes, for the financial assistance provided in the framework of its activities to support the promotion of works by francophone researchers across Canada. Finally, this book could not have been written without the contributions of my students, many of whom, over the years, have asked me questions and proposed avenues for further thought. Teaching is certainly one of the greatest sources of inspiration for academic research.

Geneviève Tellier
Ottawa, January 2018

CANADIAN PUBLIC FINANCE

Explaining Budgetary Institutions and the
Budget Process in Canada

Introduction

It is not particularly easy for the general public to participate in debates over public finance. The themes discussed are often abstract, deal with complex subjects, and generally use very technical terms. The result is that discussions around the state of public finance usually take place among experts (such as economists, tax experts, policy analysts, and jurists) in specialized circles (economics journals and magazines, research institutes, government departments, and similar places). Yet questions about public finance should concern us all. Our governments' budgetary choices reflect society's choices, and they have impacts on a great many of our daily activities. In addition, we contribute directly to funding the state's activities through our taxes—a financial contribution that gives us the legitimate right to discuss budgetary choices. This does not mean that all of us must take an active part in such discussions and decisions; we elect representatives to do this in our place. Nevertheless, we can certainly make our preferences known to our representatives and form our own opinions on public finance issues. The fact remains, however, that the general public has become more and more disengaged from public affairs. This democratic deficit is observed both in the marked drop in voter turnout (we rejoice when national voter turnout is above 70 per cent, even though this means that more than a quarter of those eligible have not voted) and in public opinion polls about trust in government (less than 50 per cent of the population in most industrialized countries trusts the public authorities[1]). Canada is not an exception to this rule.

When it comes to public finance, the general public's lack of interest may also be explained, in large part, by the increased concentration of decision-making power in the hands of a small group of actors. In recent years, the decision-making process has become very centralized in Canada.[2] Budgets are written by people in a few decision-making centres situated at the top of the government apparatus, close to the political power, at the expense of elected representatives' participation in the budgetary process. And yet our democratic institutions place parliamentarians at the heart of the process. Without the agreement of the elected representatives, governments can neither collect nor spend money.

Various actors therefore do—or should—participate in the budgetary process. Such participation is the result of a long parliamentary tradition. It is common to consider the adoption of the Magna Carta by King John of England (also known as John Lackland), in 1215, as the starting point of transformations that would lead to the creation of today's budgetary institutions by establishing the principle of consent to taxation—transformations that occurred as democratic institutions were developed. Over time, the responsibilities of budgetary decision makers, as well as the rules and institutions that govern their actions, were shaped to respond to emerging concerns and circumstances. Because these concerns and circumstances are not written in stone but change over time, the corresponding responsibilities, rules, and budgetary institutions may also change. The budgetary framework is thus not static, but dynamic. It reflects how government and, in the broader sense, society operate.

If we wish to better understand the budgetary process, therefore, it is not enough to describe the roles of actors and the operations of budgetary institutions. We should also examine why these responsibilities and roles were created and why they are used today. So, it seems appropriate to address the analysis of public finance not only by identifying *who* the actors in the budgetary process are, but also by describing *how* these actors participate in the process and *why* they do so. These three interrogations make it possible to look at public finance in a perspective that (1) explores the sociological and political aspects of public action,[3] (2) reveals the nature of interactions among the various actors in the budgetary process, and (3) highlights the transformations in public finance currently taking place.

I have drawn upon two separate but complementary research traditions for the analysis presented in this book. The first tradition—the study of responsibilities and behaviours of budgetary actors—is addressed via the works of Aaron Wildavsky, who fundamentally influenced research on public management in the Anglo-Saxon world.[4]

In Wildavsky's view, there are two groups of budgetary decision makers: those who are responsible for using public funds and those who impose the rules of budgetary discipline. Budgets must therefore be seen as reflecting a constant tension between these two groups. A third group has been added in the most recent works in this tradition: those with budgetary oversight, who are responsible for examining the actions of the other two types of decision makers. Although this group does not participate directly in writing budgetary policies, its influence has increased in recent years. Taking account of budgetary oversight is particularly important to the analysis of public finance in Canada, whose parliamentary system is very concerned with accountability questions.

The second tradition comes from the discipline of public policy analysis. It is common to study the processes involved in writing public policies by dividing them sequentially into general phases: first, the emergence of a problem and its placement on the government's agenda; second, identification of possible solutions and formulation of a public policy proposal; third, debate on and adoption of the public policy; fourth, implementation of the policy adopted; and fifth, assessment of the results produced by the public policy implemented.[5] The fifth phase may, in turn, become the first step in a new public policy process (when the results obtained are perceived as being problematic). The process of formulating public policies must therefore be seen as a continual and dynamic cycle.

Like other researchers, I believe that this framework for analysis does not convey a completely accurate image of the reality: public choices are not made in a sequence as ordered and precise as these five phases seem to suggest.[6] When it comes to the budgetary process, for example, government initiatives must also be assessed, in part, at the beginning of the budgetary cycle. However, this framework does offer an evaluation grid that is easy to understand and simple to use.[7] It also makes it possible to identify who, among the many decision makers, plays a preponderant role in certain phases of the budgetary process. For instance, although it is usually felt that parliamentarians exert weak influence on budgetary decisions, they are nevertheless the main players when it is time to adopt a budget tabled in Parliament. The conceptual framework regarding the public policy process thus makes it possible to refine analyses of the budgetary cycle.

This book contains five sections organized around the main phases in formulation of budgetary choices. The first section describes the

Canadian budgetary context, which may be useful for readers who lack familiarity with that context. Three main themes are addressed: the current state of public finance in Canada (chapter 1), how the rules of Canadian federalism affect the finances of the country's main levels of government (chapter 2), and the characteristics of the political institutions (including the rules of law) in the Canadian state (chapter 3). It should be noted that Canada does not have to follow international budgetary rules, as must the member countries of the European Union, for example.[8] On the other hand, the rules of the Canadian federation constrain the actions of governments in Canada, especially provincial ones. In this respect, the Canadian federation is often cited as a case study for countries in the European Union, notably when it comes to analysis of financial relations among EU member countries.[9]

The following four sections of the book are structured around the main elements of the classic public policy framework. Section 2 addresses budget preparation and presents the two first steps in the budgetary process: putting the budget on the agenda (chapter 4) and formulation of budgetary policy (chapter 5). These steps are grouped together because both are the responsibility of the "guardians of the treasury": the central agencies of the government (the Treasury Board leads the agenda-setting activities, and the Department of Finance prepares the budgetary proposals). As we shall see, the central agencies play a decisive role in the budgetary process today. Section 3 deals with adoption of the budget, a task that falls to lawmakers. This section presents the general democratic budgetary principles and the related rules (chapter 6), as well as the different budgetary functions performed by parliamentarians (chapter 7). As we shall see, the parliamentary rules currently in force correspond to a certain conception of democracy, but they do not always produce the expected results. Section 4 is devoted to implementation of budgetary decisions. This activity is the bailiwick of the government's program managers, who work in a "budgetary management system" (chapter 8). These managers must, however, respect the budgetary discipline directives issued by the government's central agencies (chapter 9). This examination of implementation highlights one of today's main budgetary issues in Canada: what the balance should be between centralization and decentralization of budgetary authority within the public service. Finally, section 5 is devoted to oversight of public finance and those responsible for auditing and evaluating how state resources are used. Some of these control functions are executed by the government (chapter 10), whereas others are executed by external monitors (chapter 11). Whether internal or external, these control functions have grown in popularity in recent years.

The Canadian federation is composed of a central government, a number of regional governments (the provinces and territories), and numerous local administrations (mainly municipalities). In this book it is not my intention to give detailed descriptions of all budgetary activities performed by these various levels of government. That project would require considerable resources – if only to compile information on each administration. On the other hand, examining just one level of government, whether federal or provincial, seems to fall a little short. Therefore, I have tried to present a general situation that prevails at both the federal level and in the provinces and territories (I will not examine the budgetary policies of municipalities in detail, because the situations are too diverse). Such an overview is both possible and desirable. On the one hand, these two levels of government have many similar traits that make it possible to study them simultaneously, without the analysis becoming too complex. On the other hand, these governments' budgetary processes are not identical, and the differences observed bring some nuances to the analysis. As a consequence, I accentuate the budgetary process in the federal government, and identify provincial specificities. As a number of observers have already noted, the Canadian provinces constitute an excellent laboratory for analysing public policies, notably in the area of budgets.

PART 1

Public Finance in Canadian Society

1 The Size and Composition of Canadian Public-Sector Budgets

Canada as we know it today is a relatively recent creation. The Canadian Confederation was established in 1867 with the British North American Act. This constitutional document, later renamed the Constitution Act, 1867, marked the unification of former British provinces and colonies in North America into a single country and established its main political and judicial institutions. These institutions followed a long-standing British tradition, as well as a French tradition in Quebec. Most of the rules and principles laid out at the time of adoption of the Constitution Act, 1867 are still in effect today.

Like many other Commonwealth countries, Canada is a constitutional monarchy with the Queen of England as the head of state and the prime minister as the head of the federal government (and premiers as heads of provincial and territorial governments). Although many Canadian public documents and symbols refer to the sovereign (*Crown* decision, *royal* assent to bills, *Queen's* Counsel, and so on), it is the prime minister (or premier) who actually exercises state power.

Above all, however, Canada is a legally constituted state and a parliamentary democracy. The powers of the first ministers (the prime minister and the premiers) are therefore exercised within limits set by the Constitution, and ordinary legislation may not infringe on the powers granted to legislators, the people's direct representatives.

Canadian political institutions were established as the country's main modern economic structures were being developed. The Canadian economic system is that of a mixed-market economy that favours the presence of private enterprise and the use of market forces to encourage production of and trade in goods and services. When deemed necessary or desirable, the state is called upon to intervene. The principles underlying a mixed economy recognize that the state plays an economic

Figure 1.1 Public expenditures by OECD countries as percentage of GDP, 1990

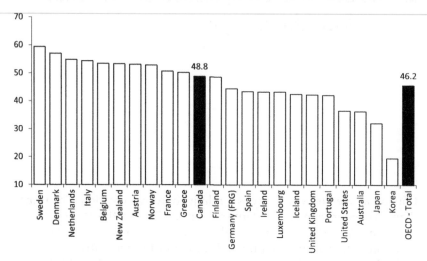

Source: OECD, *Economic outlook, analysis and forecasts*, http://www.oecd.org/eco/
outlook/ (accessed 5 July 2017).

role that is important, but not necessarily preponderant, in every sector. In this regard, Canadian economic structures are similar to those
in most industrialized countries. The Canadian government makes its
presence known in the economy mainly through the regulations that it
implements (which set out what may and may not be produced or consumed) and through direct intervention in the economy (the state itself
acting as a producer or consumer of goods and services).

Expenditures by the Canadian Public Sector

The presence of the state in society is a subject that is widely discussed
and debated these days. Many people wonder, for example, if government has simply gotten too big. To analyse this question—and, more
broadly, the state's role in society—the size of public expenditures is
often used as an indicator of the degree of intervention: the bigger
the public budget, the more interventionist the state is considered
to be. Figure 1.1 presents public expenditures as a percentage of the
gross domestic product (GDP) of member countries of the Organisation of Economic Co-operation and Development (OECD). We can see
that Canadian public expenditures are relatively low (48.8 per cent)

Figure 1.2 Public expenditures by OECD countries as percentage of GDP, 2016

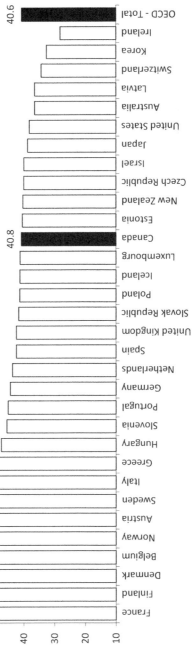

Source: OECD, *Economic outlook, analysis and forecasts,* http://www.oecd.org/eco/outlook/ (accessed 5 July 2017).

compared to those of most other countries (for some countries, the proportion is above 50 per cent). By size, the Canadian public sector is ranked twenty-first out of the thirty-one OECD member countries, behind the United Kingdom but ahead of New Zealand, the United States, and Australia (all countries, like Canada, with an Anglo-Saxon tradition).

The Canadian state has shrunk in size in recent decades. Figure 1.2 presents the public expenditures by OECD countries in 1990. We may note that public budgets have dropped in relation to GDP in most countries over the last twenty-five years. However, Canada recorded one of the greatest declines, as its expenditures fell from 48.8 per cent to 40.8 per cent of GDP from 1990 to 2016—a drop of 8.0 percentage points. For OECD countries as a whole, the reduction was from 46.2 per cent to 40.6 per cent over the same period. Some countries have a more pronounced drop than Canada during this period: Ireland (by 15.1 percentage points), New Zealand (13.1), the Netherlands (11.2), and Sweden (9.3).[1]

The Canadian Welfare State

An examination of the composition of public expenditures may provide insight into the nature of state activities. In 1959 Richard Musgrave observed that government budgets fulfil three functions: to allocate society's resources, to redistribute these resources, and to stabilize the economy.[2] Today, the state's financial resources are dedicated mainly to funding the welfare state, which corresponds closely to the redistribution function identified by Musgrave. Three general areas of public intervention are usually associated with the welfare state: health care, education, and social services.[3] Table 1.1 presents the distribution of Canadian public-sector expenditures by general category. We may note that expenditures on the welfare state account for almost two-thirds of total Canadian expenditures. This proportion has been rising constantly over the last sixty years, as Figure 1.3 shows.[4] The other major expenditure items are protection of individuals and property (which involves mainly costs linked to maintaining the armed forces, policing services, and the judiciary), transportation and communications, general services, the public administration (including expenditures by parliamentary institutions), and conservation of resources and industrial development.

Table 1.1 Public-sector expenditures by general operational category, 1965 and 2008

	1965		2008	
	Million $	%	Million $	%
Social services	3,100	18.0	190,276	30.1
Health	1,700	9.9	121,577	19.3
Education	3,000	17.4	95,732	15.2
Protection of persons and property	2,300	13.4	50,790	8.0
Debt charges	1,700	9.9	43,634	6.9
Transportation and communication	2,200	12.8	32,197	5.1
General government services	1,000	5.8	22,822	3.6
Resource conservation and industrial development	900	5.2	19,975	3.2
Environment	–	–	16,933	2.7
Recreation and culture	–	–	16,306	2.6
Foreign affairs and international assistance	–	–	6,508	1.0
Housing	–	–	6,120	1.0
Regional planning and development	–	–	2,775	0.4
Labour, employment, and immigration	–	–	2,395	0.4
Research establishments	–	–	2,268	0.4
Other expenditures	1,300	7.6	945	0.1
Total expenditures	17,200	100.0	631,253	100.0

Source: Statistics Canada, *Public Finance Historical Data, 1965/66–1991/92: Financial Management System* (Ottawa: Minister of Industry, Science and Technology, 1992), and *Table 385–0001 – Consolidated Federal, Provincial, Territorial and Local Government Revenue and Expenditures*, CANSIM database, http://www5.statcan.gc.ca/cansim (accessed 27 May 2015, link no longer valid).
Note: The hyphen (–) indicates that the category was at the time included in "Other expenditures."

Figure 1.3 The welfare state in Canada, 1950, 1970, 1990, and 2009 (expenditures by operational category as percentage of total expenditures)

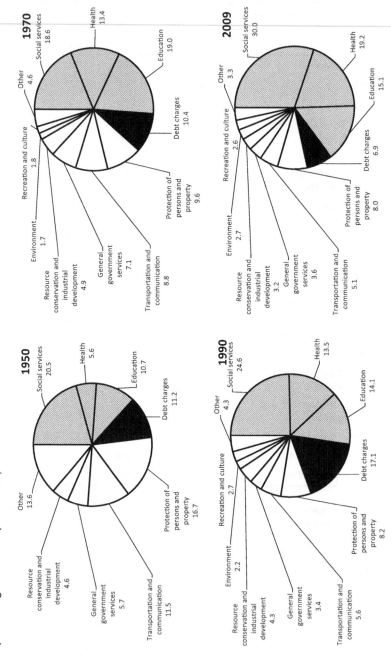

Sources: For 1950, 1970, and 1990: Tellier 2005 ; for 2009 : Statistics Canada, CANSIM, table 385.0001

The Canadian welfare state was instituted mainly during the second half of the twentieth century. Until the beginning of the Second World War, assistance to the poorest was the responsibility mostly of religious communities and municipal administrations, and health care and education services were accessible only to those who could afford them. Even though the economic crisis of the 1930s made very plain the insufficiencies of the governmental programs in existence at the time, it was only in the 1940s that Canadian governments, both federal and provincial, began gradually to adopt new social policy measures—an initiative that gained momentum in the 1950s. The federal government instituted unemployment insurance programs in 1940, family allowances in 1944, assistance to people with disabilities in 1941, old age pensions in 1952, and hospitalization insurance in 1957. The provinces played a more active role in the creation of social programs in the 1950s, especially in health care and education.[5] The Canadian welfare state model is generally seen as liberal, as its programs are intended mainly to provide minimal protection to the most vulnerable people in society when the private market is unable to do so. In this sense, the Canadian welfare state is similar to those in a number of Anglo-Saxon countries (including the United States, the United Kingdom, Australia, and New Zealand).[6]

Public Expenditures

The public programs managed by the state offer services to the population in two main forms. On the one hand, the state supplies goods and services directly to the population. For instance, governments manage hospitals, schools, and the water supply; grant permits and licences; maintain armed forces; and so on. These programs are financed by "operating" expenditures and by expenditures related to the use of "assets." Operating expenditures are made mainly to pay the salaries of civil servants and to purchase supplies and materials, professional services, and other items. Assets are goods and services whose lifespan is longer than one year. These assets include office furnishings, computer equipment, vehicles, and the like.[7] Capital consumption expenditures represent the value associated with the use of assets over a specific period, generally one year.[8] On the other hand, the state makes transfer payments—gives money to individuals, organizations (firms and not-for-profit agencies), and other levels of government (Canadian or foreign). The main characteristic of transfer payments is that the government receives no counterpart (goods or services) for the money it provides.

Table 1.2 Public-sector expenditures by economic classification, 2016

	Consolidated Canadian public sector		Federal government		Provincial and territorial governments		Local governments	
	Million $	%	Million $	%	Million $	%	Million $	%
Operating expenses	427,336	52.0	60,177	20.1	235,664	51.8	128,297	78.1
• Compensation of employees	252,527	30.7	38,234	12.8	125,873	27.7	88,420	53.8
• Use of goods and services	174,809	21.3	21,943	7.3	109,791	24.1	39,877	24.3
Consumption of fixed capital	67,667	8.2	9,247	3.1	35,728	7.9	22,692	13.8
Transfer payments	265,432	32.3	207,438	69.3	147,833	32.5	10,011	6.1
• Subsidies	17,081	2.1	2,659	0.9	10,796	2.4	3,626	2.2
• Grants, expenses	4,929	0.6	94,921	31.7	66,120	14.5	347	0.2
• Social benefits	205,932	25.1	103,138	34.5	42,764	9.4	3,421	2.1
• Other expenses	37,490	4.6	6,720	2.2	28,153	6.2	2,617	1.6
Interest	61,117	7.4	22,349	7.5	35,438	7.8	3,298	2.0
Total expenditures	821,552	100.0	299,211	100.0	454,663	100.0	164,298	100.0

Source: Statistics Canada, *Table 385–0032 – Government Finance Statistics, Statement of Government Operations and Balance,* CANSIM database, http://www5. statcan.gc.ca/cansim (accessed 5 July 2017, link no longer valid).
Note: Consolidated expenditures include data from the Canada Pension Plan (CPP) and the Québec Pension Plan. Expenditures for the Canadian public sector are not equal to the sum of federal, provincial and territory, and local expenditures, as transfer payments between governments are only counted once.

The data in Table 1.2 present the value of all expenditures made by the Canadian public sector and for each of the three main levels of government (federal administration, provincial and territorial administrations,[9] and local administrations[10]) in 2016. Operational expenditures represent more than half of total public expenditures. Major disparities, however, can be observed from level to level of government (worth a bit more than one fifth of federal expenditures, but more than three quarters of expenditures by local administrations). The consumption of fixed capital totals less than 10 per cent of total expenditures. Again, we observe some disparities among governments, as the consumption of fixed capital counts only for 3 per cent of the federal budget compared to almost 14 per cent of the budgets for local governments (which is not surprising as a larger share of local governments' budgets, especially municipal government budgets, is devoted to infrastructure spending[11]). Transfer payments by all levels of Canadian government amount to almost 30 per cent of total public expenditures (but 69.3 per cent for the federal government and less than 10 per cent for local governments). The table also includes debt servicing, which is listed as the interest paid on the debt, representing about 8 per cent of total expenditures (but significantly less for local administrations, which, in general, do not borrow to fund their current expenditures).

Governments also make use of "tax expenditures." These are not really expenditures, because they are not based on a monetary transaction. Rather, they are a cost of the government's renunciation of potential revenue. Tax expenditures involve exempting certain taxpayers from paying income or other taxes. The great majority of tax expenditures are tax credits that reduce the total value of taxable income. They are used to encourage certain behaviours deemed desirable. For example, there are tax credits for workers, families with children, charitable donations, the use of public transportation, tuition to post-secondary studies, and so on. Tax expenditures have been increasing in popularity in recent years. It is difficult, however, to know their exact value, as they are not registered in governments' financial statements or by governments' official statistical agencies (a situation that is not unique to Canada). According to certain estimates, these expenditures amount to almost $100 million per year for the Canadian federal government alone.[12] Canada is not the only country that is increasingly using tax expenditures as a public intervention tool. In a recent report, the OECD noted a significant rise in this type of expenditure in a number of European countries.[13]

Fiscal Levies

Fiscal levies may be defined as obligatory payments made to the state by individuals or organizations, usually firms. These levies provide the state with revenues. In most cases, such as levies charged through income and other taxes, the levies do not give rise to any direct consideration. That is, taxpayers who make the obligatory payments are not assured of receiving public services in exchange. This form of levy allows the state to redistribute wealth by taxing those who are better off to fund programs targeting the most vulnerable. In theory, some taxpayers may not receive public services, but in fact this situation does not arise: all taxpayers benefit, more or less directly, from some of the many services funded by the state.[14] It is worth noting that income and other taxes play a decisive role not only in formulation of budgetary policies but also in the context of democratic institutions: without taxpayers' and, more broadly, the population's consent to income tax, the modern state would not have the legitimacy necessary to justify its interventions in society.[15]

In other cases, obligatory levies are made to fund services destined only for those who make these payments. These levies are usually social security contributions, which are used to fund public insurance programs that allow contributors to protect themselves against the undesirable effects of unusual circumstances related, for example, to an accident, an illness, or loss of salary. In Canada, social contributions fund mainly two programs, both administered by the federal government with one exception for Quebec residents: Employment Insurance and the Canada Pension Plan (and its Quebec counterpart, the Québec Pension Plan). The Employment Insurance program offers financial assistance to workers who lose their job, or who want family leave (maternity or paternity leave, family caregiver leave) or sickness leave. The Employment Insurance program is funded by employees and employers, with the employers' contribution being higher than their employees'. It should be noted that the federal government also contributed directly to the Employment Insurance fund until 1990. The federal government used to set the contribution rates, but since 2017 these rates have been determined by an independent agency.[16] The Canada Pension Plan (and the Québec Pension Plan) offers income to workers who retire and to their survivors after they die. The program also offers financial assistance to workers with a long-term disability. Pension incomes are determined on the basis of age at the time of retirement, number of years worked, and contributions made. The program is funded in equal shares by employees and employers. The federal government, in consultation with the provincial governments, sets the contribution rates and pension benefits. The law requires governments to assess the plan's financial situation every three years. In 2012, the federal government under the leadership of Stephen Harper decided to gradually raise the age of retirement with a full pension from sixty-five to sixty-seven years. This decision was cancelled by the subsequent Trudeau government, in 2016.

Table 1.3 Main sources of public-sector revenues, 1965, 2008, and 2016

	1965		2008		2016	
	Million $	%	Million $	%	Million $	%
Income taxes	5,929	35.6	248,655	39.2	314,440	39.4
• Personal income taxes	3,477	20.9	189,222	29.9	240,441	30.2
• Corporation income taxes	2,282	13.7	50,277	7.9	66,796	8.4
• Other	170	1.0	9,157	1.4	7,203	1.0
Consumption taxes	4,957	29.8	107,150	16.9	–	–
• General sales taxes	2,733	16.4	67,001	10.6	–	–
• Alcoholic beverages and tobacco taxes	742	4.5	19,856	3.1	–	–
• Automotive fuel taxes	680	4.1	13,528	2.1	–	–
• Customs duties	686	4.1	4,055	0.6	5,519	0.7
• Other	116	0.7	2,710	0.4	–	–
Social security contributions	728	4.4	80,010	12.6	96,659	12.1
Return on investments[a]	1,000	6.0	57,793	9.1	46,501	5.8
Property and related taxes	2,137	12.8	54,862	8.7	78,064	9.8
Sales of goods and services	457	2.7	53,168	8.4	77,020	9.7
Other revenues	1,000	6.0	32,034	5.1	–	–
Total revenues[b]	16,660	100.0	633,672	100.0	797,361	100.0

Sources: see Tables 1.1 (for 1965) and 1.2 (for 2008), and Statistics Canada, *Table 380–0080 – National Gross Domestic Product by Income and by Expenditure Accounts*, CANSIM database, http://www5.statcan.gc.ca/cansim (accessed 6 November 2017, link no longer valid).
Note: The dash (–) indicates an amount was included in total revenues.
[a] Includes natural resource revenues.
[b] There are no inheritance taxes in Canada.

Table 1.3 shows the composition of public revenues for the entire Canadian public sector. It should be noted that some sources of revenue are used more by certain levels of government than by others. For example, property taxes are collected almost exclusively by municipalities, whereas the federal government has the authority to collect customs duties (under its constitutional powers).

As the table shows, some sources of revenue are used more today than they were fifty years ago. This is the case in particular for personal income tax, which is now the main source of public revenue, especially for the federal government (yielding almost half of its total revenues, compared to almost a quarter for all provincial and territorial governments). Canadian governments are also turning increasingly to social security contributions, which have tripled since 1965, to fund certain programs. It should be noted, however, that the use of this form of funding remains less common in Canada than in other countries. For other OECD member countries, for example, social security contributions represent on average a quarter of state revenues.[17]

Finally, the sale of goods and services is the third category of revenues, the use of which has been clearly growing for several decades in Canada; their contribution to total revenues, of the Canadian public sector has risen from 2.7 to 9.7 per cent. Rather than a tax on individuals' income and contributions to social security plans, provincial and territorial administrations make greater use of this source of funding (some provinces more than others, however[18]). These revenues come from tuition fees paid by university students, payments for public utilities (electricity, water, garbage collection, and so on), and fees for using public transportation and transportation infrastructure (public transit, tolls, and so on). The sale of goods and services by public administrations directly to users reflects a desire to institute the principle of pay for use, rather than having all taxpayers fund certain programs.

Although some sources of revenue are used more today than in the past, others have followed the opposite trend. For instance, the share of revenues drawn from corporate income tax (i.e., from private-sector firms) has dropped by almost 40 per cent since 1965. An even more marked reduction can be seen in customs duties, which now represent a marginal proportion of total public-sector revenues (less than 1 per cent). These changes may be directly attributable to the growth in international trade. Indeed, globalization has caused a drop in customs duties and encouraged greater mobility of capital. As a consequence, governments are more or less forced to turn to less mobile sources of revenue (mainly workers) to make up for the losses caused by the flight of capital abroad.[19] In Canada, the free trade movement was manifested by the implementation of the Free Trade Agreement between Canada and the United States in 1989, followed by the North American Free Trade Agreement (NAFTA) signed by Canada, the United States, and Mexico in 1994. NAFTA eliminated customs tariffs for almost all goods and services produced in and traded among these three countries and dropped barriers to investment. The United States is Canada's main economic partner, as it is the destination for 75.6 per cent of exports of Canadian goods (and the origin of 66.9 per cent of Canadian imports), followed by the European Union (7.7 per cent of exports, mainly to the United Kingdom, and 9.4 per cent of imports, mainly from Germany), China (3.9 per cent and 6.8 per cent), Japan (2.1 per cent and 1.8 per cent), and Mexico (1.3 per cent and 3.3 per cent).[20] It should be emphasized that the drop in revenues from corporations has been observed in other countries as well as Canada. The OECD noted, for example, that the taxation rate applied to firms' income in OECD countries was reduced by an average of 3 per cent just between 2000 and 2004. However, the reduction was even larger in Canada: 8 per cent for the same period.[21]

The share of public revenues related to consumption taxes is also dropping in Canada (even when customs duties are excluded from the data). This reduction involves not only taxes on certain products, the consumption of which is deemed undesirable (such as tobacco and alcohol), but also revenues drawn from the general sales tax (a tax collected, in principle, on all goods and services). The drop is attributable, in part, to a major Canadian tax reform passed in the late 1980s. In 1989, the federal government established the Goods and Services Tax (GST), a value-added tax (VAT) replacing the old tax on product manufacturers. A number of provinces, but not all, then transformed their own sales tax into a value-added tax, and "harmonized" it with the federal GST, meaning that the federal and provincial taxes are collected by one level of government only. These are the Québec Sales Tax (QST) and the Harmonized Sales Tax (HST) for Ontario, New Brunswick, Nova Scotia, Prince Edward Island, and Newfoundland and Labrador.[22] Although, in principle, the VAT applies to all goods and services in Canada, in practice certain products are taxed differently through specific taxes (generally, excise taxes), whereas others are exempted from the federal or provincial sales tax.[23]

Deficits and Public Debt in Canada

From the inception of Canadian Confederation, public administrations have had to borrow to finance their programs. Until approximately the second half of the twentieth century, these loans occurred quite sporadically and were used mainly to fund economic recovery programs,

Figure 1.4 Evolution of net public debt in G7 countries as percentage of GDP, 1970–2018

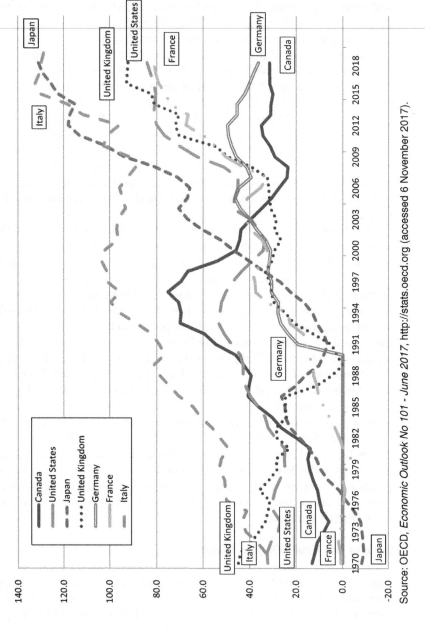

Source: OECD, *Economic Outlook No 101 - June 2017*, http://stats.oecd.org (accessed 6 November 2017).

major infrastructure projects, and the war effort. In the 1960s, however, the federal government and most provincial governments began to systematically incur annual deficits. As a consequence, the indebtedness of Canadian governments mushroomed, reaching a historical peak during the 1990s. This situation had a heavy impact on the composition of public expenditures, as debt servicing (payments related to interest on loans) became a considerable expenditure item. In 1989, for each dollar it collected, the federal government had to allocate 35 cents to debt servicing. The situation also deteriorated in all provinces and territories, as their public debt grew rapidly starting in the 1980s.

The question of stabilizing public finance was at the core of Canadian governments' budgetary concerns during the 1990s and 2000s. The federal government implemented a sweeping review of all of its programs in order to reduce state expenditures. The provinces, meanwhile, instituted legislative measures aimed at fiscal discipline. Most adopted balanced-budget statutes forbidding governments from incurring deficits.

In 2007, on the eve of the financial crisis of 2008, all provinces and the federal government posted positive budgetary balances. The financial crisis, however, forced all Canadian governments to become indebted again. The financial situation of the Canadian public sector seems enviable in comparison to those of other countries, as Figure 1.4 shows. Nevertheless, the lasting effects of the 2008 financial crisis on the Canadian public finances are not yet clearly identifiable.[24] Some provinces are having trouble emerging from the crisis, a situation that seems to suggest that the crisis had major repercussions on the industrial and economic structure and the job market in several regions of the country. Canada may well face new regional inequalities that could have an impact on the fragile fiscal balance observed in the Canadian federation.

KEYWORDS

Public expenditures • *Welfare state* • *Public revenues* • *Fiscal policies* • *Public debt*

TO FIND OUT MORE

Reading suggestions

Bird, R.M. *The Growth of Government Spending in Canada*. Toronto: Canadian Tax Foundation, 1970.

Doern, B.G., A.M. Maslove, and M.J. Prince. *Canadian Public Budgeting in the Age of Crises: Shifting Budgetary Domains and Temporal Budgeting.* Montreal: McGill-Queen's University Press, 2013.

Lindert, P.H. *Growing Public: Social Spending and Economic Growth since the Eighteenth Century.* 2 vols. Cambridge: Cambridge University Press, 2004.

Perry, H.J. *A Fiscal History of Canada: The Postwar Years.* Toronto: Canadian Tax Foundation, 1989.

Tanzi, V., and L. Schuknecht. *Public Spending in the 20th Century: A Global Perspective.* Cambridge: Cambridge University Press, 2000.

Tillotson, S. *Give and Take. The Citizen-Taxpayer and the Rise of Canadian Democracy.* Vancouver: UBC Press, 2017.

Periodicals

Canadian Tax Foundation. *Finances of the Nation* (annual). http://www.fcf-ctf.ca/ctfweb/fr/publications/finances_of_the_nation.aspx, link no longer valid.

Carleton University School of Public Policy and Administration. *How Ottawa Spends* (annual). https://carleton.ca/sppa/hos/

Databases

Statistics for government (Statistics Canada): https://www150.statcan.gc.ca/n1/en/subjects/Government

Government (OECD): https://data.oecd.org/government.htm

2 Canadian Federalism

Canada is a federation with three main levels of government: central, provincial and territorial, and local. The Constitution Act, 1867 sets out the basic principles of the Canadian federation. The main provisions adopted in 1867 are still in effect today, even though Canada has undergone major political and economic transformations since then. In 1867, Canada comprised four provinces and a central government (the federal government). Today, the Canadian federation is composed of a central government, ten provinces, and three territories. The last province to join the federation was Newfoundland, in 1949 (the province was renamed Newfoundland and Labrador in 2001), and the Northwest Territories was divided to create a new territory, Nunavut, in 1999. Canada also contains thousands of municipalities spread throughout its almost ten million square kilometres of territory.

Canadian Socioeconomic Diversity

Due to its history and geography, Canada is a very diverse country. As a consequence, demographic and economic differences, some of them quite wide, exist among the country's main regions. Table 2.1 presents some provincial and territorial indicators that highlight aspects of this diversity.

Most Canadians live in the two central provinces, Ontario and Quebec; combined, these provinces are home to more than 60 per cent of the country's total population. Almost 7 per cent of Canadians live in the Atlantic provinces (Newfoundland and Labrador, Prince Edward Island, Nova Scotia, and New Brunswick), and the western provinces (Manitoba, Saskatchewan, Alberta, and British Columbia) account for

Table 2.1 Provincial and territorial socioeconomic indicators, 2017

	Population	Area	GDP			GDP	Main industries
	Persons (thousand)	Km² (thousand)	Total (million $)	$ per capita	% of Canadian GDP	share from primary sector (%)[a]	
Newfoundland and Labrador	529	405.2	31,112	58,813	1.5	31.9	Oil and gas, fishing, hydro
Prince Edward Island	152	5.7	6,321	41,586	0.3	5.9	Agriculture, fishing
Nova Scotia	954	55.2	41,726	43,738	2.0	4.2	Shipbuilding, fishing, oil and gas, coal
New Brunswick	760	72.9	34,224	45,032	1.7	3.8	Forestry, agriculture, fishing
Quebec	8,394	1,542.1	394,819	47,036	19.4	2.7	Forestry, hydro, manufacturing (including pharmaceuticals and aerospace)
Ontario	14,193	1,076.4	794,863	56,004	39.0	2.1	Financial services, manufacturing (including motor vehicles), agriculture
Manitoba	1,338	647.8	67,863	50,720	3.3	7.2	Agriculture, mining, hydro

Saskatchewan	1,164	651.0	75,261	3.7	30.6	Oil and gas, agriculture (including grains), uranium, potash
Alberta	4,286	661.8	314,944	15.5	28.2	Oil and gas, agriculture (including grains and cattle)
British Columbia	4,817	944.7	263,706	13.0	5.9	Forestry, mining, fishing, agriculture
Nunavut	38	482.4	2,800	0.1	26.3	Mining
Northwest Territories	45	1,346.1	4,739	0.2	29.7	Mining
Yukon	38	2,093.2	2,443	0.1	12.6	Mining
Total	37,708	9,984.5	2,035,506	100.0	9.8	

Sources: Statistics Canada, *Table 051–0001 – Estimates of Population, by Age Group and Sex for July 1, Canada, Provinces and Territories*; *Table 384–0038, Gross Domestic Product, Expenditure-Based, Provincial and Territorial*; *Table 381–0030 – Gross Domestic Product (GDP) at Basic Prices, by Sector and Industry, Provincial and Territorial*, CANSIM database, and *Canada Year Book*, 2012 ed., http://www5.statcan.gc.ca/cansim (accessed 9 November 2017).
ª Data for 2014.

almost all of the rest. The territories, which include the regions of the Far North, contain less than 0.5 per cent of the Canadian population. The vast majority of Canadians live in urban centres in the southern part of the country. Some Canadian municipalities have a larger population than do certain provinces. In 2016, there were 6.2 million people living in Toronto, 4.1 million in Montreal, 2.5 million in Vancouver, 1.5 million in Calgary, and 1.4 million in Edmonton.[1] In recent years, some provinces have seen high demographic growth rates. For instance, populations in two western provinces (Saskatchewan, Alberta) and two territories (Yukon and Nunavut) have grown more than 15 per cent over the last ten years, whereas the Atlantic provinces as a whole have grown less than 3 per cent during the same period. Demographic growth was about 10 per cent in Quebec and Ontario.[2]

These demographic changes are explained, in large part, by the increase in economic activity in some regions. The oil and natural gas boom stimulated the economies of Alberta, Saskatchewan, and Newfoundland and Labrador. These three provinces have the highest per capita GDP in the country, considerably above those in Ontario and Quebec. Exploitation of other natural resources (fishing, agriculture, forestry, mining) also contributes to the country's economic growth. In fact, natural resources are an important part of the Canadian economy; the economic value of resource-related activities represents 10 per cent of Canada's GDP. These resources are beneficial to a number of provinces and to the federal government, as they generate major public revenues, thanks mainly to royalties. However, prices of raw materials fluctuate widely and unpredictably, which causes unexpected variations in revenues for governments. As a consequence, economic growth in several provinces is sometimes more volatile. Economic cycles provoked by this volatility do not occur at the same time in every such province; the federal government's revenues are therefore more stable than those of some provincial governments, because they come from all regions of the country.

Constitutional Rules Related to Sharing Fields of Jurisdiction

Canada is a federal state within which financial responsibilities are shared between the federal government, the provinces and territories, and local governments. These responsibilities are defined in the Canadian Constitution, which is composed of both written documents (the main texts of which are the Constitution Act, 1867 and the Canadian Charter of Rights and Freedoms, adopted during the 1982 constitutional reform) and conventions—that is, unwritten rules that are recognized and applied. Some of these unwritten rules are codified in ordinary laws.

The Constitution Act, 1867 sets out the provisions related to power-sharing between levels of government. In particular, it lists the respective fields of jurisdiction (i.e., the power to make legislation) of the federal government and the provinces with regard to expenditures, revenues, and borrowing (articles 91 to 95). The Constitution also gives the provinces authority to determine the responsibilities of municipalities within their borders (article 92). As a consequence, the rules governing municipalities' budgetary powers differ from province to province. Unlike the provinces, the territories have no constitutionally recognized authority; the federal government determines their powers and responsibilities. In recent years, however, these powers and responsibilities, which tend to be modelled on those of the provinces, have grown significantly.

When the Canadian federation was created in 1867, the constitutional rules that were adopted aimed to foster a strong national government. The federal government was therefore vested with the most important fields of jurisdiction at the time, such as the armed forces, external affairs, currency, the banks, criminal law, transportation, and interprovincial and international trade. The federal government also received exclusive authority over residual fields—fields that were not explicitly granted by the Constitution to one level of government. The provinces received fields of jurisdiction that allow them to maintain distinct cultural (French and Anglo-Saxon) traditions within the country and those judged to be less important: civil law, language, education, health care, and social services.[3] Finally, the federal government and the provinces exercise joint authority in some areas, including agriculture and immigration.

The Canadian Constitution also defines taxation powers for each level of government. Again, the federal government has more power than do the provinces. It may perform "the raising of Money by any Mode or System of Taxation" (article 91[3] of the Constitution Act, 1867). The provinces, for their part, may use only "direct Taxation within the Province in order to the raising of a Revenue for Provincial Purposes" (article 92[2]). Both the federal government and the provincial governments have unfettered borrowing power.

Whereas the Canadian Constitution sought, in 1867, to establish a strong central government, today the Canadian provinces have major financial responsibilities. This shift can be traced to two main factors. First, implementation of the Canadian welfare state led to an increase in provinces' responsibilities, as they manage health care, education, and social services programs. Although the federal government has obtained certain powers initially granted to the provinces through constitutional amendments (which enabled it to establish the Unemployment Insurance program[4] in 1940 and the Old Age Security program in 1951[5]), the provinces continue to provide and manage the vast majority of social welfare programs. Second, the courts have granted much financial power to the provinces over the years. For example, they have given a very broad interpretation of direct taxation, the main mode of tax collection available to the provinces. Direct taxation includes the power to charge income tax (on individuals and firms) and to collect consumption and real estate taxes. Today, only two sources of revenue are beyond the provinces' authority: customs duties and tax on the income of non-residents.[6] Furthermore, the Constitution Act, 1867 was amended in 1982 to grant provinces the exclusive right to collect taxes on non-renewable natural resources (section 92A).[7]

Canada can be considered one of the most decentralized federations. This decentralization is explained in particular by the provinces' high degree of autonomy in collecting revenues: almost 90 per cent of provincial governments' total receipts come from own-source revenues—that is, as a result of their own fiscal policies. Canadian provinces have much more autonomy in this respect than do provinces in some other federations. For example, own-source revenues represent about three-quarters of total revenues of American states and Swiss cantons, half of total revenues of German and Austrian Länder and Australian states, and a quarter of total revenues of Spanish autonomous communities.[8] This high degree of autonomy is accentuated by the absence of an organization coordinating the provinces' activities (such as the German Bundesrat). Although there are a few political bodies that oversee the provinces' and territories' interests, they have little real power within the Canadian federation. One of these bodies is the Senate of Canada, the upper chamber of the federal Parliament. The Senate's role is to provide representation of all provinces and territories in Parliament, and therefore every province and territory is represented in it. This rule also enables provinces and territories that may not have elected a member of Parliament from the party in power to nevertheless have a voice in Parliament.[9] However, senators are not elected and they deal only with dossiers submitted to the attention of Parliament. As a consequence, the Senate's real authority is weak. The second body is the Council of the Federation, an organization created by the provinces in 2003. The Council's objective is to strengthen interprovincial and -territorial cooperation by fostering discussions among provincial and territorial premiers. At least once a year, the premiers meet to try to work out common positions on various topics. The prime minister is invited to take part in these discussions but does not always participate. In fact, the Council of the Federation has had difficulty reaching strong consensuses that would force the federal government to act, because the positions of the provinces and territories sometimes diverge widely due to their different economic and financial realities.

Canadian Fiscal Federalism

Provinces' and territories' budgetary policies are also sometimes very diversified. The data presented in Table 2.2 illustrate this situation. Provincial and territorial public expenditures vary widely from one region to another; for instance, per capita expenditures in Ontario and British Columbia are only two-thirds as high as those in Newfoundland and Labrador. There are also differences in fiscal policies. For example, the highest marginal tax rate applied to individuals is 25.75 per cent (in New Brunswick and Quebec); the lowest is 11.25 per cent (in Alberta). In addition, indebtedness rates vary from one place to another (Alberta has not had a net debt since 2004).

Although their budgetary policies differ in numerous ways, all provinces and territories receive transfer payments from the federal government. These payments are intended to guarantee the availability of basic public services to all inhabitants of the country, no matter where they live. Transfer payments may be unconditional or conditional. Unconditional transfers are made in the form of equalization payments with the goal of redistributing the federal government's revenue to the poorer provinces.[10] Because these payments are not subject to any conditions, the provinces do not have to account for how they use the funds. Conditional transfer payments are made in the context of specific programs. These transfers enable the federal government to participate in initiatives in provincial fields of jurisdiction by assuming part of their cost. All provinces and territories may receive these transfers

Table 2.2 Budgetary indicators of provincial and territorial public administrations, 2015

	Total expenditures			Top personal income tax rate	Net debt		
	Million $	$ per capita	% provincial GDP		Million $	$ per capita	% provincial GDP
Newfoundland and Labrador	8,180	15,463	26.3	14.30	12,654	23,921	40.7
Prince Edward Island	1,772	11,658	28.0	16.70	2,170	14,276	34.3
Nova Scotia	9,944	10,423	23.8	21.00	15,076	15,803	36.1
New Brunswick	8,647	11,378	25.3	25.75	13,660	17,974	39.9
Quebec	96,502	11,497	24.4	25.75	185,025	22,043	46.9
Ontario	139,663	9,840	17.6	13.16	295,372	20,811	37.2
Manitoba	15,900	11,883	23.4	17.40	21,433	16,019	31.6
Saskatchewan	15,153	13,018	20.1	15.00	7,899	6,786	10.5
Alberta	49,061	11,447	15.6	11.25	(3,919)	(914)	(1.2)
British Columbia	46,791	9,714	17.7	16.80	39,597	8,220	15.0
Nunavut	1,763	46,395	63.0	11.50	(320)	(8,421)	(11.4)
Northwest Territories	1,724	38,311	36.4	14.05	666	14,800	14.1
Yukon	1,199	31,553	49.1	15.00	(153)	(4,026)	(6.3)

Sources: Department of Finance (Canada), *Fiscal Reference Tables 2017*; Statistics Canada, *Table 051–0001 and Table 381–0030*; Canada Revenue Agency, *Canadian Income Tax Rates for Individuals – Current and Previous Years*, https://www.canada.ca/en/revenue-agency (accessed 27 October 2017).

Table 2.3 Transfers from the federal government to provincial and territorial administrations, 2017

	Equalization	CHT[a]	CST[b]	Others	Total		
	Million $				Million $	$ per capita	% Total spending[c]
Newfoundland and Labrador	0	536	198	0	734	1,388	8.5
Prince Edward Island	390	154	57	0	601	3,958	31.2
Nova Scotia	1,779	966	357	(8)	3,094	3,246	30.7
New Brunswick	1,760	769	285		2,814	3,707	42.3
Quebec	11,081	8,496	3,144	0	22,720	2,710	21.1
Ontario	1,424	14,362	5,315	0	21,101	1,489	14.6
Manitoba	1,820	1,354	501		3,675	2,751	21.6
Saskatchewan	0	1,177	436	0	1,613	1,388	9.8
Alberta	0	4,338	1,605	0	5,943	1,388	11.2
British Columbia	0	4,875	1,804	0	6,680	1,388	13.1
Nunavut	1,530	38	14	0	1,583	41,745	85.2
Northwest Territories	1,294	45	17	0	1,294	29,044	74.9
Yukon	919	39	14	0	973	25,299	77.0
Total	21,936	37,150	13,748	(8)	72,826	1,986	18.4

Source: Department of Finance (Canada), *Federal Support to Provinces and Territories*, https://www.fin.gc.ca/access/fedprov-eng.asp (accessed 9 November 2017), and *Fiscal Reference Tables 2017*.
Note: Total amounts may not add due to rounding.
[a] Canada Health Transfer.
[b] Canada Social Transfer.
[c] For 2015.

as long as they agree to respect certain conditions set out by the federal government.

The data presented in Table 2.3 show that the federal government pays large sums to the provinces. In 2017, the total redistributed from the federal to the provincial and territorial level was $73 billion, representing an average of almost $2,000 per capita. The per capita amounts are not identical in every province. The highest amounts are given to the Maritime provinces (Prince Edward Island, Nova Scotia, New Brunswick), which have the right to sizeable equalization payments (these constitute more than 60 per cent of all federal transfer payments received by these three provinces). In contrast, four provinces do not receive any equalization payments (Newfoundland and Labrador, Saskatchewan, Alberta, and British Columbia). In total, the federal government made equalization payments of almost $22 billion in 2017. However, conditional payments amount to more than twice as much, at $51 billion. Countrywide, federal transfer payments fund 18 per cent of provincial and territorial budgets. This percentage is significantly higher in the Maritimes (but almost twice as low in Newfoundland and Labrador). The territories benefit the most from these payments, which fund almost their entire budgets.

The Constitution does not define any rule or procedure for determining how much is paid in federal transfers to the provinces. The Constitution has recognized the principle of unconditional transfer payments since 1982,[11] but no provision exists for conditional transfers. The dollar amount of both kinds of transfers is left completely to the discretion of the federal government, which consults the provinces but does not always feel obliged to reach agreement with them when it sets the amounts to be allocated.[12] Equalization payments, however, are calculated according to a specific formula that is relatively complex, as it attempts to estimate the fiscal base—the value of all resources that may be taxed—of each province. Equalization is thus determined as a function of what the provinces could collect (i.e., their wealth, or tax base) and not according to what they do collect (their fiscal policies). To determine the equalization amounts, the federal government measures the value of about thirty sources of revenue (individuals' income, firms' revenues, asset values, land values, reserves of natural resources, and so on). It then estimates the income per capita that would be taken from each source if the tax rates were identical in all provinces in order to establish a national standard. Provincial estimates are then aggregated and compared to the national standard. The provinces whose results are below the standard receive equalization payments to make up the difference.[13]

Conditional payments are calculated a different way. For many years, participation by the federal government consisted of paying a certain percentage of the budgets of programs eligible to receive the funding— in general, 50 per cent of the total cost. The provinces were responsible for managing these programs and determining their budgets. This contribution method did not allow the federal government to control costs, and, as a consequence, its own financial contribution—nor, in fact, did it encourage the provinces to limit the growth of their programs, as they assumed only half the funding cost. The way that conditional payments work thus underwent in-depth reviews in 1977 and 1995. Today, the federal government is committed to "block funding" of provincial programs by paying a set amount every year. Aside from cash payments, federal assistance takes the form of tax-point transfers. According to an agreement concluded between the federal government and the provinces, federal income tax rates were dropped so that provincial governments could increase their rates. The transfers have no impact on the money paid by Canadian taxpayers, as the loss in the federal government's revenue is exactly compensated for by the extra revenue collected by the provincial governments.

Conditional transfers by the federal government are paid to the provinces and territories as part of two programs: the Canada Health Transfer (CHT) and the Canada Social Transfer (CST).[14] In exchange for these payments, the provinces and territories agree to respect certain conditions. These conditions are stiffer for the CHT than for the CST, as the Canada Health Act requires five conditions to be respected for the former, whereas the Federal-Provincial Fiscal Arrangements Act, which governs the latter, requires only one. Figure 2.1 below shows these conditions. Non-compliance with one or more conditions may cause a reduction in transfers.[15]

The main objective of the CHT and the CST is to ensure that all Canadian residents, no matter which province they live in, can obtain similar services within the programs covered by the transfers. The CHT covers a single field of activities, health care, whereas the CST encompasses three: post-secondary education, assistance to children, and social services. The federal transfers enable the provinces to fund part of the programs associated with one or another of these major sectors. Although in theory transfer payments standardize how services are provided throughout the country, in fact differences exist because the provinces have claimed the right to manage their own programs, as the Constitution allows. Therefore, the provinces use federal funds to further their own priorities more than the federal government's. It has proved difficult to find a true balance between the federal government's intended requirement of national control (notably with regard to standards and costs) and the autonomy provinces demand to manage their own

Figure 2.1 Conditions related to federal transfer payments

Canadian Social Transfer (CST)

To receive federal funding, each province or territory must meet the following condition, set out under the *Federal-Provincial Fiscal Arrangements Act* (R.S.C., 1985, c. F-8):

- Minimal period of residency: provinces and territories cannot impose any period of residency (art. 25(1)).

Canadian Health Transfer (CHT)

To receive federal funding, each province or territory must meet the five following conditions (R.S.C. (1985), c. C-6):

- Public Administration: The provincial and territorial plans must be administered and operated on a non-profit basis by a public authority accountable to the provincial or territorial government.

Comprehensiveness: The provincial and territorial plans must insure all medically necessary services provided by hospitals, medical practitioners, and dentists working within a hospital setting.

Universality: The provincial and territorial plans must entitle all insured persons to health insurance coverage on uniform terms and conditions.

Accessibility: The provincial and territorial plans must provide all insured persons reasonable access to medically necessary hospital and physician services without financial or other barriers.

Portability: The provincial and territorial plans must cover all insured persons when they move to another province or territory within Canada and when they travel abroad.

Source: Health Canada, 2017, *Canada's Health Care System*, accessed 11 July 2017, https://www.canada.ca/en.html.

programs. The First Ministers' Accord on Health Care Renewal, signed in 2003, gives a good illustration of this difficulty. For the federal government, the objectives were to increase its financial assistance in order to improve the funding of specific services in the health care sector (primary care, home care, and access to certain medications), to reduce waiting times, and to establish accountability. However, the provinces did not commit to anything but producing an annual report giving the results obtained for these services. No commitment was made to guarantee the achievement of specific results (e.g., reducing waiting times for receiving certain medical treatments). In fact, Quebec refused to comply even with the commitment to produce a report. The province nevertheless receives federal funds.

Quebec has always been more reluctant than the other provinces to accept federal funding for programs under provincial jurisdiction. Although Quebec's opposition seems the most visible, it is not the only province to question the federal presence. Federal-provincial relations are currently characterized by debates bearing on two general themes: federal spending power and fiscal imbalance.[16] Discussions about federal spending power arose when the federal government sought to institute its own programs in fields of jurisdiction exclusive to the provinces after the Second World War. A number of these programs involved sending transfer payments to individuals, firms, and local governments either directly or via the provincial governments. A recent example of such a program is the financial assistance now paid directly to Canadian municipalities by the creation of the Gas Tax Fund in 2007. This fund conveys the federal government's commitment to provide a portion of the revenues that it collects through the gas tax to municipalities so that they can fund infrastructure programs. Since the Canadian Constitution provides that the provinces have exclusive power to define their municipalities' powers to spend and tax, the Gas Tax Fund therefore infringes on provinces' constitutional jurisdiction.[17] The Canadian courts have repeatedly upheld the federal government's power to spend provided that it offers a right of withdrawal to provinces that do not wish to participate in the projects it institutes. The provinces' position is that the right of withdrawal must be accompanied by monetary compensation: provinces that do not participate in the federal program should not be penalized financially compared to the other provinces and should receive supplementary funds from the federal government. The question of the federal government's spending power still is not resolved.[18]

The question of fiscal imbalance came under real scrutiny starting in the mid-1990s, when the federal government set up a major financial recovery program. Among the measures adopted to reduce public spending, the government unilaterally cut its transfer payments to the provinces considerably, by a total of $10 billion over two years (1996 and 1997), representing a reduction of almost 20 per cent.[19] However, these cuts only accelerated a trend already underway: a constant drop in the federal share of funding provincial budgets. Federal transfers represented 25 per cent of total provincial revenues in 1983, 20 per cent in 1995, and 16 per cent in 1997.[20] The main reason for this reduction was an increase in expenditures by provincial administrations, which were facing a steep rise in the number of users of public services. There was therefore a structural vertical fiscal imbalance engendered by the fact that the federal government's taxation powers were out of proportion to its fields of jurisdiction. A number of provinces demanded that the sharing of financial resources, as structured in 1867, now had to be modified. However, there was no unanimity on the solutions proposed. Some provinces (Manitoba, New Brunswick, Ontario) wanted the federal government to show a lasting and growing commitment through its transfer payments, whereas one (Quebec) was asking the federal government to transfer some of its taxation powers to the provinces.[21] The 2008 financial crisis relegated the debates on fiscal imbalance to the back burner, but the issue still is not resolved.

The Canadian Municipalities

Because the Canadian Constitution delegates to the provinces the authority to determine the financial responsibilities of their municipalities, the principles and budgetary rules of local administrations may vary widely from one province to another. It is therefore difficult to paint a complete portrait of the public finances of local administrations. However, it is possible to present some general characteristics. The main observable difference among the provinces concerns the extent of powers that they grant to local administrations. Some provinces provide municipalities with great latitude, whereas others try to limit their range of action as much as possible. However, all Canadian cities offer certain basic services: fire protection, garbage collection, planning and maintenance of the road system and traffic control, territorial planning, economic development, libraries, parks, and tourism promotion, among others.[22]

Unsurprisingly, the extent of municipalities' responsibilities has a direct influence on the size of their budgets. However, cities with more responsibilities do not necessarily have greater taxation power. Some provinces prefer to collect the public revenues and distribute them to municipalities rather than delegating taxation powers to local administrations. The data in Table 2.4 present the size of local administrations' budgets and the sources of their revenues. As the table shows,

Table 2.4 Local administrations' revenues, per capita ($), 2006

	Own-source revenues			Federal government transfers[a]	Provincial government transfers	(% total revenues)	Total
	Property taxes	Sales of goods and services	Other				
Newfoundland and Labrador	521.50	179.46	29.77	7.08	186.27	(20.2)	924.08
Prince Edward Island	366.84	122.77	14.30	56.25	123.78	(18.1)	683.94
Nova Scotia	1,017.26	258.32	48.86	42.27	71.09	(4.9)	1,437.80
New Brunswick	614.86	289.80	19.83	32.29	145.95	(13.2)	1,102.73
Quebec	1,018.02	275.99	66.07	2.42	198.14	(12.7)	1,560.64
Ontario	1,137.43	512.73	166.04	75.38	540.12	(22.2)	2,431.70
Manitoba	562.65	339.84	119.67	69.03	276.73	(20.2)	1,367.92
Saskatchewan	714.85	335.83	166.19	42.33	162.42	(11.4)	1,421.62
Alberta	1,051.06	658.86	450.42	30.24	338.37	(13.4)	2,528.95
British Columbia	741.83	446.08	156.99	17.63	86.44	(6.0)	1,448.97
Total	984.87	434.43	159.80	41.64	331.03	(17.0)	1,951.77

Source: Andrew Sancton and Robert Young, eds, *Foundations of Governance: Municipal Governments in Canada's Provinces* (Toronto: IPAC/IAPC and University of Toronto Press, 2009), appendixes.
[a] Conditional transfer payments.

provincial transfers are lowest in Nova Scotia and British Columbia and the highest per capita expenditures are made in Alberta and Ontario.

Despite the great diversity of fiscal arrangements between the provinces and their municipalities, all provinces are faced with similar public funding issues. Among these issues, the theme of centralization and decentralization of budgetary decisions has been abundantly discussed in recent years. Most provincial governments, observing an appreciable growth in municipal budgets, established major programs for restructuring local public utilities in the last fifteen years. Many cities, large or small, urban or rural, were merged with neighbouring cities in order to centralize management of certain services and thus to reduce costs (by creating economies of scale). These mergers did not take place without opposition; a number of them were forced through by provincial governments. Furthermore, it seems that restructuring did not have the desired results. Studies have shown that the costs of municipal services have not dropped.[23] In fact, the growth in the cost of municipal services seems to have been the same in merged and non-merged cities of comparable size. Many people blame the provincial governments for having created cities that are too complex to manage, run by elected officials who are now less attentive to local residents' concerns.

KEYWORDS

Constitution Act, 1867 • *Fields of jurisdiction* • *Transfer payments* • *Equalization* • *Federal spending power* • *Fiscal imbalance* • *Municipal mergers*

TO FIND OUT MORE

Reading suggestions

Atkinson, Michael M., Daniel Béland, Gregory P. Marchildon, Kathleen Mcnutt, Peter W.B. Phillips, and Ken Rasmussen. *Governance and Public Policy in Canada: A View from the Provinces*. North York: University of Toronto Press, 2013.
Béland, Daniel, André Lecours, Gregory P. Marchildon, Haizhen Mou, and M. Rose Olfert. *Fiscal Federalism and Equalization Policy in Canada: Political and Economic Dimension*. Toronto: University of Toronto Press, 2017.
Commission on Fiscal Imbalance. *A New Division of Canada's Financial Resources: Final Report*. Quebec City: Government of Quebec, 2002.
Richer, K. *The Federal Spending Power*. Ottawa: Parliament of Canada, 2007.

Websites

The Council of the Federation: http://www.canadaspremiers.ca/en/
Department of Finance (Canada), *Federal Support to Provinces and Territories*: http://www.fin.gc.ca/access/fedprov-eng.asp
Forum of Federations: http://www.forumfed.org/en/index.php
Institute of Intergovernmental Relations at Queen's University, http://www.queensu.ca/iigr/

Statutes

Federal-Provincial Fiscal Arrangements Act (R.S.C., 1985, c. F-8)
The Constitution Act, 1867 (30 & 31 Vict, c. 3)

3 Canadian Budget-Making Authorities

Numerous actors participate in the formulation of public-sector budgets, and they play a number of different roles. Some are tasked with determining the government's general budgetary orientations, for example, whereas others must use the state's financial resources to offer goods and services to the population. However, budgetary decisions must comply with certain basic principles inherent to all democracies. For instance, governments may not spend or collect revenues without having obtained prior authorization to do so, are required to follow sound financial management practices, and must be transparent. To understand the role of each participant in the budgetary process, we must begin by understanding general parliamentary principles and the legal framework built upon them.

The Canadian Parliamentary System

Like all democracies, the Canadian state is composed of three branches, each endowed with important decision-making power: the legislative branch, the executive branch, and the judiciary. These three components exist in the Canadian federal government and in each of the ten provinces and three territories,[1] and were established on the basis of certain fundamental constitutional principles. One of these principles is that of responsible government, under which the executive branch (the government) is answerable to the legislature (Parliament[2]). It is the government's ministers who exercise this responsibility, both individually and collectively. Individually, each minister is accountable to Parliament for his or her own decisions and actions and those of his or her department. Together, all ministers must assume and defend the decisions of the Cabinet (or executive council), which is the senior

executive decision-making body. A second constitutional principle is
that of cooperation between the executive and legislative branches.
This principle is different from that of separation of powers, which is
found in a number of presidential systems that are based on the notion
of weight and counterweight (which characterizes, for example, the
relationship between the president and the Congress in the United
States). Canadian constitutional custom has it that the first minister (the
federal prime minister and the provincial and territorial premiers) and
the ministers sit in the legislature. This means that they are members of
both the executive and the legislative branches. A third principle is that
a party must have the confidence of the House to govern. As a consequence, the party that forms the government is the one that receives the
support of the largest number of members of the legislative assembly.
The confidence of the House is easier to obtain if the party in power
holds the majority of seats. Finally, Canada is a state of laws. As a consequence, all public decisions must be legal and disputes are adjudicated
completely independently by judges or arbitrators.

On the basis of these general principles, the executive branch, the
legislature, and the judiciary fulfil various financial and budgetary
responsibilities.

The Executive Branch

In Canada, the executive branch is the only one that may propose budgets. As a consequence, any bill submitted to Parliament that commits
public funds or authorizes the collection of revenues must be presented
by a minister. The executive branch is also responsible for implementation and management of governmental programs. In this role, it thus
controls the entire governmental apparatus—that is, the civil service.
Executive power is assumed by the Cabinet (or executive council),
which is composed of ministers responsible for various portfolios. The
ministers are appointed by the first minister, who is the leader of the
party in power. The ministers (including the first minister) must, however, be elected and thus sit in the legislature.[3] The size of the Cabinet
is also determined by the first minister. The federal Cabinet usually has
between thirty and forty ministers. Provincial and territorial executive
councils are generally smaller, even in the most populous provinces.

Once approved, the decisions made by the Cabinet are implemented
by the public administration, which is composed of a multitude of

administrative units grouped by minister. Some ministers are also responsible for public bodies – entities with some independence from government departments. Among these bodies are the Bank of Canada, Statistics Canada (the federal public statistical agency), Export Development Canada (which offers insurance programs for exporters), and the Canadian Human Rights Commission. Some of these entities must function on a cost-recovery basis (i.e., they must generate sufficient revenue to fund all the costs related to their activities), but not all. The top administrator in each government department (also called "ministry" in some provinces; here I will use the generic term "department" for both) is the deputy minister, a career senior civil servant appointed by the first minister.

The first minister also has his or her own department, which is the Privy Council Office, or PCO, at the federal level and the Office of the Premier in the provinces and territories. This department has considerable influence on the budgetary process due to its close ties to the first minister and the resources at its disposal. Currently, the Privy Council Office comprises almost one thousand civil servants who advise the prime minister and oversee coordination of the activities of the public sector as a whole. The first minister's department also works in close collaboration with the Cabinet. First ministers decide the responsibilities of their own department, which usually reflect their personal concerns or interests and the major issues faced by the civil service. Figure 3.1 presents the current structure of the federal Privy Council Office. The senior administrator is the Clerk of the Privy Council Office, who is both a deputy minister to the first minister and the hierarchical superior of all other deputy ministers in the civil service.

Aside from their own department, first ministers may also count on the support of a small group of political advisors. In Ottawa, these advisors (fewer than one hundred) are grouped within the Prime Minister's Office, or PMO. Unlike employees in the Privy Council Office, those in the Prime Minister's Office are not considered regular civil servants and therefore are not subject to the administration management rules (pay, assignments, job security, and so on). However, the Prime Minister's Office and the Privy Council Office are in frequent contact. Most provinces have adopted an administrative model similar to the federal Privy Council Office and Prime Minister's Office.[4]

Figure 3.1 Organizational structure of the federal government's Privy Council Office

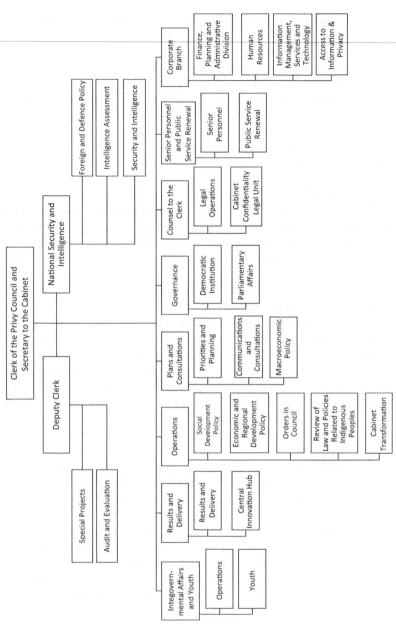

Source: Privy Council Office, *About the Privy Council Office*, accessed 12 July, 2017, http://www.pco-bcp.gc.ca/index.asp?lang=eng&page=about-apropos (link no longer valid).

The Legislative Branch

In Canada, the mandate of the legislature is articulated around four main functions: to represent the interests of the public, to give the government the resources necessary to govern, to oversee the government's actions, and to choose the government.[5] Members of Parliament who are not ministers may present bills as long as they do not have financial implications for the public purse.[6] This means that their options are limited, as very few initiatives do not require the use of public funds. On the other hand, the government may not spend or collect taxes without the explicit consent of Parliament. In addition, any legislative vote directly concerning the government's general budgetary policy is a vote of confidence. The legislature is also responsible for examining the government's actions. In this role it may ask questions about the government's intentions and initiatives, conduct a detailed probe of the activities of all departments and public bodies, and verify compliance with the law.

Legislative power is normally exercised by representatives elected directly by universal suffrage. Each province has its own legislative assembly and elects its own representatives. The federal Parliament is the only Canadian legislative assembly formed of two chambers: the House of Commons (the lower chamber), composed of members elected by universal suffrage, and the Senate (the upper chamber), formed of appointed senators. Budgetary review and control are performed by all parliamentarians. However, certain legislative committees (or parliamentary commissions) have received the mandate to execute particular tasks. In the House of Commons, these are the following three committees:[7]

- The Standing Committee on Finance, responsible for analysing the budgetary policies of the Department of Finance, notably its economic forecasts (including the forecasts of the Bank of Canada)
- The Standing Committee on Government Operations and Estimates, which analyses issues related to the effectiveness of governmental programs and the quality of budgetary information transmitted by the government
- The Standing Committee on Public Accounts, which is charged with the task of reviewing the reports of the Auditor General. This committee is an agent of Parliament, the mandate of which is to audit the government's operations

In addition, the Standing Senate Committee on National Finance conducts various in-depth studies on themes related to the government budget and public finance.

Aside from these committees, Parliament also receives support from two senior civil servants: the Parliamentary Budget Officer and the Auditor General of Canada. The mandate of the Parliamentary Budget Officer is to examine the accuracy of budget forecasts presented by the government. This position exists only in the Canadian and Ontarian legislatures (in Ontario the title for this position is the Financial Accountability Officer). The Auditor General of Canada examines the accuracy and compliance of the financial results presented by the government. All provinces and territories have their own auditor general. Both the Parliamentary Budget Officer (and Financial Accountability Officer) and the Auditor General oversee budgetary operations on behalf of the members of Parliament. However, this oversight is not accomplished simultaneously during the budgetary cycle: the Parliamentary Budget Officer and Financial Accountability Officer examine budgetary issues as policies are being formulated—thus, at the beginning of the budgetary cycle, or "ex ante"—and the Auditor General exercises budgetary control after policies are implemented—thus, once the cycle is complete, or "ex post."

The organizational chart in Figure 3.2 presents a synthesis of the structures in the federal Parliament and the main actors participating in the budgetary process. As noted above, the provinces and territories do not have an upper chamber. All, however, have legislative committees that deal with public finance and budgets, a public accounts committee, and an auditor general.

The Judiciary

The third branch of the Canadian state is the judiciary. Judicial power is granted to judges who are appointed by the government and thereafter enjoy great independence. There are a number of judicial bodies, both federal and provincial. The Supreme Court of Canada is the court of last resort in the Canadian judicial system; its decisions are final and cannot be appealed. The Supreme Court rules on budgetary questions when constitutional principles are in play. There is also a federal tax court that decides on tax disputes between the federal government and taxpayers. In 2007, the federal government created the Office of the Taxpayers' Ombudsman. This office is responsible for receiving complaints from

Figure 3.2 The legislative branch of the federal government

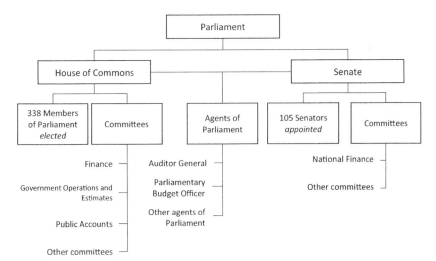

taxpayers, whose rights are protected by the Taxpayer Bill of Rights. However, it is not a judicial body, and the ombudsman reports to the minister of revenue. Finally, unlike in other countries (such as France, Italy, and Brazil), there is no Canadian judicial body mandated specifically to rule or bring lawsuits against people who have allegedly misused or misappropriated public funds (similar to a Court of Accounts, for example). Such cases are decided according to the usual judicial process.

The Legal Framework for the Budgetary Process

The Canadian Constitution, the fundamental law of the land, is composed, as mentioned above, of written documents and unwritten conventions. Certain clauses and conventions of the Constitution have a major impact on the budgetary process. For instance, the Constitution defines the sharing of budgetary powers between levels of government and the responsibilities of the legislative, executive, and judicial branches. However, it is silent with regard to the internal budgetary process that rules the government's decisions. This process is framed by a few ordinary laws and numerous regulations (policies, directives, internal standards) established by the governments themselves. Unlike the situation in some countries, Canadian laws regarding the budget do not have distinct legal status giving them precedence over other laws (such as the French *loi organique relative aux lois de finances* or the German framework law governing the budgets of the *Länder*, for example[8]).

The Financial Administration Act

The federal government and each provincial and territorial government must comply with their respective Financial Administration Act (called the Provincial Finance Act in Nova Scotia), which is the legal framework that governs their budgetary process. These statutes, which set out the financial responsibilities and obligations of various governmental bodies,[9] have existed since the very beginning of Canadian Confederation, although they have been amended many times in order to adapt to the changing circumstances of the public-sector universe. The federal, provincial, and territorial Financial Administration Acts all cover the following six major themes:

- Administrative organization of the budgetary process
- Collection and management of public funds
- Payments from public funds
- Powers to lend, borrow, and manage the public debt
- Preparation of financial statements
- Definition and delineation of the public sector

Administrative organization of the budgetary process. The administrative organization of the budgetary process is characterized by the presence of central agencies responsible for defining the government's budgetary policy and ensuring that public funds are used correctly and efficiently. The Financial Administration Act delegates the main budgetary responsibilities to two central agencies: the Department of Finance and the Treasury Board. The Department of Finance is responsible for formulating and presenting the government's budgetary policy. As such, it determines the government's budgetary priorities, which will lead to the preparation of spending plans and fiscal policies. It is also responsible for establishing projections regarding the economic and financial situation of the country, province, or territory and its government. Finally, it sees to financial agreements between the federal government and the provinces and territories (and with municipalities in the case of provincial and territorial governments). The federal government's Department of Finance also performs certain functions that the provincial and territorial departments do not; among these, seeing to the operation of financial institutions and markets (as such, it is responsible for the Bank of Canada and international financial agreements), Canada's exchange-rate policy, and the signing of fiscal accords with other countries.

The Treasury Board is responsible for administering the public funds. Because it is a Cabinet committee, its chair is a government minister. In the past, the Treasury Board was run by the minister of finance. The growing complexity of state activities has led the federal government, as well as the provinces of Ontario and Quebec, to delegate the responsibilities of the Treasury Board to another minister, the president of the Treasury Board. The Treasury Board has its own department, or administrative branch, the Treasury Board Secretariat—or Treasury Board division in the provinces in which the tasks of the Treasury Board are still assumed by the ministry of finance—to help it fulfil its functions. The main duties of the Treasury Board and its administrative branch are to ensure that public funds are distributed and used in compliance with the budgetary policy formulated by the government and approved by the legislature. In this role, the Treasury Board Secretariat or division sets out the different rules and mechanisms governing all departments and public bodies. For backup, it may turn to the expertise of the Comptroller General, who is responsible for internal audits of governmental activities (external audits are performed by the legislature's auditor general). The Treasury Board is also the employer of the civil service. It is responsible for negotiating collective agreements with employees and setting rules for the assignment and management of human resources.

Collection and management of public funds. A number of departments are involved in the process of collecting and managing public funds. The Department of Finance formulates the government's fiscal policy, which makes it possible to identify sources of revenue. The federal government's Canada Revenue Agency implements this fiscal policy by establishing mechanisms for collecting appropriate taxes through various laws, including the Income Tax Act (a tome more than three thousand pages long) and the Excise Tax Act (which includes the provisions governing the sales tax). These mechanisms concern individuals' and firms' tax returns, the collection of sales taxes and customs duties, and policies for fighting fraud and tax evasion. It should be noted that the Canada Revenue Agency also collects income taxes and certain other taxes on behalf of provincial governments, with the exception of Quebec.[10] The Treasury Board is responsible for determining the spending authority required for public funds to be used by the managers of public departments and agencies.

Payments from public funds. The Receiver General is responsible for making payments and receiving revenues on behalf of the government. It acts, however, according to directions issued by the Treasury Board. Its main responsibility is to make sure that expenditures have been authorized beforehand.

Powers to lend, borrow, and manage the public debt. Like expenditures and revenues, loans must be authorized beforehand by Parliament. Once these authorizations are obtained, the Department of Finance is responsible for formulating the various borrowing mechanisms (issuance of various receivables such as Treasury bills and bonds). The Department of Finance is also responsible for developing and implementing a strategy for managing the public debt. The main objective is to ensure that the government benefits from the best possible borrowing conditions.

Preparation of financial statements. The Receiver General is also responsible for recording all the activities of the administration's treasury— that is, funds entering and leaving the government accounts. The Receiver General must maintain a general register in which all transactions are accounted for. This register is then used to establish the Public Accounts that the government is required to submit to Parliament. The Public Accounts are accompanied by a notice from the Auditor General.

Definition and delineation of the public sector. All public organizations (government departments and other bodies created by the government) must follow the financial management rules stated in the legislation. Compared to departments, public agencies (e.g., the central bank, universities, hospitals) benefit from greater independence, which enables them to adopt management policies of their own. Many of these organizations are Crown corporations (or government business enterprises) with a commercial vocation—that is, their activities must generate sufficient revenues to cover their operating costs. In some cases, governments ask them to fulfil profitability objectives (this is the case notably for Crown corporations responsible for selling alcoholic beverages or lottery games). The financial management rules may thus be different for some public organizations and for Crown corporations. It should be noted, however, that governments are trying more and more to standardize the rules governing these various organizations.

Table 3.1 Canadian legislation relating to financial and budgetary policy of governments, in force as of 1 July 2017

	Financial Administration Act	Balanced budget	Budgetary transparency	Taxpayer consent	Results-based management framework
Newfoundland and Labrador	Yes	No	Yes	No	No
Prince Edward Island	Yes	No	No	No	No
Nova Scotia	Yes	No[a]	Yes	No[a]	No
New Brunswick	Yes	No[a]	No[a]	No[a]	Yes
Quebec	Yes	Yes	No	No	Yes
Ontario	Yes	Yes	Yes	Yes	No
Manitoba	Yes	Yes	Yes	Yes	No
Saskatchewan	Yes	No[a]	No[a]	No	No[a]
Alberta	Yes	No[a]	Yes	Yes	Yes[b]
British Columbia	Yes	Yes	Yes	No	No
Nunavut	Yes	Yes	No	No	No
Northwest Territories	Yes	Yes	No	No	No
Yukon	Yes	Yes	No	Yes	No
Federal government	Yes	No[a]	No	No	No
Total	14/14	7/14	6/14	4/14	3/14

[a] Previously in force but now repealed.
[b] Result-based management legislation adopted in 2012 for a period of five years. The legislation was not extended.

Other Statutes Related to Budgets

Over the last few years, new statutes relating to the budgetary process have been adopted in Canada. These laws reflect governments' increasingly clear desire to show transparency and accountability. Some of them may also be seen as conveying certain governments' desire to limit the power of elected officials. Among the most popular of these are balanced-budget laws, which forbid governments from incurring deficits. As we can see from the information presented in Table 3.1, balanced-budget laws are in force in seven of the fourteen Canadian jurisdictions. The commitment of Canadian governments to balanced-budget rules has declined in recent years; before the 2008 global financial crisis, balanced-budget laws were in force in twelve jurisdictions. Although less widespread, other laws have been added to balanced-budget measures. For instance, budget-transparency statutes force governments to publish reports and information on different budgetary issues (such as budgetary objectives, multi-year budgetary plans, economic perspectives, progress reports and updates, and long-term financial viability). Taxpayer-consent statutes require that governments obtain the agreement of the population (by holding a referendum) before raising certain taxes or income taxes. Finally, laws covering management of results force governments to undertake regular in-depth examination of their programs, in order to eliminate those that are the least effective. Although they are still not widespread, these additional laws are gaining popularity today (especially, since the 2008 financial crisis, laws affecting management results).

The Government Apparatus

The public sector is composed of a large number of departments, public agencies, and Crown corporations. In total, Canadian public administrations employ more than 3.3 million people.[11] The provincial and territorial administrations employ the greatest number of these workers, providing 48.2 per cent of public-sector jobs, followed by local administrations at 38.9 per cent, and the federal government at 12.9 per cent. The vast majority of employees in provincial and territorial administrations work in public agencies in health care and social services (hospitals, long-term residential facilities, and other institutions receiving beneficiaries—53.8 per cent of jobs) and education (schools, colleges, professional training centres, universities—23.9 per cent). A good proportion of jobs is also found in Crown corporations, which employ almost 10 per cent of public-sector workers countrywide. Here, once again, the highest proportion of employees is in provinces and territories (46.4 per cent of total Crown corporation jobs), followed by the federal government (32.1 per cent) and then local administrations.

Although the great majority of jobs are found in government departments, public agencies (which report to departments), and Crown corporations (which also report to departments), the responsibility for establishing the government's budgetary plans (general orientations

Figure 3.3 The structure of the federal government apparatus

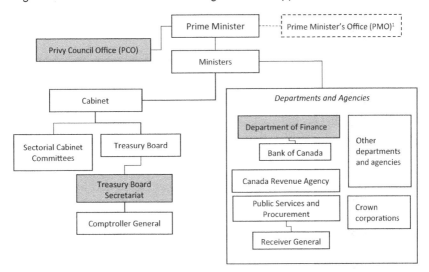

Notes: [1]Prime Minister's political staff, which are not part of the regular public service. Central agencies are identified by a grey area.

and the programs flowing from them) falls to a small group of decision makers. The diagram in Figure 3.3 presents the main decision-making centres in the federal government. The provinces have instituted very similar structures, although the names are sometimes different (furthermore, the provinces do not have a central bank and some have delegated the task of collecting taxes to the Canada Revenue Agency).

The diagram in Figure 3.3 highlights three organizations that are mainly responsible for formulating budgetary policy: the Privy Council Office, the Treasury Board Secretariat, and the Department of Finance. These organizations are the government's central agencies. Their decisions directly influence the activities of all other entities in the governmental apparatus. The Comptroller General also exerts some influence, but not as much. Acting under the authority of the Treasury Board Secretariat, the Comptroller is responsible for instituting internal audit policies with which all departments and public agencies must comply. Other units also provide services to the civil service as a whole, but they have a limited role in the process of formulating budgetary policies. The Canada Revenue Agency collects most government revenues. The

Department of Public Services and Procurement Canada[12] is responsible for public procurement and management of the building inventory. The Receiver General manages cash flow (issuing payments and receiving funds) and keeps the accounts.

In recent decades, the influence of the central agencies and the budgetary process has grown considerably in both the federal and provincial government apparatuses.[13] Today, they are the true centres of power in these administrations.[14] They set the government's general budgetary orientations; dictate the policies, directives, and budgetary standards that all financial administrators and program managers must adhere to; and establish mechanisms for program assessment and review as well as control mechanisms. According to Wildavsky, it is easier to understand the budgetary process and the responsibilities and influences of each actor if we distinguish between two main groups: on the one hand, the "spenders," which are the departments and public agencies responsible for execution of the budget—that is, whose main function is to use public funds to finance public programs; and on the other hand, the "guardians" of the public budget, whose task is to see to prudent management of public funds.[15] The central agencies act as guardians. During the decades following the Second World War, when it seemed that public funds would always be plentiful, the spenders exerted an undeniable influence. The guardians began to direct budgetary choices in the 1980s, when it was becoming more and more difficult for governments to find sources of funding for public programs. The guardians' predominance is particularly evident when the agenda is set for the budgetary initiatives that constitute the first stage of the budgetary cycle.

FEATURE BOX: ARE BALANCED-BUDGET RULES EFFECTIVE?

Balanced-budget statutes have existed in Canada for twenty-five years now. They have been gradually adopted by the majority of provinces and territories (the first jurisdiction to do so was British Columbia in 1991), and in 2015 the federal government adopted its own balanced-budget legislation.

Have the balanced-budget statutes kept governments from making systematic use of deficits? Research shows that there is indeed a correlation between the presence of strict budgetary rules and the absence of public deficits. What is less clear, however, is the direction of the correlation. The results of a number of studies suggest that favourable financial conditions (i.e., the presence of budgetary surpluses) lead to adoption of balanced-budget statutes, rather the reverse. These results would be explained by governments' propensity to use balanced-budget statutes to demonstrate their good management skills. These laws provide them with an effective tool (based on compliance with laws) to communicate to the population that they manage budgets prudently and responsibly.

What happens if deficits occur? Once again, the behaviour of Canadian provincial governments supports the explanation that balanced-budget statutes are the result and not the cause of balanced budgets. Governments prefer to amend the legislation to bend the rules that are the most difficult to comply with, rather than breaking the law. The financial crisis of 2008 and the subsequent unprecedented decline of oil prices both illustrate this point very well: all provinces that incurred a deficit contravening the legislation amended (Quebec, Manitoba, British Columbia) or abrogated (Nova Scotia, New Brunswick, Saskatchewan, Alberta, and the federal government) their statute. Today, governments are explicitly forbidden to run deficits in two provinces only: Quebec and British Columbia. The federal government also repealed its own legislation in 2016, once it became clear it would run a deficit.

Source: Geneviève Tellier, "Balanced-Budget Legislation: The Rationale, Consequences and Lessons the Federal Government Can Draw from the Experiences of Canadian Provinces," in *How Ottawa Spends, 2015–2016: The Liberal Rise and the Tory Demise*, ed. C. Stoney and B.G. Doern (Montreal/Kingston: McGill-Queen's University Press, 2016), 228–59.

KEYWORDS

Executive power • *Privy Council Office* • *Legislative power* • *Financial Administration Act* • *Balanced-budget statutes* • *Civil service*

TO FIND OUT MORE

Reading suggestions

Forsey, Eugene A. *How Canadians Govern Themselves*. 9th ed. Ottawa: Library of Parliament, 2016. https://lop.parl.ca/About/Parliament/senatoreugeneforsey/book/preface-e.html
Organisation for Economic Co-operation and Development. "The Legal Framework for Budget Systems: An International Comparison." Special issue, *OECD Journal on Budgeting* 4, no. 3 (2004).
Organisation for Economic Co-operation and Development. Government at a Glance 2017. Paris: OECD, 2017.
Rigaud, Benoît, and Paul-Émile Arsenaul. "Budget Governance in Canada: Comparing Practices within a Federation." *OECD Journal on Budgeting* 13, no. 1 (2013): 9–30.

Periodicals

The Library of Parliament publishes many research notes (current publications and legislative summaries) that explain how federal political institutions work; these can be accessed on the Library website: https://lop.parl.ca/sites/PublicWebsite/default/en_CA/ResearchPublications
Canadian Public Administration (quarterly publication edited by the Institute of Public Administration of Canada): https://www.ipac.ca/iPAC_EN/Programs_Services/Research/CPA_Journal/iPAC_EN/Programs/CPA_Journal/CPA.aspx?hkey=d8175053-3dea-4415-b2f1-8e82e39c1b68
Canadian Public Policy (quarterly publication, edited by the University of Toronto Press): https://economics.ca/cpp/en/index.php

Database

International Budget Practices and Procedures Database (OECD): http://www.oecd.org/governance/budgeting/internationalbudgetpracticesandproceduresdatabase.htm

Websites

List of federal departments and agencies (Canada): https://www.canada.ca/en/government/dept.html

List of provincial government websites: https://www.canada.ca/en/
intergovernmental-affairs/services/provinces-territories.html
Privy Council Office (Canada): https://www.canada.ca/en/privy-council.
html
Library of Parliament of Canada: https://lop.parl.ca/sites/PublicWebsite/
default/en_CA
Institute of Public Administration of Canada: https://www.ipac.ca

Statutes

Financial Administration Act, R.S.C., 1985, c. F-11 (Canada)
Financial Administration Act, RSNL. 1990 c. F-8 (Newfoundland and
Labrador)
Financial Administration Act, RSPEI. 1988, c. F-9 (Prince Edward Island)
Provincial Finance Act, RSNS. 1989, c. 365 (Nova Scotia)
Financial Administration Act, RSNB. 2011, c. 160 (New Brunswick)
Financial Administration Act, CQLR. c. A-6.00 (Quebec)
Financial Administration Act, RSO. 1990, c. F.12 (Ontario)
The Financial Administration Act, CCSM. c. F55 (Manitoba)
The Financial Administration Act, SS. 1983, c. F-13.3 (Saskatchewan)
Financial Administration Act, RSA. 2000, c. F-12 (Alberta)
Financial Administration Act, RSBC. 1996, c. 138 (British Columbia)
Financial Administration Act, RSNWT. (Nu) 1988, c. F-4 (Nunavut)
Financial Administration Act, SNWT. 2015, c. 13 (Northwest Territories)
Financial Administration Act, RSY. 2002, c. 87 (Yukon)

PART 2

Budget Preparation

4 Setting the Agenda for Budget Actions

In the Canadian political system, the responsibility for formulating the government's budgets falls to the executive branch. It is therefore the ministers who jointly determine the government's orientations and make the resulting budgetary decisions. The ministers meet regularly (usually every week when Parliament is in session) in Cabinet and committee meetings. The committees are formed of small groups of ministers, whereas the Cabinet brings them all together. The first minister determines the number, mandate, and members of the committees. The exceptions to this rule are the statutory committees, the existence of which is required by law. The federal Cabinet has one statutory committee, the Treasury Board, composed of six members, including the president of the Treasury Board and the minister of finance. Provincial and territorial cabinets have structures similar to the federal government's, although the number of statutory committees and the power and composition of the Treasury Board may vary from jurisdiction to jurisdiction.[1]

The responsibilities of the Treasury Board are set out in the Financial Administration Act. These responsibilities cover a wide range of fields, the main ones being:

- The general orientations and organization of the public administration
- Financial management (including determination of accounting methods)
- Reviews of spending plans and programs (annual and multi-year)
- Management of the administration's human resources
- Internal audit of the public administration

Given the extent of its powers, the Treasury Board is called upon to intervene in almost all portfolios reviewed by the Cabinet. In fact, the Treasury Board reviews all actions analysed by the committees. It must sometimes deal with complex and highly technical budgetary questions. For this reason, it operates differently from other Cabinet committees. Whereas most committees deal only with subjects in sectors associated with their mandate (foreign affairs, social policy, and economic development, for example), the Treasury Board is involved in all aspects of the government's positions. Furthermore, the ministers in the sector policy committees act as spokespeople for their respective departments, whereas the members of the Treasury Board are responsible for seeing to the interests of government as a whole. Finally, senior

Figure 4.1 Organizational branches and sectors of the Treasury Board of Canada Secretariat

Office of the Comptroller General	Expenditure Management Sector
• Office of the Comptroller General history	• Expenditure management
• Comptroller General's Priorities	**Government Operations Sector**
• Financial management	**Chief Information Officer Branch**
• Internal audit	
• Professional audit support services	• Information and privacy policy
• Departmental audit committees	• Information management
• Assets and acquired services	• Information technology
• Accountability	• IT project review and oversight
• List of Chief Financial Officers	• Security and identity management
• List of Chief Audit Executives	
Office of the Chief Human Resources Officer	
• Awards, recognition and special events	• Pensions and benefits
• Collective agreements	• Performance and talent management
• Diversity and employment equity	• Professional development
• Labour management	• Terms and conditions of employment
• Official languages	• Values and ethics

(*Continued*)

Figure 4.1 (Continued)

Priorities and Planning	Regulatory Affairs Sector (RAS)
• Management Accountability Framework • Risk management	• Federal regulatory management • Canada-United States Regulatory Cooperation Council
Social and Cultural Sector **Strategic Communications and** **Ministerial Affairs** • Access to information and privacy office • Federal Identity Program • Government communications • Proactive disclosure • Treasury Board submissions	**Economic Sector** **International Affairs, Security and** **Justice Sector** **Internal Audit and Evaluation Bureau** **Human Resources Division** **Corporate Services Sector** **Legal Services Branch**

Source: Treasury Board Secretariat (Canada). *Treasury Board of Canada Secretariat Organization*, accessed 23 October 2017, https://www.canada.ca/en/treasury-board-secretariat/corporate/organization.html.

civil servants frequently participate in Treasury Board meetings, but never (or very rarely) in the meetings of the sector policy committees.

To discharge its various duties, the Treasury Board uses the resources of an administrative branch of the civil service, the Treasury Board Secretariat or division. The minister in charge of the Treasury Board administrative branch is the president of the Treasury Board or the minister of finance. The federal government's secretariat currently has almost eighteen hundred employees in fifteen management areas. Figure 4.1 presents these areas.

The Role of the Treasury Board Administrative Branch

The Treasury Board administrative branch may be seen as the liaison between the cabinet and the civil service—that is, between elected officials and the administrative apparatus of the state. It ensures that the Cabinet's decisions are properly transmitted to and implemented by the various bodies of the public administration, and that requests from departments are sent to the Cabinet.

Although the government's fiscal stance is defined by the Cabinet, and more particularly by the first minister and the minister of finance, the Treasury Board administrative branch also participates actively in its formulation. Its primary responsibility consists of ensuring that the Cabinet has all the information it needs to make decisions. This information falls into three general categories:

- The performance of the government's budget-management systems
- The performance measurements for each department's and public agency's programs
- The results expected for all new budget actions or reallocations requiring the approval of the Cabinet and the Treasury Board

To perform these activities, the Treasury Board administrative branch must be able to count on a set of reliable, detailed financial data. One of its main tasks therefore consists of gathering data from the departments and public bodies. It must ensure that its data accurately represent the government's activities in all fields and that the information gathered is uniform and coherent for the public administration as a whole. The Treasury Board administrative branch has therefore instituted a series of directives, with varying degrees of detail and restrictiveness, that senior executives and managers of the government's financial branches must follow. Table 4.1 gives an overview of the nature of these directives and their respective roles within the federal apparatus. Together, these rules form the Foundation Framework for Treasury Board Policies of the federal government.

The Treasury Board administrative branch plays a predominant role in the adoption of new expenditures or the redistribution of existing expenditures among programs by helping senior civil servants prepare requests that must be submitted to the Treasury Board. Every new spending plan must be approved by the Treasury Board, even if it has received prior approval from the Cabinet. In fact, all budget requests must be approved twice. First, the Cabinet decides if the request corresponds to the government's priorities; second, the Treasury Board examines the feasibility of implementing the project. Requests for approval submitted to the Treasury Board must be accompanied by detailed documentation that clearly presents the project's objectives and the financial resources required. Requests are evaluated according to a number of criteria: relevance, feasibility of implementation, optimal use of resources, available financial sources, and establishment of evaluation instruments

Table 4.1 Classification of directives issued by the Canadian government's Treasury Board Secretariat

Instrument	Description	Application	Target audience	Example
Policy framework	Explains why a policy is set	Architectural		Policy framework for the management of assets and acquired services
Policy	Explains what is expected to be achieved	Mandatory	Ministers & deputy heads	Policy on financial management
Directive	Explains how policy objectives are to be attained	Mandatory		Directive on payments
Standard	Provides detailed information on how to conduct certain tasks	Mandatory		Standard for project complexity and risk
Guideline	Provides guidance, advice, or explanation	Voluntary	Managers & functional specialists	Guideline on the application of Goods and Services Tax/ Harmonized Sales Tax
Tool	Disseminates examples such as best practices, handbooks	Voluntary		Guide to using the project complexity and risk assessment tool

Source: Adapted from Treasury Board Secretariat (Canada), *Foundation Framework for Treasury Board Policies*, http://www.tbs-sct.gc.ca/pol/doc-eng.aspx?id=13616&section=html (accessed 25 July 2017).

to measure the effects obtained.[2] The Treasury Board administrative branch ensures that the documentation presented addresses all the elements required for the evaluation. Figure 4.2 summarizes the respective roles of the departments, the Treasury Board Secretariat, and the Cabinet in the presentation of budget requests at the federal level.

Figure 4.2 The federal Treasury Board submission process

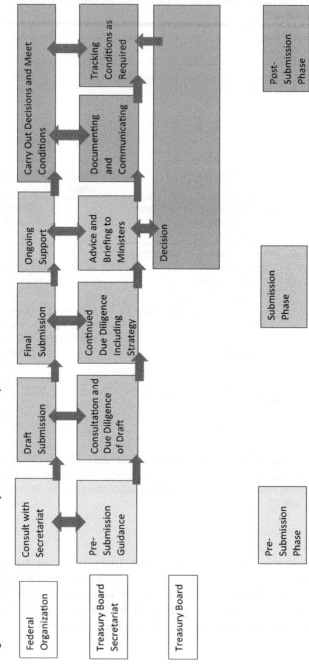

Source: Treasury Board Secretariat (Canada). *Treasury Board Submissions Overview*, accessed 23 October 2017, https://www.canada.ca/en/treasury-board-secretariat.

To assess whether departments' and agencies' programs are managed efficiently and to determine whether the budgetary resources could have been used in another way, the federal Secretariat conducts "strategic reviews."[3] These reviews are conducted periodically and cover all programs of all departments in the federal civil service. They evaluate whether resources are being optimally used, whether each program is satisfying its mandate, and whether the program corresponds to the government's principal orientations. To ensure that these objectives are achieved, the Secretariat has established a permanent mechanism for reallocation of resources. Each department must determine which of its programs have low priority or are not performing well. The funding for these programs will be reallocated to other programs that the government (i.e., the Cabinet) deems more effective or higher priority. Currently, programs to be identified for reallocation must represent 5 per cent of the respective department's total spending.

Finally, the Secretariat ensures the uniformity and compliance of the budgetary rules under which the financial reports for all programs are written. These reports are public, and a good number of them are submitted to Parliament. The information that they contain is broken down by budget classification, corresponding to various kinds of transactions: payroll, purchases of supplies and equipment, capital costs, grant payments, accounts receivable, and so on. This information is compiled for each decision-making unit, by department, and finally for the civil service as a whole. For example, Figure 4.3 presents the financial report for current spending by the federal government's Department of Justice for the quarter ending 30 June 2017. All departments are required to publish a similar report every quarter. This report is only one of the many budget reports prepared by federal departments.

The Government's Budgetary Choices

Today, budgetary choices have grown in number and complexity, and they thus require the participation of a large number of decision makers. This was not always the case. In his memoirs, Walter Gordon, the minister of finance in the Pearson government (1963–68), noted that the Cabinet was informed of the content of the budget only the morning it was presented (or, if possible, the previous day) and that no minister was truly in a position to express reservations about its direction and content.[4] The current situation is very different, as the Cabinet and the Treasury Board regularly discuss budgetary questions. Budget actions

Figure 4.3 Quarterly financial report by the Department of Justice of the Government of Canada, 2017

	Fiscal year 2017–2018			Fiscal year 2016–2017		
(In thousands of dollars)	Planned expenditures for the year ending 31 March 2018	Expended during the quarter ended 30 June 2017	Year to date used at quarter end	Planned expenditures for the year ending 31 March 2017	Expended during the quarter ended 30 June 2016	Year to date used at quarter end
Expenditures						
Personnel	531,325	138,480	138,480	535,275	134,041	134,041
Transportation and communications	8,492	1,236	1,236	7,732	1,593	1,593
Information	3,231	377	377	3,308	430	430
Professional and special services	37,217	4,236	4,236	38,158	4,701	4,701
Rentals	7,063	832	832	6,237	912	912
Repair and maintenance	4,437	98	98	5,964	192	192
Utilities, materials, and supplies	4,418	664	664	4,648	602	602
Acquisition of machinery and equipment	5,401	261	261	6,028	401	401
Transfer payments	390,315	7,848	7,848	365,234	10,815	10,815
Other subsidies and payments	6,357	1,366	1,366	2,479	494	494
Total gross budgetary expenditures	998,256	155,398	155,398	975,063	154,181	154,181
Less revenues netted against expenditures (Revenues)	(296,200)	(18,805)	(18,805)	(296,200)	(41,510)	(41,510)
Budgetary expenditures	702,056	136,593	136,593	678,863	112,671	112,671

Table header: Department of Justice — Departmental Budgetary Expenditures by Standard Object (unaudited)

Source: Department of Justice (Canada). *Quarterly Financial Report for the Quarter Ended June 30, 2017*, accessed 23 October 2017, http://www.justice.gc.ca/eng/rp-pr/cp-pm/qfr-rft/index.html.

are continually put on the agenda, driving a process that requires sustained attention by ministers throughout the year.

The complexity of budgetary issues also influences how budget-related decisions are made. Governments do not have the necessary resources to review every program every year. As Wildavsky amply demonstrated a number of years ago, budgetary decisions are usually incrementalist in nature—that is, current budgets are the result of "incremental" adjustments being made to preceding budgets in order to respond to new problems, requests, and priorities.[5] Thus, governments do not put every program into play (or reset the meter at zero, as some would recommend[6]) every year. The program review conducted by the Treasury Board Secretariat gives a good illustration of the incrementalism of the federal government's budgetary process. Even though program reviews have become more common today so that program spending can be monitored more closely, reviewing every program every year has not been proposed.

Every year, the Cabinet examines a large number of proposed budget actions. After an exhaustive analysis of the various proposals submitted, it decides which actions will be presented in the next budget. The proposals submitted to the Cabinet come from ministers, who are trying to obtain funds for their respective portfolios. Not every Cabinet member is equally influential, however: some opinions hold more weight than others. This is certainly the case for the first minister, who is responsible for determining the government's general strategic direction, and the minister of finance, who establishes the government's fiscal framework by making an inventory of the financial resources available to implement the budget. Although Cabinet decisions are supposed to be consensual, they are still the result of the complex (and usually difficult) negotiations among the members.[7]

The Cabinet must also deal with multiple budgetary constraints, some of which are imposed by the Cabinet itself. The government may, for example, impose spending-reduction programs as part of a restrictive budgetary policy. Other constraints may be totally beyond its control, such as the occurrence of natural disasters or the need to comply with international commitments (a free-trade agreement, for example). These constraints define the government's margin of manoeuvre.

Budget requests examined by the Cabinet fall into four general categories, each related to a specific issue:[8]

• General necessities
• General directions

- Essentials
- Wish list

General necessities are budget actions that attempt to correct a major problem in public policy. The first minister must approve them, in both form and content. These actions require large sums of money and usually reduce the funds available for other initiatives. However, they do not occur every year. An example of such an action would be a new agreement for sharing of financial resources between the federal government and the provinces.

General directions are budget actions that result directly from the government's priorities, which were usually presented in the government's political platform in the previous election. They therefore implement the government's commitments. The budgets allocated to them are usually quite large. Although the first minister must approve these initiatives, the departments are responsible for designing them and having them approved by the Cabinet. Under this category, a number of distinct actions are presented in each annual budget. Programs focusing on reduction of the fiscal burden, environmental protection, fighting crime, international aid, and improvements to social services are actions that fall under general directions.

The essentials are inevitable expenditures that the government knows will arise during the year. What is less certain, however, is the specific moment when the funds will have to be used, their exact use, and the sums required. The minister of finance is responsible for establishing the budgets associated with these events. Over the last few years, governments have gotten into the habit of adding contingency reserves to their budgets to deal with certain unforeseen expenditures (including unanticipated drops in revenue). Essential expenditures concern public health programs (in case of a pandemic, for example), emergency assistance (natural disasters, humanitarian crises), and security (terrorist attacks).

Items on the wish list are small-scale initiatives that convey cabinet ministers' concern with satisfying the needs of certain groups of citizens. These initiatives are not necessarily chosen as a function of the government's priorities. In fact, they usually express other considerations, such as wanting to please a particular voter faction, easing tensions in the Cabinet by ensuring that everyone benefits from the government's budgetary policy, and so on. The first minister decides which initiatives are chosen. Although the budgets are small, the accumulation of initiatives may become significant. In recent years, a number of these initiatives have taken the form of tax expenditures, such as tax credits targeting specific taxpayer groups. This type of initiative is most likely to be implemented just before an election.

Requests for approval that are reviewed and approved by the Cabinet come from the ministers themselves (including the first minister). This does not mean, however, that only internal requests—those formulated within the governmental apparatus—are examined by the Cabinet. In fact, individuals, organizations, firms, and pressure groups are constantly lobbying ministers and their managers to adopt specific budgetary policies. It is not unusual for the government to ask the opinion of users or stakeholders when it formulates its policies. Communications between the public administration and external groups are, however, ruled by codes of conduct and a legal framework (code of ethics for civil servants and laws governing lobbying).

In recent years, a new form of communication specific to the budgetary process has appeared: prebudget consultations conducted by ministers of finance. These consultations are not new in themselves. It has long been customary for ministers of finance to consult with certain key stakeholders in socio-economic and business circles to obtain their opinion on particular envisaged budgetary measures. These consultations are private. What is more recent is the broadening of these consultations to the general public and their being conducted publicly in various forms. For instance, governments institute online surveys, discussion forums, and even citizen assemblies to discuss various budgetary issues and gauge public opinion.[9] These new mechanisms are intended to make the budgetary process more transparent and inclusive. Today, all the provinces and the federal government use these types of prebudget consultations. It is worth noting, however, that private prebudget consultations continue to exist.

The Government's Budgetary Calendar

The formulation of federal and provincial budgets is a complex task requiring the participation of all administration organizations. Preparing the budget requires a full year of work. Thus, the preparation of the next budget begins as soon as the budget for the current year is presented to Parliament. The fiscal year of federal and provincial and territorial public administrations begins on 1 April. Most budgetary documents must therefore be ready for this date. The diagram

Figure 4.4 The budget-planning schedule, Canadian federal government

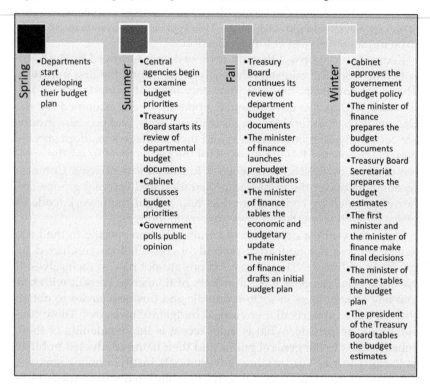

Spring
- Departments start developing their budget plan

Summer
- Central agencies begin to examine budget priorities
- Treasury Board starts its review of departmental budget documents
- Cabinet discusses budget priorities
- Government polls public opinion

Fall
- Treasury Board continues its review of department budget documents
- The minister of finance launches prebudget consultations
- The minister of finance tables the economic and budgetary update
- The minister of finance drafts an initial budget plan

Winter
- Cabinet approves the governement budget policy
- The minister of finance prepares the budget documents
- Treasury Board Secretariat prepares the budget estimates
- The first minister and the minister of finance make final decisions
- The minister of finance tables the budget plan
- The president of the Treasury Board tables the budget estimates

presented in Figure 4.4 shows the main steps in the cycle of preparation of the federal budget. The federal budget calendar provides a good illustration of the decision-making process also observed in the provinces and territories.

As the figure shows, managers of the departments and public bodies begin by preparing the budget documents that they must submit to the Treasury Board in the spring. These documents must present an update to their current budget that takes account of decisions already made by Cabinet but not yet implemented, an estimate of the funding needed for the next year, and an analysis of the performance of programs for the year that has just ended. Although these tasks concern preparation of the budget for the next year, the departments must also make multi-year projections covering the next few years.

During the summer, the central agencies begin to identify the general themes of the next budget. The prime minister's advisors (such as the Privy Council Office and Prime Minister's Office) review the government's priorities, including those that have already been announced publicly (during election campaigns, at the opening of Parliament, during important debates, and so on) and the actions adopted to date. The Treasury Board begins to examine the budget reports transmitted to it by the departments. The Cabinet also begins its own reflections during meetings that often take place in less-formal settings than other meetings during the year. In addition, the government takes advantage of the summer break in parliamentary work to float some trial balloons—that is, to put forth some ideas in public to gauge the public's reaction.

In the fall, the government formulates its fiscal framework. The Department of Finance establishes, then presents, its economic projections, which inform the population of the resources available, as planned by the government, and sets out the obligations that the government will have to meet for the next year. Once these projections are published, the government begins its formal prebudget consultations. These consultations are private and are usually conducted with economic forecasters from the private sector, representatives of major business sectors and other socio-economic sectors, and representatives from other levels of government. Also in the fall, governments ask citizens to send them suggestions regarding the content of the next budget.

At the beginning of winter, all of the lines of thinking of the various bodies are discussed as a whole. The Cabinet approves the government's general fiscal stance. However, the prime minister and the minister of finance may still modify the budget, even after it is accepted by the Cabinet. Therefore, important decisions may still be made at the very end of the budgetary cycle, sometimes just a few hours before the budget is publicly tabled. But before tabling its budget, the government must formulate its fiscal framework. This task falls under the responsibility of the Department of Finance.

KEYWORDS

Cabinet • Treasury Board • Treasury Board Secretariat • Budget requests • Government's budgetary schedule

TO FIND OUT MORE

Reading suggestions

Bernier, Luc, Keith Brownsey, and Michael Howlett, eds. *Executive Styles in Canada: Cabinet Structures and Leadership Practices in Canadian Government.* Toronto: University of Toronto Press/Institute of Public Administration of Canada, 2005.

Good, David A. *The Politics of Public Money.* 2nd ed. Toronto: University of Toronto Press, 2014.

Savoie, Donald J. *Governing from the Centre: The Concentration of Power in Canadian Politics.* Toronto: University of Toronto Press, 1999.

Wildavsky, Aaron, and Naomi Caiden. *The New Politics of the Budgetary Process.* 5th ed. New York: Pearson Longman, 2004.

Database

Infobase (Treasury Board Secretariat of Canada):   http://www.tbs-sct.gc.ca/ems-sgd/edb-bdd/index-eng.html#start (data on staff and financial operations collected by Treasury Board Secretariat)

Websites

Treasury Board Secretariat (Canada): https://www.canada.ca/en/treasury-board-secretariat.html

Treasury Board Secretariat (Ontario): https://www.ontario.ca/page/treasury-board-secretariat

Treasury Board Secretariat (Quebec): http://www.equipevisage.ca/en/ressources/secretariat-du-conseil-du-tresor-quebec-treasury-board/

Treasury Board Secretariat of other provinces and territories: see provincial and territorial Finance Department websites.

5 Formulation of the Fiscal Framework

Putting the government's initiatives on the agenda is an important step in the budgetary cycle. However, this agenda setting is incomplete unless the government knows that it has the resources needed to implement its initiatives. The fiscal framework enables the government to estimate whether it will have the financial resources required to implement its budgetary policy. Once these resources have been estimated, the government can finalize the policy. The fiscal framework also indicates whether revenues will be sufficient to cover spending, whether the economy is in a risky situation that could engender major fluctuations in government spending or revenues, and whether the financial markets are inclined to fund the government's borrowing, if necessary. Budget actions are put on the agenda by the Cabinet, assisted by the Treasury Board administrative branch, based on a review of the internal activities of the civil service, whereas formulation of the fiscal framework is based on an analysis of the environment beyond the public sector. The minister of finance is responsible for conducting this analysis and making the final decisions.

The Responsibilities of the Minister of Finance

The Department of Finance may be seen as the government's main central agency. Although other central bodies are also influential (first minister's department, Treasury Board administrative branch), the Department of Finance enjoys an unequalled stature and reputation in the government apparatus, at both governmental levels, federal as well as provincial and territorial. Its expertise, its resources, and the prestige of the position of minister of finance make it the most prominent actor in the budgetary process. The following exchange between a lawyer and the former federal minister of finance during the Gomery Commission's[1] public hearings gives a good illustration of the central role of the department and its minister:

> MR FINKELSTEIN: So I am the minister. I have come to you as Finance Minister. I have said "I would like to do this program." What happens if you say no?
>
> THE RT. HON. PAUL MARTIN: Well it is pretty well over unless – I mean, the Finance Minister can be overruled by the Prime Minister, but essentially, if the Finance Minister says "no" then you are going to have a long year ahead of you.[2]

There are a number of reasons that the minister of finance plays such a prominent role. One is the presence of solid economic and financial expertise within his or her department.[3] The federal government's Department of Finance has almost 750 employees, most of whom are involved with formulating the framework for economic and budgetary policies. In comparison, the parliamentary director of the budget, an agent of Parliament responsible for reviewing the accuracy of budget and financial forecasts made by the Department of Finance, has a team of only a dozen analysts.

Figure 5.1 below presents the organizational diagram of the federal government's Department of Finance. The department focuses on developing policies rather than the implementation and current management of government financial activities—activities that are performed by other departments or public bodies. For instance, although the department is responsible for formulating fiscal policy, it is the Canada Revenue Agency that implements this policy (notably by collecting income and most other taxes[4]). The federal Department of Finance also oversees monetary policy to ensure that the country has enough cash in circulation to fulfil its economic needs. However, the Bank of Canada formulates and implements Canada's monetary policy, and minting the coins and bills in circulation is the responsibility of the Royal Mint of Canada. The department also works with the Bank of Canada to develop and implement the strategy for managing government debt. The Bank of Canada executes borrowing and investment transactions. Finally, the federal Department of Finance is responsible for formulating the policies and regulations that frame the activities of the Canadian financial sector (banks, insurance and trust companies, credit cooperatives, private pension funds). The superintendent of financial institutions sees to the proper operation and accountability of the financial sector.

Figure 5.1 Organizational chart of the Department of Finance of the Government of Canada, 2017

Economic Development and Corporate Finance Branch

  Microeconomic Policy Analysis Division
  Sectoral Policy Analysis Division

Economic and Fiscal Policy Branch

  Fiscal Policy Division
  Economic Studies and Policy Analysis Division
  Economic Analysis and Forecasting Division

Federal-Provincial Relations and Social Policy Branch

  Federal-Provincial Relations Division
  Social Policy Division

Financial Sector Policy Branch

  Economic & Fiscal Policy Branch
  Economic Development & Corporate Finance Branch
  Federal-Provincial Relations & Social Policy Branch
  Financial Sector Policy Branch
  International Trade & Finance Branch
  Tax Policy Branch
  Law Branch
  Corporate Services Branch
  Consultations & Communications Branch

Internal Audit and Evaluation
Financial Sector Division
Financial Institutions Division
Funds Management Division
Capital Markets Division

International Trade and Finance Branch

  International Finance and Development Policy Division
  International Policy and Analysis Division
  International Trade Policy Division

Law Branch

  Office of the Assistant Deputy Minister and Counsel to the Department of Finance
  General Legal Services Division
  Tax Counsel Division
  Access to Information and Privacy Division
  Values & Ethics Division

Tax Policy Branch

  Personal Income Tax Division
  Sales Tax Division
  Business Income Tax Division
  Intergovernmental Tax Policy, Evaluation and Research Division
  Tax Legislation Division

(Continued)

Figure 5.1 (Continued)

Consultations and Communications Branch	Internal Audit and Evaluation
Communications Strategy and Parliamentary Affairs Division Public Affairs and Operations Division Web and Multimedia Services	Internal Audits Evaluations External Audits
Corporate Services Branch Corporate Planning Division Financial Management Division Human Resources, Security and Planning Directorate Information Management and Technology Division	

Source: Department of Finance (Canada), Our Branches, accessed 26 October 2017, http://www.fin.gc.ca/afc/branches-eng.asp.
Reproduced with the permission of the Department of Finance, 2018

It is worth noting that certain responsibilities of the federal Department of Finance are not assumed by provincial and territorial governments. For example, only the federal government deals with the Bank of Canada. As we know, the Canadian Constitution gives the federal government exclusive jurisdiction over monetary policy. The provinces and territories have developed their own programs and institutions for activities related to debt management and regulation of financial markets (including the real estate market), as their departments of finance are usually responsible for these activities. In fact, the roles and functions of provincial departments of finance are as extensive within their respective jurisdictions as are those of the federal government. As an illustration, Figure 5.2 presents the organizational diagram of a provincial government's department of finance (Newfoundland and Labrador).

Among the many responsibilities granted to the Department of Finance, those concerning preparation of budgetary estimates play an essential role in the budget-writing phase. These forecasts are used to define the fiscal framework that will enable the government to institute (or not) its budgetary initiatives.

Figure 5.2 Organizational chart of the Department of Finance of the Government of Newfoundland and Labrador, 2017

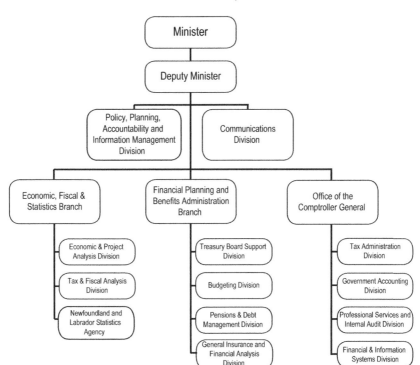

Source: Department of Finance (Newfoundland and Labrador), *About the Department*, accessed 27 October 2017, http://www.fin.gov.nl.ca/fin/department/index.html.

Budget Forecasts

The budget is the result of a constant forecasting process. The government (i.e., the Cabinet) must be able to estimate which needs will have to be met under the budgetary policy and what resources will be available to respond to these needs. Many of these forecasts are closely linked to the country's economic situation. For example, an increase in unemployment will have an impact on the number of beneficiaries of the Employment Insurance program and on the total revenue from personal income tax. To measure the potential effect of fluctuations in economic activity, the Department of Finance performs sensitivity testing. Table 5.1 shows the federal government's

Table 5.1 Estimate of the effect on federal revenues, expenses, and budgetary balance of a one-percentage-point decrease, over one year, of growth in real GDP

	Year 1	Year 2	Year 5
Federal revenues			
Tax revenues			
Personal income tax	−3.3	−3.2	−3.5
Corporate income tax	−0.4	−0.4	−0.5
Goods and Services Tax	−0.4	−0.4	−0.4
Other	−0.2	−0.2	−0.2
Total tax revenues	−4.2	−4.1	−4.6
Employment Insurance premiums	0.1	0.6	0.6
Other revenues	−0.1	−0.1	−0.1
Total budgetary revenues	−4.1	−3.6	−4.0
Federal expenses			
Major transfers to persons			
Elderly benefits	0.0	0.0	0.0
Employment Insurance benefits	0.8	0.7	0.5
Children's benefits	0.0	0.1	0.1
Total	0.8	0.8	0.6
Other program expenses	−0.2	−0.3	−0.5
Public debt charges	0.0	0.1	0.5
Total expenses	0.6	0.6	0.6
Budgetary balance	-4.7	-4.2	-4.6

Source: Department of Finance (Canada), *Budget 2017: Building a Strong Middle Class* (Ottawa: Her Majesty the Queen in Right of Canada, 2017), 262.
Note: Totals may not sum due to rounding. Estimation based on the assumption that any decrease in economic activity is proportional across income and expenditure components.

estimates of the effect of an economic slowdown on its budget balance. As we can see, an economic slowdown equivalent to a 1 percentage point drop in GDP increases the government's deficit by $4.7 billion the first year, by $4.2 billion the second year, and by $4.6 billion the fifth year.

Table 5.2 Forecasters consulted by the federal government to establish its budgetary estimates (2017 budget plan)

BMO Capital Markets	Industrial Alliance Insurance and Financial Services Inc.
Caisse de dépôt et placement du Québec	Laurentian Bank Securities
Canadian Federation of Independent Business	National Bank Financial Markets
CIBC World Markets	Royal Bank of Canada
The Conference Board of Canada	Scotiabank
Desjardins	TD Bank Financial Group
IHS Global Insight	University of Toronto, Policy and Economic Analysis Program

Source: Department of Finance (Canada), *Budget 2017*, 243.

The Department of Finance's estimates summarize the country's main macroeconomic aggregates, which give a picture of the vigour of economic activity in the country: variation in GDP and its main components (consumption, investment, exports and imports, and so on), inflation, the unemployment rate, and exchange rates. Because the Canadian economy is heavily dependent on international trade, the department also pays close attention to the strength of foreign markets, and especially to the American economy. Finally, the department also analyses certain specific industries, such as those in the natural resources sector (particularly the oil industry), because of their considerable contribution to national revenues.

The Department of Finance establishes its own budgetary estimates. Lately, however, finance ministers have been in the habit of consulting private-sector forecasters (mainly from the banking sector) to help them establish the economic hypotheses that will be used to formulate the budget plan. For the last few years, the federal government has held annual meetings with private- and public-sector economists to discuss their projections. The list of organizations consulted for preparation of the 2015 budget is presented in Table 5.2. The government is under no obligation to follow these projections to the letter. For example, in its 2015 budget the government forecasted slightly weaker economic growth than that anticipated in the private sector. The use of consultations with private forecasters and publication of the results of these consultations mark a significant change in attitude within the Department of Finance. Canadian governments, and in particular departments of finance, seem increasingly inclined to find ways to make the budgetary process more open and transparent. The Canadian provinces are innovating the most in this area. British Columbia and Ontario have adopted legislation that requires their governments to form an advisory economic forecast committee. Although the governments are not obliged to follow their respective committee's revisions to the letter, they must now explain publicly why they have decided, or not, to use the committee's forecast.[5] On the other hand, Canadian governments have not yet followed the example of Great Britain's Office for Budget Responsibility, formed in 2010, which is in charge of preparing the economic and financial estimates that the government must use to prepare its budgets. Notably, the Ontario statute also requires the minister of finance to present "a comprehensive discussion of the risks that, in the Minister's opinion, may have a material impact on the economy or the public sector during the period of the [budgetary] plan" (Fiscal Transparency and Accountability Act, 2004, SO 2004, c. 27, section 5).

Another recent innovation with regard to budgetary estimates is the systematic taking into account of unpredictable events in the budgetary planning exercise. Most Canadian governments now include in their budgetary plan a contingency reserve, the goal of which is to enable the government to deal with unanticipated economic circumstances that might arise during the year. The federal government is not required by law to form such a reserve, although it usually does so. On the other hand, a majority of provinces have passed legislation to force the government to create contingency reserves or reserve funds. Reserve funds are distinguished from contingency reserves by their duration: they are established to enable governments to make up deficits that might arise in coming years and not just for the year underway (only the federal government and the governments of Newfoundland and Labrador, Prince Edward Island, and British Columbia have not adopted such legislation). In recent years, contingency reserves and reserve funds have proved useful in helping Canadian governments to balance their budgets. We should remember that seven provinces, three territories, and the federal government must now comply with balanced-budget laws.

Because budgetary estimates exert such a great influence on public decisions, one might think that the government would try to use the most exact estimates possible. In the past, however, Canadian governments have often deliberately used estimates that overestimate or underestimate those formulated by the private sector or international agencies (the OECD and International Monetary Fund, for example, frequently publish their own economic-growth estimates for Canada). Under the federal Progressive Conservative government in power between 1984 and 1993, budgetary deficits were regularly higher than projected. In contrast, the Liberal government that succeeded it systematically underestimated its budgetary surpluses.[6] How can such systematic errors be explained? They are no doubt the result of a political calculation by elected leaders, at least in part. In the view of certain governments, it is preferable to present the budgetary situation in a favourable light, even if estimates subsequently have to be revised downward. Other governments feel that it is better to alert public opinion to the presence of difficult economic circumstances and reserve the possibility of revising its decisions later. The goal of the actions aimed at improving budgetary estimates (including adoption of laws requiring balanced budgets and increased transparency of the budgetary process) is to correct this situation.[7]

Fiscal Policies and Debt Management

Aside from budgetary estimates, the Department of Finance must also formulate fiscal policies (or taxation policy)—that is, determine where its revenues will come from. The Canadian state collects revenues from numerous sources. It also uses the financial markets to fund some of its activities.

Although taxpayers usually react loudly to changes in tax rates,[8] the actual formulation of fiscal policies has remained relatively sheltered from public debate, at least until recently. In the past, it was felt that fiscal decisions had to be made behind closed doors by a small group of analysts in the Department of Finance so that they would not be influenced by external pressure. Today, governments are showing greater openness, and some agree that fiscal reforms should be debated in the public square. This was the case for adoption of the carbon tax in British Columbia in 2008 and the VAT (or HST) in Prince Edward Island in 2013. Budgetary initiatives regarding taxation that are presented in annual budget plans are increasingly announced and discussed before the budget is tabled. However, it would be inappropriate for the government to formally announce the details of certain tax changes before the budget is presented (e.g., an increase in consumption taxes on certain goods). The content of the budget plan must remain secret until it is presented to Parliament. A leak may force the minister of finance to resign.

Fiscal policies are formulated taking account of two general principles. On the one hand, the government wants to avoid having its fiscal policies create undesirable economic distortions. By taxing certain products or activities more, the government may influence taxpayers' behaviour. High taxation rates, for example, may lead to tax evasion or avoidance.[9] Based on this principle, the federal government has lowered corporate income tax in recent years, arguing that firms can easily transfer their activities elsewhere if tax rates are too high. In contrast, certain fiscal policies may provoke behaviours seen as desirable. A carbon tax, for example, is an instrument of public policy that reduces the production of greenhouse gases and thus protects the environment. The government is turning increasingly to user fees for public goods and services in an effort to change the behaviours of those who use some public programs.

On the other hand, fiscal policies must respect equity principles. Each taxpayer must feel that he or she is paying his or her fair share, in line with his or her resources and needs. There are several forms of taxation equity:

• Horizontal equity: people in similar situations must contribute similarly
• Equity and diversity: people in different situations must contribute differently
• Vertical equity: people with more resources must contribute more
• Procedural equity: taxpayers are all equal before the tax authorities
• Generational equity: future generations must not assume the entire tax burden of the current generations

Most Canadian governments adhere to these general principles.[10] This is manifested mainly in the use of progressive tax rates—that is, tax rates modulated according to income: people with higher incomes contribute more to the state's revenue. The data in Table 5.3 present the distribution of Canadian taxpayers who pay federal income tax, by income category, and those in Table 5.4 present the marginal tax rates in force in Canada. As Table 5.3 shows, 23.1 per cent of total federal revenue from income tax paid by individuals comes from the wealthiest people, who represent only 1.5 per cent of taxpayers. All provinces and territories use a progressive taxation plan, as Table 5.4 shows.[11]

Table 5.3 Federal income tax on individuals, by category of taxable income, 2015

| | Number of taxable returns | | Net federal tax | |
	Number	%	$ Million	%
All taxpayers	17,918,250	100.0	135,226	100.0
Less than $10,000	157,610	0.9	8.5	0.01
$10,000 to 24,999	2,372,220	13.2	1,257	0.9
$25,000 to 49,999	6,773,740	37.8	15,885	11.7
$50,000 to 99,999	6,323,000	35.3	46,594	34.5
$100,000 to 149,999	1,456,330	8.1	23,611	17.5
$150,000 to 249,999	560,180	3.1	16,645	12.3
$250,000 and more	275,170	1.5	31,226	23.1

Source: Canada Revenue Agency, *Preliminary Statistics 2017 Edition* (for the 2015 Tax Year), https://www.canada.ca/en/revenue-agency.html (accessed 27 October 2017).

Aside from taxation, the government may also obtain financial resources by borrowing on the financial markets. Unlike revenues from fiscal policies, loans must eventually be paid back. In addition, an extra cost is incurred: interest charged by the lenders (payment of which is known as servicing the debt). The minister of finance must thus determine in the budget if part of the state's activities will be funded by loans (unless the law bans recourse to borrowing). If so, the budget balance is in deficit. Two main factors explain the presence of deficits. First, the government may judge that increasing taxes would have undesirable effects on the economy. For example, a rise in the sales tax might cause consumers to purchase less, causing economic growth to slow. Second, unforeseen events might cause an unanticipated rise in public spending or an equally unexpected drop in revenues. The government might prefer to borrow instead of modifying the composition of its budget. The use of deficits thus has advantages and disadvantages.[12] The Department of Finance is responsible for assessing the consequences of incurring deficits and determining the government's borrowing level.

In addition to deficits, the government must manage wisely its borrowing programs and its debt, which is the accumulation of past deficits that have not yet been paid back. In general, when a loan comes

Table 5.4 Tax rate by income category, tax on individuals' income, 2017

	1st tax bracket[b]	2nd tax bracket	3rd tax bracket	4th tax bracket	5th tax bracket
Newfoundland and Labrador	8.70	14.50	15.80	17.30	18.30
Prince Edward Island	9.80	13.80	16.70		
Nova Scotia	8.79	14.95	16.67	17.50	21.00
New Brunswick	9.68	14.82	16.52	17.84	20.30
Quebec	16.00	20.00	24.00	25.75	
Ontario	5.05	9.15	11.16	12.16	13.16
Manitoba	10.80	12.75	17.40		
Saskatchewan	11.00	13.00	15.00		
Alberta	10.00	12.00	13.00	14.00	15.00
British Columbia	5.06	7.70	10.50	12.29	14.70
Nunavut	4.00	7.00	9.00	11.50	
Northwest Territories	5.90	8.60	12.20	14.05	
Yukon	6.04	9.68	10.90	12.80	15.00
Federal government[a]	15.00	20.50	26.00	29.00	33.00

Source: Canadian Revenue Agency, *Canadian Income Tax Rates for Individuals – Current and Previous Years*, https://www.canada.ca/en/revenue-agency.html (accessed 27 October 2017).

[a] Quebec taxpayers receive a refundable tax abatement of 16.5% on their federal basic tax.
[b] Tax bracket categories differ among the provinces. For instance, the second tax bracket is applied for annual revenues ranging from $29,590 to $59,180 in Nova Scotia and from $126,625 to $151,950 in Alberta.

to term, the government does not reimburse it but refinances it—that is, borrows again. It is easier to refinance loans if the financial markets judge that the state's financial health is solid. Governments are therefore concerned with obtaining favourable assessments by financial rating agencies (e.g., Moody's, Standard & Poor's, Dominion Bond Rating Service), which examine the government's capacity to repay.[13] The objective is to find secure sources of funding at the lowest possible interest rates. The Financial Administration Act grants the minister of finance the authority to formulate the government's strategy

Figure 5.3 Proportion of the debt contracted on markets by G7 countries that is held by non-residents

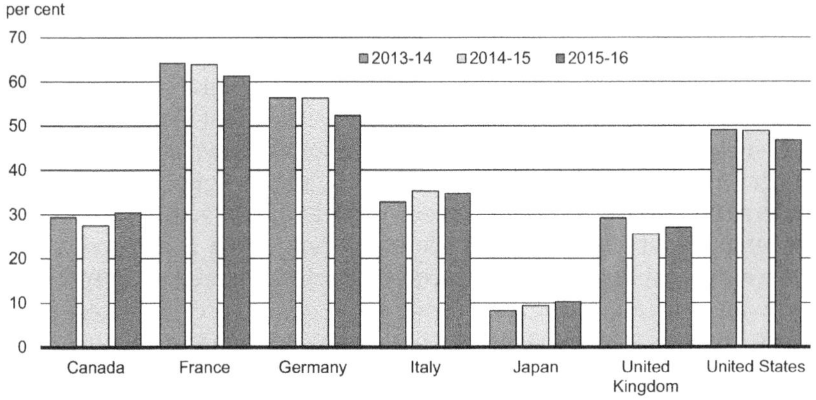

Source: Department of Finance (Canada), Debt Management Report, 2015-2016 (Ottawa: Her Majesty the Queen in Right of Canada, 2016). Reproduced with the permission of the Department of Finance, 2018, https://www.fin.gc.ca/dtman/2015-2016/dmr-rgd1601-eng.asp.

with regard to managing the debt. At the federal level, the strategy is designed in close collaboration with the Bank of Canada, the "financial right arm of the government," which advises the federal government and executes financial operations on its behalf (but not for the provinces and territories, which have their own debt-management mechanisms). The main sources of government financing are bonds (securities issued by the government that usually pay interest to those holding them; these securities are negotiable, which means that they may be traded on financial markets), savings bonds (bonds reserved for Canadians, non-negotiable), Treasury bills (securities with very short terms), and Canada bills (similar to Treasury bills but issued on American markets). About 30 per cent of the federal government's debt is held by foreigners, which is comparable to the situations of Italy and the United Kingdom, but higher than Japan, as Figure 5.3 shows. Despite the 2008 financial crisis and the ensuing growth in public indebtedness, the federal government has been able to maintain its borrowing capacity at a low interest rate. In 2015, the effective interest rate on its debt contracted on financial markets was 2.0 per cent, compared to 3.2 per cent in 2008 (and 10.7 per cent in 1990).[14]

Macroeconomic Policies

In addition to formulating the government's fiscal framework, the Department of Finance is responsible for ensuring that the Canadian (or provincial or territorial) economy runs smoothly. There is no consensus on the role of the state as an economic agent, and governments with different ideologies may have divergent views on the nature of the government's interventions in the economy (right-wing parties generally have a clear preference for a reduced state role compared to centrist and left-wing parties). However, despite these divergences, it is generally agreed that the state must intervene from time to time to regulate certain economic activities. The Department of Finance sets the general orientations of public intervention, and the Bank of Canada implements policies required to attain the government's objectives. It is normally accepted that the Bank of Canada's decisions must not be influenced by political pressure. The minister of finance and the governor of the central bank regularly discuss common strategies to institute. The minister of finance is the hierarchical superior of the governor: the former appoints the latter, and if there is disagreement with regard to the general orientation of monetary policy, the minister's opinion prevails. However, the minister does not intervene in the everyday management of the bank's activities, and the Bank of Canada independently sets its key interest rates.[15]

Since 1991, the federal government has emphasized inflation control. This position is based on the hypothesis that knowledgeable prediction of variations in future prices creates a stable economic environment propitious to economic growth. The federal government and the Bank of Canada have therefore agreed that the annual inflation rate should be 2 per cent. The Bank of Canada uses its key interest rate (the rate that Canadian banks must follow[16]) to hit this target. Since 1991, all elected governments have committed to respecting this target.[17]

The priority given to controlling inflation has relegated other considerations to the background. For instance, the Canadian government adopted a policy of floating exchange rate (market forces determine the rate) and set no precise parity target with other currencies for the Canadian dollar. The last time the central bank intervened to influence the evolution in the value of the Canadian dollar was 1998. Since then, the bank has acted occasionally to correct sudden, large variations on the exchange rate that were felt to be short term, but no more than that. The bank has liquidity reserves equal to at least 3 per cent of the Canadian GDP to be used for intervention on the exchange market.

Nor does the government have employment targets. Although it follows the employment situation closely, the government generally intervenes only if the country's economic situation deteriorates considerably. Some governments are more inclined to adopt budget actions targeting job creation (notably by offering grants or tax credits for job creation and research and development and by creating labour training programs).[18] On the other hand, more sustained and targeted public interventions take place if the economic situation worsens. These interventions are inspired by Keynesian economics, which calls for the state to step in when the private sector is not able to relaunch the economy and create jobs. During the financial crisis of 2008, all Canadian governments, without exception, set up major economic-recovery programs funded by public deficits. Although initially opposed to such an intervention, the conservative federal government adopted a recovery plan based on infrastructure spending (construction or renovation of public works and structures, such as bridges, roads, and buildings).[19] The recovery plan ended up costing $62 billion, increasing the public deficit by the same amount.

FEATURE BOX: ARE BUDGETS FAIR? AN OVERVIEW OF GENDER-SENSITIVE BUDGETS

Governments try to formulate budget policies that are fair. To date, the search for equity has taken account of only one factor: the income of taxpayers. Thus, all citizens with comparable incomes must be treated similarly, and wealthier citizens must contribute more to funding state activities.

In recent years, a second criterion for equity has begun to be discussed and analysed by budgetary policy analysts: gender. This reflection is based on the observation that governments' budgetary policies have different repercussions for men and for women, because of their respective responsibilities and needs. For instance, tax credits for workers and contributions to social security plans (such as pension funds) do not take account of the fact that many women leave the labour market for a number of years to take care of family members. These women receive fewer benefits from the state than do men who have been active on the labour market for longer.

This situation has led a number of people to state that government budgets are not neutral; rather, they are "blind" to women's condition. To better understand the repercussions of budgetary policies, it has been suggested that governments compare the effects of their policies on men and on women. Gender-sensitive budgets try not to impose similar policies on both groups, but to inform the population of the differences that exist between the two sexes.

The presentation of gender-sensitive budgets is an initiative that received the support of the United Nations in its 1995 Declaration. According to the UN, sixty countries implemented gender-sensitive budget measures in 2010. Australia is a pioneer in the area, having adopted its Women's Budget Program in 1984.

Governments in Canada (both federal and provincial) have not yet manifested serious interest in presenting gender-sensitive budgets. The Standing Committee on the Status of Women of the House of Commons looked at the question in 2008. It recommended that the government set up and fund an advisory group that would be responsible for implementing a gender-sensitive budget. The government has not yet followed up on the committee's recommendations. It should be noted, however, that for the first time the federal government presented "A Gender Statement" in its 2017 budget plan; the statement provides and contrasts some macro-level data on women and men for some socio-economic indicators (education, wages, poverty, and so on). The federal government has also indicated that it would adopt further initiatives in the coming years.

> *Sources*: Clara Morgan, *Gender Budgets—An Overview* (Ottawa: Parliament of Canada, Political and Social Affairs Division, 2007); Laura Munn-Rivard, *Gender-Sensitive Parliaments: 2. The Work of Legislators* (Ottawa: Library of Parliament, 2012).

KEYWORDS

Department of Finance • *Minister of finance* • *Canada Revenue Agency* • *Budget estimates* • *Taxation* • *Macroeconomic policies* • *Bank of Canada*

TO FIND OUT MORE

Reading suggestions

Hale, Geoffrey. *The Politics of Taxation in Canada*. Peterborough: Broadview, 2002.

Larson, Marc, and Étienne Lessard. "Developing a Medium-Term Debt-Management Strategy for the Government of Canada." *Bank of Canada Review* (Summer 2011): 43–50.

Organisation for Economic Co-operation and Development. *Recent Tax Policy Trends and Reforms in OECD Countries*. Paris: OECD, 2004.

Testimony of the Right Honorable Paul Martin. *Public Hearings*, vol. 73, Commission of Inquiry into the Sponsorship Program and Advertising Activities, 10 February 2005.

Database

Economic Accounts (Statistics Canada): https://www.statcan.gc.ca/eng/subjects/economic_accounts

Websites

Bank of Canada: http://www.bankofcanada.ca
Canadian Revenue Agency: https://www.canada.ca/en/revenue-agency.html
Department of Finance (Canada): http://www.fin.gc.ca/fin-eng.asp
Department of Finance (Newfoundland and Labrador): http://www.fin.gov.nl.ca/fin/
Department of Finance (Prince Edward Island): http://www.gov.pe.ca/finance/index.php3

Department of Finance and Treasury Board (Nova Scotia): http://www.novascotia.ca/finance/en/home/default.aspx

Department of Finance (New Brunswick): http://www2.gnb.ca/content/gnb/en/departments/finance.html

Ministère des Finances (Québec): http://www.finances.gouv.qc.ca/index_en.asp

Ministry of Finance (Ontario): https://www.ontario.ca/page/ministry-finance

Department of Finance (Manitoba): http://www.gov.mb.ca/finance/index.html

Ministry of Finance (Saskatchewan): http://www.saskatchewan.ca/government/government-structure/ministries/finance

Ministry of Treasury Board and Finance (Alberta): http://www.finance.alberta.ca/index.html

Ministry of Finance (British Columbia): http://www2.gov.bc.ca/gov/content/governments/organizational-structure/ministries-organizations/ministries/finance

Department of Finance (Nunavut): http://www.gov.nu.ca/finance

Department of Finance (Northwest Territories): http://www.fin.gov.nt.ca

Department of Finance (Yukon): http://www.finance.gov.yk.ca/index.html

PART 3

The Budget Vote

6 Parliamentary Rules

The roles played and powers exercised by Canadian legislators in the budgetary process are the result of the evolution of parliamentary practices used in Canada and other countries over centuries. Some authors trace the origins of modern parliamentarianism to the adoption in 1215 of the Magna Carta, an agreement that limited the British Crown's spending power.[1] Because Canada was a British colony, it is not surprising that many of its political institutions follow the Anglo-Saxon model. In fact, the political institutions in Canada and the United Kingdom are similar, though not identical.

The influence of British parliamentary principles on Canadian parliamentary rules and institutions is undeniable; in fact, the preamble to the Canadian Constitution states that Canadian constitutional rules "are similar in Principle to that of the United Kingdom."[2] Some of these rules are clearly stated in the Constituton Act, 1867. Others are conventions that have been codified in the regulations of the House of Commons and the Senate and in ordinary laws, including the Parliament Act. Provincial legislatures have adopted analogous rules and conventions originating in the British tradition (including the National Assembly of Quebec, despite the influence of French law in certain areas under the authority of the provincial government).[3] Therefore, the various legislatures in Canada operate in a relatively similar way.

The principles underlying Canadian parliamentary rules and institutions have changed little since Confederation.[4] Even the 1982 constitutional reform did not modify Canadian parliamentary procedure, although the regulations and statutes have been amended a number of times to ensure better application of the constitutional principles, notably by strengthening the capacity of parliamentarians to examine the government's budget policies. At the federal level, the Canadian Parliament adopted a major reform granting parliamentary commit- tees more responsibilities in 1968 (most provinces and territories would eventually initiate similar reforms to their committee system). Other important reforms have been instituted since. For instance, the Stand- ing Committee on Finance of the House of Commons was given respon- sibility to undertake annual prebudget consultations in 1994 (similar consultations also exist in Ontario and British Columbia); the content of financial reports submitted to Parliament was profoundly altered in 1996 to improve the quality of the budgetary information presented; the Standing Committee on Government Operations and Estimates was established in 2002; and the position of Parliamentary Budget Offi- cer was created in 2006 (a similar position, the Financial Accountability Officer, was established in Ontario in 2013). Today, a number of voices are being raised to demand further changes to the parliamentary rules, and it is not impossible that such changes will take place fairly quickly.[5] This phenomenon is not unique to Canada; more and more observers are urging that the legislative branch be given a larger role in the bud- getary process.[6]

Constitutional Budgetary Principles

Five general constitutional principles form the framework for the Cana- dian parliamentary budgetary procedure, for both the federal govern- ment and the provincial and territorial governments:[7]

- The need for the government to obtain the authorization of Parliament to incur expenses or levy taxes
- The government's exclusive power to initiate the budget process
- In-depth parliamentary assessment of all legislative measures requiring an expenditure or a tax
- The precedence of the House of Commons over the Senate in Parliament (only for the federal government)
- The universality of budgets

The constitutional rules clearly set out the respective responsi- bilities of the executive branch (the government) and the legislative branch (Parliament). The first three principles establish that only the government has the authority to formulate the government's budget- ary policy. However, the budgetary policy must be assessed and then assented to by the legislature before it is implemented.[8] In other words, Parliament's role consists of examining, debating, and criticizing—but not crafting—the government's budgetary policy. As a well-informed observer of Canadian parliamentarianism reminded members of Parliament in his comments on a study of the parliamentary budget process, "Parliament holds the government accountable; it does not govern."[9] The fourth principle gives precedence to the elected representatives in the Canadian Parliament. The senators, recall, are not elected, and they should therefore play a smaller role in examining the budgetary policy. Finally, the fifth policy, universality of budgets, requires the constitution of a single money fund, the Consolidated Fund. All revenues collected must be deposited in the Consolidated Fund and all expenses must be paid from it. As a consequence, it is not possible to allocate a specific source of revenue to a particular expenditure (principle of non-allocation of revenues) or to record financial transactions on a net basis, for example by presenting only the budget balance rather than gross expenditure and revenue amounts (principle of non-contraction). The principle of universality reinforces parliamentarians' oversight capacity by allowing them to examine the government's budget measures as a function of the general interest and not particular interests, and to have exhaustive budgetary data available to them.

These fundamental principles have led to the establishment of a precise parliamentary procedure for adoption of the government's budget measures. For instance, only parliamentarians who are Cabinet members (ministers) have the authority to present bills that contain financial provisions (or finance bills[10]) in Parliament. Furthermore, in the Canadian Parliament all bills with a financial impact must be submitted to the House of Commons before being examined by the Senate, and only parliamentarians participate in the debates that follow the government's tabling of the budget and can authorize the government to raise the funds necessary to implement its budget plan. Finally, all votes on budget measures (tabling of the budget, raising of income or other taxes, bills requiring the use of financial resources) constitute votes of confidence. Rejection of a financial initiative triggers the resignation of the executive.

The government must obtain the assent of parliamentarians to implement its budget plan. In the Canadian parliamentary system, there are four categories of assent, each governed by a distinct procedure. The first category concerns budget requests presented with *appropriation bills* (or *supply bills*[11]). At the beginning of the budget year, the government asks Parliament to give it authorization to spend funds drawn from the public purse for the entire fiscal year. These requests enable the government to fund the current activities of the public administration. The budgetary requests of the federal government are examined and approved by both chambers of Parliament. The second category of assent is related to revenues. Any increase of public revenue through taxation must be authorized by Parliament via the business of *ways and means*. The government's revenues do not have to be approved every year; only initiatives that impose a new tax or increase an existing one must be presented to the legislature. In the Canadian Parliament, only members of the House of Commons assent to ways and means requests. The third category concerns the adoption of the general orientations of the government's budgetary policy. These orientations are presented in the minister of finance's *budget speech*. The parliamentarians then debate and adopt the speech. Senators do not participate in this activity. Finally, the fourth category of approval applies to ordinary bills that create new financial responsibilities for the government (some of these bills are called *budget implementation bills*). These bills create new programs with confirmed funding for a number of years. There is therefore no need to authorize these programs every year. In Ottawa, the House of Commons and the Senate assent to these bills.

The distinction between appropriation and ways and means procedures is the outcome of a long series of events in the evolution of British parliamentarianism. Historically, Parliament assented only to funding requests submitted by the Crown (the monarch). Over time, parliamentarians were granted supplementary power to authorize government expenditures. The process of distinguishing between appropriation and ways and means followed the creation of the Consolidated Fund. The very fact that the fund exists establishes the principle of non-allocation of revenues. This means that an expense cannot be financed from a specific source of revenue. Ways and means requests serve to fill the Consolidated Fund, and appropriation bills ask for authorization to use the fund's financial resources.

The central activity of parliamentarians in terms of accountability is to examine in detail the government's financial initiatives. Over time, this activity has become difficult to carry out due to the growing complexity of government programs and their budgetary issues and to the growing centralization in the decision-making process in the government apparatus. This situation is not unique to Canada. Recent reforms have tried to correct this problem by granting more means to legislators to exercise their oversight function (resources, responsibility, expertise). In particular, these reforms have sought to give more responsibility to parliamentary committees. Parliamentarians on these committees have an opportunity to develop their budgetary expertise with respect to specific issues. Since the 1968 reforms, the federal committees have had the task of examining in detail the budgets of departments and agencies placed under their aegis.[12] Legislators may also have access to the expertise of agents of Parliament, notably the Auditor General, as well as the Parliamentary Budget Officer on the federal level and the Financial Accountability Officer in Ontario. Finally, a number of financial reports must now be tabled in Parliament by the government in order to give detailed explanations of its budgetary policies and the activities that they fund. Although these reforms are welcome, many—including parliamentarians—view them as incomplete.[13] Some Canadian governments (the federal government and several provincial and territorial governments) still seem to be reluctant to devote more resources to legislators for accountability.

The Parliamentary Rules Resulting from Constitutional Principles

The constitutional principles that frame the budgetary procedure have given rise to the institution of a series of supplementary parliamentary rules meant to define lawmakers' constitutional responsibilities. Unlike constitutional principles, parliamentary rules may be amended relatively frequently. The current rules are the result of a number of reforms made since the beginnings of Confederation. These rules are still examined and discussed, and some were recently modified; it is not impossible that other rules will be modified in the near future. However, these changes are not intended to challenge constitutional principles.

The Canadian parliamentary rules (federal, provincial, and territorial) involve the following aspects:

• Annuality of budgets
• Budgetary unity
• Scope of budgetary appropriations
• Controls over budget implementation

These rules are spelled out in the Financial Administration Act (and similar provincial and territorial statutes).

Annuality of Budgets. The objective of annualizing budgets is to force governments to periodically submit a budget to legislators. Without this rule, the government would not be required to regularly obtain the assent of the legislature for implementation of its budget policy, nor would budget actions be examined periodically. This periodicity is annual—that is, examination and assent apply to budgets for a single year.

Although the annuality rule has advantages, it also has disadvantages. Its main flaw is its weak capacity to address budgetary issues, the effects of which last several years. Lawmakers must frequently examine budget actions without knowing if they are financially viable over the medium or long term (questions of financial viability are particularly important in the areas of health care and pension policy as the population ages), and parliamentary rules rarely allow debates on or analyses of these questions. However, there have been certain innovations in recent years. For instance, Canadian governments more frequently publish multi-year budget reports, which provide data on the projected activities of the government and its departments and agencies, usually for the following two or three years. The Ontario legislation is very restrictive in this respect. Figure 6.1 shows the legal provisions with which the government must comply. The statute requires the government to present a report on the government's financial viability covering a twenty-year period. Ontario is the only province that holds its government to such a requirement. On the federal level, the Parliamentary Budget Officer publishes a report on the financial viability of the Canadian public sector every year. In fact, the Auditor General of Canada has strongly recommended to the federal government that the Office of the Auditor General prepare such a report every year,[14] and the minister of finance complied, in part, in 2012.[15]

Budgetary Unity. The budgetary unity rule came into effect at the same time as the annuality rule. For lawmakers to have a robust capacity to analyse budgets, they must have access to complete, uniform, and definitive budgetary information. The government must therefore present exhaustive budget reports that contain all expenditures, revenues, and borrowings. In addition, the information presented in the different documents must be prepared according to identical rules. Finally, budget documents must not be subject to later modifications, which might lead to undue manipulation. The objective of these criteria is to increase the transparency of governments' budgetary activities.

Figure 6.1 Ontario legislation regarding publication of multi-year budget reports

---

Fiscal Transparency and Accountability Act, 2004

S.O. 2004, CHAPTER 27

[Excerpts]

Information for the Public

Multi-year fiscal plan

5 (1) Each year, the Minister shall release a multi-year fiscal plan in the Budget papers that are laid before the Assembly.

Period of the plan

(2) The fiscal plan must address the fiscal year of the Budget and the following two years, and it may address a longer period.

Contents

(3) The fiscal plan must include the following information:
1. Ontario's fiscal policy objectives for the period of the plan.
2. The macroeconomic forecasts and assumptions used to prepare the Budget and the plan and a description of any significant differences from the forecasts and assumptions used to prepare the previous Budget and plan.
3. An estimate of Ontario's revenues and expenses for the period of the plan, including estimates of the major components of the revenues and expenses.
4. Details of the reserve described in subsection (4).
5. A comprehensive discussion of the risks that, in the Minister's opinion, may have a material impact on the economy or the public sector during the period of the plan.
6. A description of the intended effects of the plan on the province.
7. Information about the ratio of provincial debt to Ontario's gross domestic product.
8. If a deficit is anticipated, the details of the recovery plan required by subsection 4 (3).

[...]

Long-range assessment of the fiscal environment

9 (1) Within two years after each provincial election, the Minister shall release a long-range assessment of Ontario's fiscal environment.

Content

(2) The long-range assessment must include the following information:
1. A description of anticipated changes in the economy and in population demographics during the following 20 years.
2. A description of the potential impact of these changes on the public sector and on Ontario's fiscal policy during that period.
3. An analysis of key issues of fiscal policy that, in the Minister's opinion, are likely to affect the long-term sustainability of the economy and of the public sector.

Source: https://www.ontario.ca/laws/statute/04f27

Although these rules seem relatively simple, their application is not completely satisfactory, even in the opinion of parliamentarians.[16] For example, parliamentary procedure does not require the government to present to Parliament the state of its tax expenditures (i.e., revenues uncollected due to tax exemptions).[17] Because the use of such expenditures has burgeoned in recent years, it would be appropriate for them to be examined by MPs.[18] There have also been discussions regarding the accounting rules used in the public sector. Whereas the government uses accrual accounting to prepare its own financial statements and the Public Accounts submitted to Parliament, the budgetary estimates present budget information according to the principles of cash basis of accounting. These two methods record financial information by different criteria (see the feature box at the end of this chapter). It would therefore be a good idea to standardize the methods so that costs and revenues associated with public programs can be more easily comprehended.

Scope of Budgetary Appropriations. The Canadian Constitution requires the government to ask Parliament for spending authorization. The statutes and regulations adopted subsequently by lawmakers were aimed mainly at forcing the government to give a detailed justification for its requests. As a result, use of budgetary appropriations is governed by the following rules:

- Allocation of funds (earmarking): appropriations must be assigned to specific items of expenditure (for a given program or service); each appropriation requested must indicate the amount and its use
- Exclusivity of appropriations: appropriations are not transferable from one item to another
- The limited nature of appropriations: appropriations indicate the maximum amount that the government is authorized to spend
- The optional nature of appropriations: the government is not obliged to use a budgetary appropriation in whole or in part
- The cancellation of unused appropriations: the appropriations unused at the end of the fiscal year disappear

Recently, the rule of cancellation of unused appropriations has been made somewhat more flexible in order to enable the federal government to request that certain unused appropriations, up to 5 per cent of a department's or agency's operating budget, be transferred to the following fiscal year. This provision was adopted to discourage managers from spending their entire budget at the end of the year. However, these transfers must be authorized by the Treasury Board.

Controls over budget implementation. Rules were also established to enable lawmakers to ensure that the budgetary authorizations they grant to the government are respected. This parliamentary control arises during analysis of the government's Public Accounts. The purpose of the Public Accounts is to present all of the government's budgetary and financial activities for one year. The Public Accounts are submitted to Parliament once the financial year has ended; they are audited by the Office of the Auditor General, which issues a notice of compliance of the government's financial transactions with the authorizations granted. Once submitted, the Public Accounts are automatically sent to the Public Accounts Committee of the legislative assembly to be examined. After the committee completes its analysis, it reports its results to the House.

Parliamentary Control Rules in Other Countries

In all democratic regimes, governments are obliged to present their budgetary policies to the legislators, who have the authority to publicly debate budgetary issues and adopt the government's initiatives. However, lawmakers do not have the same influence in every regime. In some countries, they may participate actively in formulation of the budget policy—that is, propose their own budgetary initiatives to the government. This mechanism acts as a counterweight to executive power (this is the case in the United States and most presidential regimes in the Americas) or as a means to establish a budgetary policy intended to be consensual (as it does in the Nordic countries—Sweden, Denmark, Norway, and Finland). In most countries, however, the legislative branch plays a much more limited role. In some cases, lawmakers may influence the government's budgetary policy by amending its proposals (this is the case in most European countries and in Japan). In other countries, lawmakers' influence is exerted through accountability. They must assent (or not) to the government's budgetary policy as presented, without possibility of amendments (except marginal ones). But their assent is crucial: rejection of the budget causes the government to fall. This is the case in the United Kingdom and in most countries with rules descended from the British tradition, including Canada.

It is generally considered that parliamentary systems in the British tradition grant fewer powers to lawmakers than do other democratic parliamentary systems (notably presidential regimes). To better understand the effect of parliamentary business on budgetary policy in Canada, it is useful to draw comparisons with other countries. The OECD has conducted a number of studies in recent years that examine the role

Table 6.1 The role of Parliament in the budgetary process: Legal constraints

Are there any restrictions on the right of the legislature to modify the budget proposed by the government?

	No	Can only approve or reject the budget in whole	Can only decrease funding levels	May reallocate or increase spending yet without changing total deficit/surplus
Australia		X		
Belgium	X			
Brazil				X
Canada			X	
France			X	
Germany	X			
Japan			X	
Mexico				X
South Africa		X		
Sweden	X			
United Kingdom			X	
United States	X			

Sources: Organisation for Economic Co-operation and Development, "The OECD Budgeting Database," *OECD Journal on Budgeting* 1, no. 3 (2002): 155–71, and *International Budget Practices and Procedures Database*, http://www.oecd.org/gov/budgeting/internationalbudgetpracticesandproceduresdatabase.htm (accessed 27 October 2017).

of parliaments in various countries. These studies have addressed the following themes:

• The capacity of lawmakers to change the budget
• The impact of lawmakers' vote on keeping the government in power
• The respective roles of the parliament's upper and lower chambers
• The respective roles of parliamentary committees (or parliamentary commissions)

Tables 6.1 to 6.4 present the characteristics of certain rules for a selection of countries. With the exception of the vote of confidence rule

Table 6.2 The role of Parliament in the budgetary process: The vote of confidence

	No	Yes
Is a vote on the budget considered a vote of confidence in the government?		
Australia		X
Belgium		X
Brazil	X	
Canada		X
France	X	
Germany	X	
Japan	X	
Mexico	X	
South Africa	X	
Sweden	X	
United Kingdom		X
United States	X	

Source: see sources, Table 6.1.

Table 6.3 The role of Parliament in the budgetary process: The role of the chambers

	Upper house has no role	Lower house can override any vote of upper house	Both houses enjoy similar stature	Additional rules
What is the respective role of each house of the legislature in approving the budget?				
Australia			X	The upper house can only approve or reject the entire budget
Belgium	X			
Brazil			X	
Canada			X	Upper house may not introduce expenditure or taxation measures

(*Continued*)

Table 6.3 (Continued)

	What is the respective role of each house of the legislature in approving the budget?			
	Upper house has no role	Lower house can override any vote of upper house	Both houses enjoy similar stature	Additional rules
France		X		
Germany		X		
Japan		X		
Mexico		X		The upper house must approve tax measures; has no direct role in approving expenditures
South Africa		X		
Sweden	n/a			There is no upper house
United Kingdom		X		
United States			X	Tax legislation must originate in the lower house, but can be amended by both houses

Source: See sources, Table 6.1.

(Table 6.2), which is more or less exclusive to countries in the British parliamentary tradition, there are a variety of parliamentary roles and attributes in various democratic regimes.

This diversity was corroborated in a study that measured the capacity of lawmakers to influence budget decisions using an index based on two general dimensions: (1) the powers granted to lawmakers to participate in formulating budgetary policies; and (2) the organizational structures and resources available to lawmakers to examine the government's initiatives.[19] This index ranges from 0 = no capacity to 100 = full capacity. Unsurprisingly, Canada, like other countries with a British parliamentary tradition, is at the bottom of the scale, with a

Table 6.4 The role of Parliament in the budgetary process: The role of commissions

What best describes the committee structure for dealing with the budget?		
A single budget committee deals with all budget-related matters	A single budget committee deals with budget aggregates	No budget committee in place
Sectoral committees may make recommendations, but budget committee does not have to follow them	Sectoral committees deal with appropriations for each respective sector	Sectoral committees deal with appropriations for each respective sector
Australia			X
Belgium*			
Brazil		X	
Canada		X	
France	X		
Germany	X		
Japan	X		
Mexico	X		
South Africa		X	
Sweden		X	
United Kingdom		X	
United States		X	

Sources: See sources, Table 6.1, and Information Services Section, Research Unit (South Africa), *Budget Analysis Manual* (Cape Town: Parliament of the Republic of South Africa, 2011).

Note: *Data for Belgium not available.

score of 25.[20] In contrast, lawmakers in the United States and the Scandinavian countries are able to exert a strong influence (with a score of 89 for the United States and above 55 for Scandinavian countries[21]). Although parliamentary systems in the Anglo-Saxon tradition are similar, there are nevertheless certain significant differences with regard to the source of their influence. For example, Canada offers greater organizational capacity to its lawmakers (in terms of time, responsibility of committees, and financial data) than do New Zealand, Ireland, and Australia, and is similar to the United Kingdom in this respect. In fact, on this dimension, Canada is rated higher than a number of other countries.

FEATURE BOX: ACCRUAL ACCOUNTING OR CASH BASIS OF ACCOUNTING?

Financial transactions are usually recorded in budget documents by one of two methods: cash basis of accounting or accrual accounting. Cash basis of accounting records transactions when payments are made and revenues collected—that is, when cash actually changes hands—whereas accrual accounting records transactions when the goods or services purchased are consumed and the revenues are generated—that is, when expenses and revenues are incurred. For instance, income tax is recorded when it is paid into the public purse under cash basis of accounting and when the tax is due under accrual accounting.

In the past, public budget documents presented financial transactions under the cash basis of accounting. Today, however, most Canadian governments use both methods. In the federal public sector, budget estimates presented to Parliament use the cash basis of accounting, whereas the government's internal accounting rules, used mainly to prepare end-of-year financial reports, including the Public Accounts, use accrual accounting. The use of two different accounting methods is problematic, as the financial results may diverge widely. This is the case for acquisition of assets—goods or services with a lifespan of longer than one year. Under the cash basis of accounting, the full purchase value of an asset is recorded in the year in which it was acquired (and paid for), whereas under accrual accounting, only a portion of the total value, corresponding to the depreciation of the asset, is recorded in the financial statements for each year of its lifespan.

In recent years, a number of public management experts (including the Auditor General of Canada and OECD analysts) have tried to encourage public administrations to use only accrual accounting. This method would present a more accurate portrait of the state of the public finances, notably with regard to the government's future obligations, and would therefore permit better long-term planning of budgetary resources. Not everyone shares this opinion, however. Some note that under accrual accounting, financial data are more easily manipulated (even falsified) and subject to the uncertainty of forecasting errors (what is the lifespan of an asset? what is its depreciation rate? how can adjustments be performed? and so on). In addition, financial results prepared using the cash basis of accounting are simpler to understand. This is a not-insignificant fact given that non-experts must analyse the government's financial statements. The question is still under consideration in Canada.

Source: Standing Committee on Government Operations and Estimates (Canada), *Strengthening Parliamentary Scrutiny of Estimates and Supply*, 41st Parliament, 1st session (Ottawa: Parliament of Canada, 2012).

KEYWORDS

Constitutional parliamentary principles • *Parliamentary examination* • *Appropriations procedures* • *Ways and means procedures* • *Consolidated Fund* • *Annuality of budgets*

TO FIND OUT MORE

Reading suggestions

McGee, David G. *The Budget Process: A Parliamentary Imperative*. London: Commonwealth Parliamentary Association with Pluto Press, 2007.

Standing Committee on Government Operations and Estimates (Canada). *Strengthening Parliamentary Scrutiny of Estimates and Supply.* 41st Parliament, 1st session. Ottawa: Parliament of Canada, 2012.
Wehner, Joachim. *Legislatures and the Budget Process: The Myth of Fiscal Control.* New York: Palgrave Macmillan, 2010.

Periodicals

Canadian Parliamentary Review: http://www.revparl.ca/english/index. asp?param=231

Database

Legis-info (Parliament of Canada): http://www.parl.ca/LegisInfo/Home. aspx?ParliamentSession=41-2&Language=E (provides information on all legislation before Parliament)

Websites

Parliament of Canada: http://www.parl.gc.ca/Default.aspx?Language=E
House of Assembly of Newfoundland and Labrador: http://www.assembly. nl.ca/
Legislative Assembly of Prince Edward Island: https://www. princeedwardisland.ca/en/information/legislative-assembly-prince- edward-island
Nova Scotia House of Assembly: https://nslegislature.ca/about
Legislative Assembly of New Brunswick: http://www.gnb.ca/legis/ index-e.asp
Assemblée nationale du Québec: http://www.assnat.qc.ca/en/index.html
Legislative Assembly of Ontario: https://www.ola.org/en/node/3771
Legislative Assembly of Manitoba: http://www.gov.mb.ca/legislature/index. html
Legislative Assembly of Saskatchewan: http://www.legassembly.sk.ca
Legislative Assembly of Alberta: https://www.assembly.ab.ca/
Legislative Assembly of British Columbia: https://www.leg.bc.ca/
Legislative Assembly of Nunavut: http://www.assembly.nu.ca
Legislative Assembly of the Northwest Territories: http://www.assembly. gov.nt.ca
Yukon Legislative Assembly://www.legassembly.gov.yk.ca/index.html

7 The Parliamentary Calendar

Parliamentarians' work on budget questions follows a procedure well established through House regulations and, secondarily, regulations of the Senate, which, as we have seen, plays an incidental role in the federal government's financial procedure.[1] Certain aspects of the procedure are also regulated by ordinary laws (notably, the federal Act of Parliament, the Public Administration Act, the Auditor General Act, and the corresponding provincial statutes). In some cases, parliamentarians must respect specific deadlines. For instance, federal members of Parliament (MPs) must report on the results of their examination of the budgetary appropriations by 31 May. In other cases, the government and lawmakers have more flexibility. For example, federal pre-budget consultations may begin when the House deems appropriate.[2] It should be noted that the Canadian budgetary calendar is not as rigid as that in other countries (the United States, for example). Figure 7.1 shows the main phases of the federal government's parliamentary budgetary calendar. The provinces and territories follow a similar cycle, but the deadline dates may differ. For clarity of presentation, this chapter will focus on the federal parliamentary process, as an illustration of the various rules in force in Canada. Particular provincial or territorial rules will be presented when useful.

Parliamentary activities are organized around the documents submitted to the attention of legislators. Most of these documents are presented by the government. The budgetary process is a continuous cycle, and activities related to a given budget year in fact take place over a longer period. As Figure 7.1 shows, the budgetary cycles for different years overlap. For instance, in winter, Parliament examines the government's general budgetary orientations for the next year, when

Figure 7.1 The parliamentary calendar for the Canadian federal government's budgetary cycle

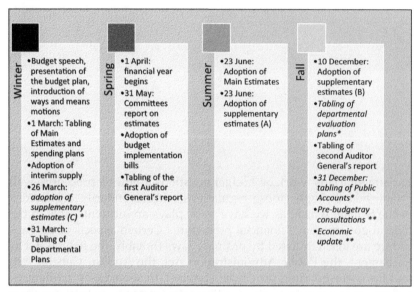

Note: * the activity concerns the budget tabled the previous year; ** the activity concerns the budget that will be table the next year.

the minister of finance gives his or her budget speech, at the same time as they approve the final budgetary appropriations for the fiscal year that is ending, when the Supplementary Estimates (C) are adopted.

Parliamentary work is concentrated around four main activities:

- Analysis of the government's budgetary directions
- Analysis of budgetary appropriations
- Analysis of the Public Accounts and the Auditor General's reports
- Analysis of outside budget requests

Each of these activities has a specific purpose.

Analysis of the Government's Budgetary Orientations

The presentation of the budget is, of all of the government's budgetary activities (not to mention all parliamentary activities), certainly the event the most heavily covered by the media. Presentation begins with the budget speech and continues with the introduction of a number of bills related to the budget.

The Budget Speech

Each parliamentary session begins with a speech from the throne given by the government to the legislature. The speech announces to parliamentarians, and the population at large, the initiatives that the government wishes to submit for parliamentary assent during the session. The government is not, however, bound to implement all the measures presented in its throne speech. The budget speech plays the same role as the throne speech, but concentrates solely on budgetary initiatives. Unlike the throne speech, which must be made at the beginning of a legislative session, the budget speech does not have to be presented on a specific date.[3] In fact, no rule obliges it to be made before 1 April, the first day of the fiscal year. However, Canadian governments are more and more inclined to present their budget several weeks before the fiscal year begins. The goal is to make the public-sector budget cycle more predictable. The federal government usually presents its budget in February. Some provincial governments have adopted stricter parliamentary rules in recent years. The British Columbia government is required to present its budget on the third Thursday of February; the Manitoba government must do so by 30 April. Most provinces prefer to wait until the federal government tables its budget before submitting their budgets to their respective legislative assemblies so that they can take into account the federal government's intentions with regard to transfer payments.

The government may also present an economic statement later in the year if deemed appropriate. This statement (or mini-budget) enables it to present new fiscal initiatives if necessary, especially if economic circumstances have changed since the budget speech. The budget statement must not be confused with an economic update, which occurs at the end of the fiscal year and is intended to summarize the government's economic, financial, and budgetary situation. The update informs parliamentarians of the progress made in implementing budgetary policies and underpins the work related to preparation of the next budget (notably via prebudget consultations). Economic updates are not obligatory in all legislatures, but they are becoming more and more frequent.

The budget speech is given by the minister of finance to the House of Commons.[4] The speech usually indicates that more specific legislative measures will be presented to parliament:

> Mr. Speaker, I rise before this House today to table the budget documents for 2015, including notices of ways and means motions.
>
> The details of the measures are contained in these documents, and I am asking that an order of the day be designated for consideration of these motions.
>
> I also wish to announce that the Government will introduce legislation to implement the measures in the budget. (Budget speech of the federal minister of finance, 2015)

The minister's statement usually covers four general themes:

- The country's current economic situation and future prospects
- The government's proposed new spending initiatives
- New tax initiatives, also proposed by the government
- The government's financial position (deficit, debt, debt service)

The budget speech should be seen above all as a communication tool used by the government to present the general outline of budget-related bills that it intends to have adopted by lawmakers. It is not intended to deliver detailed information on these initiatives or on the government's fiscal framework. The fiscal framework, more technical in nature, is presented in the government's budget plan, which is published at the same time as the budget speech.

The budget plan usually contains supplementary information on the following subjects:

- The composition of budgetary expenditures (expenditures related to provision of goods or services, such as salaries, purchases of supplies, transfer payments, and so on) and non-budgetary expenditures (that arise when the composition of the government's assets is modified—advances, loans, loan guarantees, changes to the value of employee pension plans, and so on)
- Description of new fiscal measures
- Update of the government's financial situation
- Presentation of macroeconomic hypotheses used to establish economic forecasts
- Balance sheet on past initiatives

Over the years, the government's budget plan has become a voluminous document. The budget plan presented to Parliament in 2015 was 518 pages long.

The budget speech and plan are accompanied by a third category of document: notices of ways and means motions. The notices announce that bills presenting new tax measures (or modifying existing measures) will soon be tabled. Under legislative rules, tax measures come into effect when they are presented in a notice of ways and means motion and not when they are approved by the House. This procedure makes it possible to institute tax measures immediately so that taxpayers are not encouraged to change their behaviours (e.g., a tax increase on a product that does not take effect for several months might encourage consumers to hoard that product). The presentation of notices of ways and means motions does not, however, remove the obligation from the government to obtain assent from the House. The initiatives presented in ways and means notices must subsequently be approved through adoption of the ways and means bill.[5]

Adoption of the Budget

Several votes are required to approve the government's budget. A first vote takes place to approve the government's general policy. Presentation of the budget (budget speech, budget plan, and notice of ways and means motions) is followed by four days of debates in the House of Commons. During these debates, MPs from all parties discuss the initiatives proposed by the government. The opposition parties will thus have an opportunity to comment on the government's budget and present their own budgetary initiatives, if applicable. To limit debate, MPs are allowed to propose only a small number of amendments. At the conclusion of these debates, it is proposed "that the House approve the government's general budgetary policy." The vote that follows is a vote of confidence. A motion presented to amend the budget is also considered a vote of confidence.[6] Once the budget is adopted, the government presents various bills to proceed with implementation:

- Enabling bills, which are common bills that the government uses to create new programs or modify existing programs with recurring funding
- Appropriation bills authorizing the government to pay funds out of the Treasury (the Consolidated Fund)

Table 7.1 Main budget for expenditures, money appropriated, and statutory items (federal government)

	2015–2016	2016–2017		2017–2018
	Expenditures	Main estimates	Estimates to date	Main estimates
1. Budgetary (billion $)				
Voted	85.17	89.85	103.18	102.14
Statutory	156.21	160.29	153.98	155.78
Total	241.38	250.14	257.17	257.92
2. Non-budgetary				
Voted	0.04	0.03	0.06	0.03
Statutory	55.55	0.34	(0.09)	(0.25)
Total	55.59	0.37	(0.03)	(0.22)
Total (1+2)				
Voted	85.21	89.88	103.24	102.17
Statutory	211.76	160.63	153.89	155.53
Total	296.97	250.51	257.13	257.70

Source: Treasury Board Secretariat (Canada), *2017–18 Estimates: Parts I and II. The Government Expenditure Plan and Main Estimates* (Ottawa: Her Majesty the Queen in Right of Canada, 2017).
Note: Totals may not add due to rounding.

- Ways and means bills that enable the government to raise income and other taxes
- Borrowing authority bills that authorize the government to borrow funds[7]

There are two categories of expenditures, each subjected to different parliamentary rules: *non-statutory expenditures* and *statutory expenditures*. Non-statutory expenditures must be authorized every year. They cover most salaries, investments, purchases, and similar expenses. Statutory expenditures have already been authorized in preceding years by previous laws. These expenditures fund major transfer programs, such as Employment Insurance and Old Age Security. Statutory expenditures are thus deemed to be permanent, although they may be amended or even abolished by a new bill. Table 7.1 presents the distribution of the federal government's expenditures between non-statutory and statutory expenditures. The latter count for almost two-thirds of total government expenditures. As noted above, parliamentary financial procedure does not allow lawmakers to examine tax expenditures.[8]

Statutory expenditures are authorized when ordinary bills are adopted. The government presents several bills of this nature (four or five, usually) per year. Each of these bills covers a specific field of activities.[9] Appropriation expenditures are approved through appropriation bills (also called supply bills). Parliamentary procedure provides for adoption of five such bills during the year. The first grants the government interim appropriations that it needs to use government money during the first months of the fiscal year. The interim appropriations are necessary to allow parliamentarians the time to complete a detailed analysis of the budgetary appropriations requested by the government at the beginning of the year. The second bill is for the actual budget (or Main Estimates). This bill contains the vast majority of authorizations requested by the government. Debate on this bill may also deal with the previously adopted interim appropriations. The three other appropriation bills enable the government to obtain supplementary authorizations, either to make expenditures not foreseen at the beginning of the year or to transfer funds already authorized from one program to another. Each of these bills must be tabled within a precise time frame. Table 7.2 presents the dates and authorizations granted for each appropriation bill submitted to Parliament in the 2016–2017 fiscal year.

Ways and means bills and borrowing authority bills provide the government with the authorizations necessary to obtain revenues. Ways and means bills must be used when the government is considering raising income and other taxes. These bills cover neither drops in income and other taxes nor sales of goods and services. Borrowing authorization bills are required when the government wishes to increase its borrowing. They are not used when the government refinances its debt or when its financial reserves cover additional borrowing.

Except for ways and means statutes, it is not necessary for a bill to have been announced in the budget ahead of time. At any time during the year, the government may table new bills regarding its budgetary policy. In addition, in compliance with constitutional principles, only the House of Commons is required to adopt the government's public policy and its ways and means bills. Ordinary budgetary bills, appropriations bills, and borrowing bills are examined and approved by both chambers. They must, however, be presented to the House of Commons first.

Table 7.2 Federal government's appropriation bills for the fiscal year ending 31 March 2017

Appropriation act	Adoption date	Total sum granted (million $)
Appropriation Act No. 1, 2016–17 Interim supply for Main Estimates	21 March 2016	26,423
Appropriation Act No. 2, 2016–17 Full supply for Main Estimates	14 June 2016	63,449
Appropriation Act No. 3, 2016–17 Supply for Supplementary Estimates (A)	14 June 2016	7,014
Appropriation Act No. 4, 2016–17 Supply for Supplementary Estimates (B)	1 December 2016	3,881
Appropriation Act No. 5, 2016–17 Supply for Supplementary Estimates (C)	21 March 2017	2,472
Total Estimates for 2016–2017		103,239

Source: Treasury Board Secretariat (Canada), *Appropriation Acts*, https://www.canada.ca/en/treasury-board-secretariat/services/planned-government-spending/appropriation-acts.html#further (accessed 27 October 2017).
Note: Totals may not add due to rounding.

Consideration of Budgetary Appropriations

One of the main financial responsibilities of parliamentarians is to examine and approve the government's current activities. Much of this work is done in the context of studying the government's budget appropriations. The appropriations are presented in the Main Estimates[10] and must be submitted to Parliament before the fiscal year begins—by 1 March at the latest. Each appropriation grants an authorization to spend a certain amount for a specific activity. The Main Estimates document is accompanied by another document, the government's *Expenditure Plan*, which presents budget forecasts for all expenditures, including statutory expenditures.

The appropriations detail the amounts and expenditure categories (operating expenses, capital expenses, subsidies, and so on) requested for each department or agency. Table 7.3 presents the appropriations of the Department of Foreign Affairs, Trade and Development presented

Table 7.3 Main Estimates, Department of Foreign Affairs, Trade and Development

		2015–2016	2016–2017		2017–2018
		Expenditures	Main Estimates	Estimates to date	Main Estimates
		($)			
Budgetary—voted					
1	Operating expenditures	1,529,980,770	1,458,048,856	1,602,891,841	1,557,659,937
5	Capital expenditures	135,740,375	124,444,220	177,876,478	106,313,014
10	Grants and contributions	3,834,875,859	3,529,676,551	4,251,965,821	3,903,486,753
15	Payments, in respect of pension, insurance, and social security programs or other arrangements for employees locally engaged outside of Canada, or in respect of the administration of such programs or arrangements	64,032,14	50,779,000	64,706,000	66,273,000
20	Pursuant to ss. 12(2) of the International Development (Financial Institutions) Assistance Act, payments to international financial institutions – direct payments	. . . . .	1	1	1
—	Debt forgiveness – loans to the government of the Republic of Cuba	. . . . .	. . . . .	18,009,733	. . . . .

(Continued)

Table 7.3 (Continued)

Total voted	5,564,629,151	5,162,948,628	6,115,449,874	5,633,732,705
Total statutory	432,223,415	352,592,269	359,929,125	368,393,362
Total budgetary	432,223,415	5,515,540,897	6,475,378,999	6,002,126,067
Non-budgetary—voted				
L25 Pursuant to ss. 12(2) of the InternationalDevelopment (Financial Institutions) Assistance Act,payments to international financial institutions – capitalsubscriptions	.....	1	1	1
— Working capital advance – Loans and advances	1,864,632	.....	.....	.....
— Working capital advance – Advances to posts abroad	(3,449,639)	.....	.....	.....
Total voted	(1,585,007)	1	1	1
Total statutory	53,481,420	3,098,450	3,098,450	39,860,000
Total non-budgetary	51,896,413	3,098,451	3,098,451	39,860,001

Source: Treasury Board Secretariat (Canada), *2017–18 Estimates: Parts I and II. The Government Expenditure Plan and Main Estimates* (Ottawa: Her Majesty the Queen in Right of Canada, 2017), II-101–02.

in the Main Estimates of 2017–2018. The number for each appropriation refers to a specific vote.

It is expected that the appropriations will be examined by parliamentarians. The parliamentary committees assume this function.[11] Each standing committee conducts a detailed analysis of the appropriations for the departments and agencies under its responsibility. For example, the House of Commons Standing Committee on Agriculture and Agri-Food examines the appropriations of the Department of Agriculture and Agri-Food, the Canadian Grain Commission, the Canadian Dairy Commission, and Farm Credit Canada. Appropriations are examined by both the House and Senate committees (in the Senate, however, only one committee, the Standing Committee on National Finance, studies appropriations). The committees have the power to accept, reduce, or reject an appropriation.[12] They cannot increase appropriations or transfer them from one item to another, as this would contravene the principles of primacy of the executive branch with respect to public expenditures. Once the committee adopts the appropriations, it reports its decisions to the House. The House then examines the Estimates and adopts them (with or without the amendments proposed by the committees). The House's powers of amendment are the same as those of the committees. If no report is tabled on 31 May, the committee is deemed to have submitted a report and approved the appropriations requested.

To complete their examination of appropriations, the committees usually summon the minister responsible (accompanied by his or her senior civil servants) to obtain further information on the activities covered by the appropriations. The committee members may also take advantage of information contained in two other documents that the government is required to table in Parliament: the Departmental Plans (DPs) and the Departmental Results Reports (DRRs).[13] These reports are prepared under the supervision of the Treasury Board Secretariat for each department and agency (except Crown corporations) and presented to Parliament by the president of the Treasury Board. The DPs are published at the beginning of the fiscal year (by 31 March) and give detailed descriptions of the respective department's current activities (objectives, programs, human resources, financial resources) and projected activities (expected strategic results and performance indicators, by program and subprogram) for each of the next three years. The DRRs are tabled at the end of the fiscal year (in the fall) and present results achieved compared to the projections in the DPs. It should be

noted that the information contained in these two reports covers all
ministerial expenditures and not just expenditures targeted by appropriations (or non-statutory expenditures). These reports therefore offer
more complete descriptions and analyses of the budgetary situation of
each department and public agency.

Although, in principle, the adoption of appropriations is one of the
most important budgetary responsibilities granted to parliamentarians,
in fact, they are generally not very interested in this activity. As a House
of Commons parliamentary committee observed:

> Each year, some 87 departments and other government organizations
> provide parliamentary committees with separate spending estimates
> and related reports, and many of these receive no formal attention
> in committee meetings. And when meetings occur, they are typically
> dominated by partisan exchanges with ministers that shed minimal light
> on the estimates. Consideration of the supplementary estimates, which
> allow departments to obtain additional funding at specified intervals
> during the year, has been even less satisfactory. With only a few exceptions,
> committees regularly fail to examine them at all.[14]

There are two reasons for this situation. First, Canadian political parties impose very strong discipline on their officeholders, who, especially
if they are members of the party in power, have very little margin for
manoeuvre in influencing budgetary choices. Second, the debates surrounding examination of the appropriations often have to do with very
technical subjects, which are not very interesting to the public (nor, by
extension, to the media). Further, the budget documents submitted to
Parliament often lack clarity and transparency. The members therefore
hesitate to devote time and resources to activities with so few positive
returns.[15] To provide parliamentarians with greater latitude in examining the appropriations, many have asked that new parliamentary rules
be adopted to reduce the parties' influence and improve the quality of
information contained in the budget documents.[16]

Examination of the Public Accounts and the Auditor General's Reports

When the fiscal year has ended, the government must prepare a detailed
balance sheet of all financial transactions that took place during the year.

This report is presented in the form of Public Accounts, which must be submitted to Parliament by 31 December following the end of the fiscal year. In fact, however, the Public Accounts are presented earlier, in the fall.[17] The Auditor General is responsible for auditing and approving the Public Accounts prepared by the government. Examination of the Public Accounts is an important accountability task that parliamentarians must execute. It involves verifying whether the money spent was previously approved by Parliament. The Public Accounts documents usually comprise three sections (or volumes). The first paints a general portrait of the government's financial position, including assets, liabilities, and government debt, as well as the Auditor General's report and observations. (Figure 7.2 shows an excerpt of the Auditor General's 2013 report regarding the Public Accounts of Canada.) The second presents the financial transactions of each department and public agency by appropriation. The third provides detailed financial information on activities not covered by appropriations.

The Public Accounts are examined by the Standing Committee on Public Accounts of the House of Commons. The committee may issue recommendations to improve the efficiency of the government's budgetary and accounting rules. These recommendations result from the observations made by the Office of the Auditor General in its report and when the Auditor General testifies to the committee. The Standing Committee on Public Accounts does not, however, give an opinion regarding the relevance or merits of a given program. It is common for the government to respond to these recommendations. Its responses are generally favourable to the committee's recommendations, which are suggested by the Auditor General's observations. This sense of cooperation conveys the credibility built by the Office of the Auditor General of Canada over the years and the non-partisan nature of the work done by the Standing Committee on Public Accounts – so non-partisan that Parliament changed the House regulation so that the committee chair would be chosen from among opposition MPs and not MPs in the majority in the House, as is the custom for the other committees.[18]

The Auditor General also submits audit reports to Parliament on various facets of internal management. The reports are usually submitted twice a year, in spring and fall. Again, the Standing Committee on Public Accounts is responsible for examining the reports and making recommendations to the government. The committee often submits reports to the House following the Auditor General's examinations.

Figure 7.2 Auditor General of Canada's report and comments, Public Accounts, 2016–2017

Public Accounts of Canada, 2016–2017

Office of the
Auditor General
of Canada

Bureau du
vérificateur général
du Canada

Independent Auditor's Report

To the House of Commons

Report on the consolidated financial statements

I have audited the accompanying consolidated financial statements of the Government of Canada, which comprise the consolidated statement of financial position as at 31 March 2017, and the consolidated statement of operations and accumulated deficit, consolidated statement of change in net debt and consolidated statement of cash flow for the year then ended, and a summary of significant accounting policies and other explanatory information.

The Government's Responsibility for the Consolidated Financial Statements

The Government is responsible for the preparation and fair presentation of these consolidated financial statements in accordance with the stated accounting policies of the Government of Canada set out in Note 1 to the consolidated financial statements, which are based on Canadian public sector accounting standards, and for such internal control as the Government determines is necessary to enable the preparation of consolidated financial statements that are free from material misstatement, whether due to fraud or error.

Auditor's Responsibility

My responsibility is to express an opinion on these consolidated financial statements based on my audit. I conducted my audit in accordance with Canadian generally accepted auditing standards. Those standards require that I comply with ethical requirements and plan and perform the audit to obtain reasonable assurance about whether the consolidated financial statements are free from material misstatement.

An audit involves performing procedures to obtain audit evidence about the amounts and disclosures in the consolidated financial statements. The procedures selected depend on the auditor's judgment, including the assessment of the risks of material misstatement of the consolidated financial statements, whether due to fraud or error. In making those risk assessments, the auditor considers internal control relevant to the Government's preparation and fair presentation of the consolidated financial statements in order to design audit procedures that are appropriate in the circumstances, but not for the purpose of expressing an opinion on the effectiveness of the Government's internal control. An audit also includes evaluating the appropriateness of accounting policies used and the reasonableness of accounting estimates made by the Government, as well as evaluating the overall presentation of the consolidated financial statements.

I believe that the audit evidence I have obtained is sufficient and appropriate to provide a basis for my audit opinion.

Opinion

In my opinion, the consolidated financial statements present fairly, in all material respects, the financial position of the Government of Canada as at 31 March 2017, and the results of its operations, changes in its net debt, and its cash flows for the year then ended in accordance with the stated accounting policies of the Government of Canada set out in Note 1 to the consolidated financial statements, which conform with Canadian public sector accounting standards.

Report on Other Legal and Regulatory Requirements

As required by Section 6 of the *Auditor General Act*, I report that, in my opinion, the stated accounting policies of the Government of Canada have been applied on a basis consistent with that of the preceding year.

Michael Ferguson, CPA, CA
FCPA, FCA (New Brunswick)
Auditor General of Canada

6 September, 2017
Ottawa, Canada

Source: Receiver General for Canada, *Public Accounts of Canada, 2016–2017. Volume 1. Summary Report and Consolidated Financial Statements* (Ottawa: Minister of Public Services and Procurement, 2017), 2.4.

Examination of External Budget Requests

Prebudget consultations are certainly one of the most interesting innovations in the parliamentary budget cycle in recent decades. This procedure, however, is still not widespread in the parliaments of other countries.[19] The Canadian Parliament and two provincial legislative assemblies, those of Ontario and British Columbia, conduct such consultations.[20] It is important to emphasize that these consultations are separate from the prebudget consultations conducted by ministers of finance. The objective is to encourage the population to make recommendations on the content of the next budget. Both citizens and organizations (public, private, and not-for-profit) are invited to participate in the consultation exercise, but over the years it has been observed that representatives of various organizations are most often the participants. Prebudget consultations are conducted by a parliamentary committee (the committee responsible for finance), which then submits a report containing its recommendations to the House once the consultations have ended. The consultations take place in the fall. A few weeks before work begins, the committee asks for written submissions from all individuals or groups interested. For example, the notice of the Standing Committee on Finance of the House of Commons is presented in Figure 7.3. The committee then invites a certain number of the participants that provided a written submission to testify at public hearings that take place in different regions of the country or province. The public hearings will enable committee members to learn more about certain topics. The committee also invites other witnesses with specific expertise on the economic situation of the country or the province, including the minister of finance or his or her representatives, the governor of the Bank of Canada, and the Parliamentary Budget Officer. In addition, the committee takes account of the most recent estimates of the country's and provinces' economic and financial situation. In this respect, it has become normal for the federal government and all provincial governments to present such updates to their respective legislatures in the fall (such as the updated economic and budgetary projections of the federal government).

The government is not required to implement the committee's recommendations. We may therefore wonder if these prebudget consultations are really useful. A study conducted on prebudget consultations in British Columbia shows that despite the non-restrictive nature of these consultations, they are nonetheless relevant. First, the committee reports

Figure 7.3 Notice of prebudget consultations for the 2018 budget by the Standing Committee on Finance

Comité permanent des finances   Standing Committee on Finance

CHAMBRE DES COMMUNES
HOUSE OF COMMONS
CANADA

<u>For immediate release</u>

NEWS RELEASE

CANADIANS ARE INVITED TO SHARE THEIR PRIORITIES FOR THE 2018 FEDERAL BUDGET

Ottawa, June 02, 2017 -

On 2 June 2017, the House of Commons Standing Committee on Finance launched its pre-budget consultations process for this year, and is inviting Canadians to participate in this important process. The process will result in a report to be tabled in the House of Commons in December 2017, and this report will be considered by the Minister of Finance as the 2018 federal budget is developed.

"The House Finance Committee's pre-budget consultations process is a critical means by which Canadians are able to express their priorities for forthcoming budgets, and I'm pleased to be announcing the launch of the Committee's consultations in advance of the 2018 budget," said the Honourable Wayne Easter, P.C., M.P. for Malpeque and Chair of the House of Commons Standing Committee on Finance. "The pre-budget consultation process is a very important part of the Committee's work, and Committee members are always impressed by the thoughtful and innovative proposals put forward by Canadians as potential budget measures."

Consistent with last year's theme of economic growth, and believing that more productive people and more productive and competitive businesses can lead to enhanced growth and prosperity, the Committee is interested in receiving written submissions and oral testimony on the topic of productivity and competitiveness. Specifically, the focus of submissions and testimony should be:

1. What federal measures would help Canadians to be more productive?

For example, what education and training, health, housing, and labour market participation and mobility measures would help Canadians to be as productive as possible in their workplaces and their communities?

2. What federal measures would help Canadian businesses to be more productive and competitive?

For example, what measures would help businesses to undertake research, innovation and commercialization, purchase advanced technology and equipment, invest in the training and development of their employees, participate in global value chains and increase their international market share?

The deadline for written submissions to the Committee is no later than Friday, 4 August 2017 at 11:59 p.m. Eastern Standard Time. Submissions should be no longer than 2,000 words, including an executive summary. Only one submission per individual or organization, including any of its task forces, committees, etc., will be accepted; thus, individuals or organizations shouldnot submit both individually and as part of a joint submission. Submissions that exceed this word limit or that fail to respect the stipulation that an individual or organization can make a submission individually or jointly, but not both, will not be considered by the Committee. Following translation, the submissions will be circulated to Committee members and posted on the Committee's website. Written briefs must be submitted through the study's website.

In September, on behalf of Committee members, the Clerk of the Committee will extend invitations to selected groups and individuals to appear as witnesses during the pre-budget hearings. All those who make a submission will be considered as having made a request to appear. Priority will be given to individuals and groups that address productivity and competitiveness in their submissions, and have not yet –or have not recently –appeared before the Committee. Pending approval by the House of Commons, the Committee intends to hold hearings in Ottawa and in various locations across Canada. Once those locations and the hearing dates have been confirmed, the Committee will issue a news release.

More information about this year's pre-budget consultations is available on the study's website.

Source: Standing Committee on Finance (Canada), *News Releases*, accessed 26 October 2017, https://www.ourcommons.ca/DocumentViewer/en/42-1/FINA/news-release/9002784. © House of Commons

are now expected and examined by a number of external observers, including civil servants at the Department of Finance. Second, a number of organizations now have available a public forum allowing them to present and publicly explain their recommendations, a platform that did not previously exist.[21] But without a doubt the main advantage of the prebudget consultations is that they enhance the role of parliamentarians. Granting lawmakers the responsibility to solicit and communicate the opinion of the population to the government allows them to more fully perform their role as elected representatives of the population.

FEATURE BOX: ARE CANADIAN PARLIAMENTARIANS EFFECTIVE?

Although it is undeniable that Canadian parliamentarians—the elected representatives of the population—play an important role in the budgetary process, we can wonder if they are effectively fulfilling their responsibilities. This question has been examined by two attentive observers of the federal parliamentary scene. Their conclusion: MPs are doing their job quite well, but not in every area. The table below summarizes the authors' conclusions. The coefficients presented represent their evaluation of the MPs' work based on their own observations and judgment. The coefficients represent orders of magnitude and not absolute values (5 represents the best result and 1 the worst result). They must therefore be compared to each other.

The control function (examination of the results) seems to be the best element performed by the MPs. This result indicates that they perform well one of the fundamental responsibilities of British-tradition parliamentary systems: accountability. The representation function is judged to be relatively satisfactory thanks notably to the prebudget consultations in the House of Commons that make it possible for a wide variety of groups to present their positions on the government's budgetary policy. It is the function of granting means of action that presents the least satisfactory results. The complexity of the information presented in the many budget documents and an examination procedure that is too rigid (analysis by appropriation in parliamentary committee) likely explains much of the result. The result should encourage the government, in collaboration with MPs, to conduct an in-depth review of Parliament's fiscal framework, including the role of budgetary appropriations (i.e., the materials on which parliamentarians are called upon to debate and vote).

Role	Performance indicator	Coefficient (1–5)
Represent citizens' interests	Have Canadians participate in the definition of political priorities	3
	Deliberation and synthesis	2
	Visibility of differences	4
	Relevance of committees' studies to budgetary issues	2
	Correlation among committee studies	3
Grant means of action to the government	Overall budgetary power	5
	Control framework for programs	2
	Transparency of modes of examination of appropriations	1
Examine the results	Overall effectiveness of the budget	5
	Effectiveness of management	4
	Establishment of programs and policies	1

Source: Peter Dobell and Martin Ulrich, "Parliament's Performance in the Budget Process: A Case Study," *Policy Matters* 3, no. 5 (2002): 1–24.

KEYWORDS

Parliament budgetary schedule • Budget speech • Budget plan • Estimates • Parliamentary committees' tasks • Public Accounts • Prebudget consultations

TO FIND OUT MORE

Reading suggestions

Chenier, John A., Michael Dewing, and Jack Stillborn. "Does Parliament Care? Parliament Committees and the Estimates." In *How Ottawa Spends, 2005–2006: Managing the Minority*, ed. Bruce G. Doern, 200–21. Montreal/Kingston: McGill-Queen's University Press, 2005.
House of Commons (Canada). "Financial Procedures." *Compendium of Procedure.* http://www.ourcommons.ca/About/Compendium/FinancialProcedures/c_g_financialprocedures-e.htm
Ministry of Finance (Ontario). *Ontario's Fiscal Cycle.* https://www.fin.gov.on.ca/en/budget/
Office of the Auditor General (Canada). *Parliamentary Committee Review of the Estimates Documents: 2003 March Report of the Auditor General of Canada.* Ottawa: Minister of Public Works and Government Services Canada, 2003.

Database

Treasury Board Secretariat Infobase (Canada):   http://www.tbs-sct.gc.ca/ems-sgd/edb-bdd/index-eng.html#start (tracks how budget estimates are approved and used)

Websites

The House of Commons Standing Committee on Public Accounts: http://www.ourcommons.ca/Committees/en/PACP?parl=41&session=2
The House of Commons Standing Committee on Finance: http://www.ourcommons.ca/Committees/en/FINA?parl=41&session=2
The House of Commons Standing Committee on Government Operations and Estimates: http://www.ourcommons.ca/Committees/en/OGGO?parl=41&session=2
The Senate Standing Committee on National Finance: https://sencanada.ca/en/committees/nffn/41-2
Provincial legislative committee websites can be found on their respective provincial legislature web page (see the list provided at the end of chapter 6)
Public Accounts of Canada (General Comptroller of Canada): http://www.tpsgc-pwgsc.gc.ca/recgen/cpc-pac/index-eng.html
Provincial Public Accounts can be found on respective provincial Department of Finance websites

PART 4

Budget Implementation

8 The Budgetary Management System

In the Canadian parliamentary system, the executive branch is responsible for formulating and implementing the government's budget policy. Only one small group of decision makers actively participates in formulating the budget (the Cabinet, supported by the Treasury Board administrative branch), but implementation is different: tens of thousands of civil servants assigned to a multitude of programs are responsible for using and managing public funds. Because of the vast extent of its activities, the government has no choice but to entrust some of its responsibilities to managers in the public administration. To counterbalance this delegation of power, the government needs to establish control mechanisms to ensure that the tasks performed by the civil service comply with its decisions, which will have been approved beforehand by the legislature.

Delegation of Authorizations

The federal Financial Administration Act (and the analogous provincial and territorial financial management statutes) frame the rules for delegating the federal government's (and the provincial and territorial governments') authority to spend, levy, and borrow. In every department, a senior civil servant, the deputy minister, manages administrative activities.[1] The law provides that the deputy minister is the department's deputy head. At the federal level the deputy minister is also the department's accounting officer. As deputy head, the deputy minister assumes overall management of the department, particularly with regard to human resources. As accounting officer, the deputy minister oversees the running of the department's programs, sets up the internal oversight mechanisms for financial transactions, and approves the transactions that will be recorded in the Public Accounts. The accounting officer is required to make a management statement to both Parliament and the Treasury Board.[2] The deputy minister thus assumes a role of coordination between the central agencies and his or her department or public body.[3]

One of the deputy minister's main tasks with regard to the budgetary process is to distribute the budgetary appropriations in allotments. Appropriations are authorizations to spend approved by the legislature, whereas allotments (or allocations) are authorizations approved by the Treasury Board to allow departments to use the funds. There are three general allotment categories:

- Standard allotments: for operating and capital expenses and transfer payments
- Special-purpose allotments: limited to specific programs
- Frozen allotments: unused budgetary appropriations. These allotments may be temporary (the program must fulfil certain conditions before being allowed to use them) or permanent (they expire at the end of the fiscal year)

Once the allotments are determined by the department, under the responsibility of the deputy minister, and approved by the Treasury Board, the department's program managers may use them. The deputy minister will proceed with sub-allotments of authorizations among the department's programs.

In addition to distributing budgetary allotments, the deputy minister must ensure that sound financial management strategies are established. He or she works in concert with a chief financial officer (generally with the rank of assistant deputy minister), who formulates the policies for management of the department's financial activities, oversees execution of the department's or agency's financial obligations (most of which are stated in the statutes governing its activities), makes recommendations, supports the work of other managers in the department dealing with financial questions, and negotiates with central agencies. The chief financial officer leads a team of financial officers, whose numbers vary depending on the size and extent of activities of the department or agency. The financial officers see to the financial compliance of all of the department's operations. The chief financial officer must ensure that the financial powers delegated to his or her employees comply with the Treasury Board's authorizations and directions.

Aside from the chief financial officer, a number of senior managers (assistant and associate deputy ministers) in the department also report directly to the deputy minister. These senior civil servants and their managers (executive directors, directors) are responsible for handling the department's operating budgets (covering salaries, rent, equipment, and supplies, for example), which are divided into various responsibility centres. The number and hierarchical structure of the responsibility centres are determined within the department, as a function of the number and nature of programs to be managed. The department is also responsible for determining the distribution of budgetary allotments authorized by the Treasury Board among the different responsibility centres. In the 1990s, a new management philosophy was established in the federal service: budgetary responsibilities were to be decentralized through delegation to managers. The aim is to encourage a reduction in the number of administrative levels and to increase the discretionary powers of employees, especially "front-line" employees in direct contact with users of public services.[4]

Cash-Flow Management

The counterpart of increased accountability is greater participation in implementation of budgetary policies, including ensuring that the financial resources granted to departments are used effectively. Because resource allocation is planned and approved at the beginning of the fiscal year, it might seem that tasks related to the implementation phase are relatively simple to execute. However, it is not possible to anticipate all circumstances likely to change the use of financial resources during the fiscal year. The implementation of budgetary initiatives thus consists not only of employing the financial resources as provided during the budgetary planning phase, but also of modifying the allocation of these resources if unforeseen circumstances arise. These activities are related to management of each department's respective cash position.

Table 8.1 presents the main differences between activities related to cash management (budget-implementation phase) and activities related to budgetary planning (budget-formulation phase), the latter being performed mainly by the central agencies. The table shows that cash-management activities are more involved with day-to-day decisions made in response to changing circumstances. Activities related to budgetary planning take place on a longer-term horizon, with the main goal of establishing a budget policy that is predictable and therefore stable.

Table 8.1 Differences between budgetary management and cash-position management

	Budgetary management	Cash management
Main responsibilities	• Budget: allocating resources, setting authorizations, limits, and targets	• Managing differences between projected and actual results
Main tool of intervention	• Resource allocation	• Resource reallocation
Main preoccupations	• Government priorities	• Current situation
	• Source of revenues	• Cost control and risk management
	• Performance and optimization	• Reallocation
Time horizon	• Long term and permanent	• Short term and transitory
	• Changes occurring within the usual annual budgetary cycle	• Changes occurring frequently, depending on risk and volatility
	• Decisions made before the start of the financial year	• Decisions are frequent and ongoing during the financial year

Source: Adapted from Andrew Graham, *Canadian Public-Sector Financial Management.* 2nd ed. (Kingston: School of Public Policy, Queen's University, 2014), 166.

A variety of factors force managers to revise their operating budgets during the year. For instance, the price of purchases (including wages, notably when collective agreements are renegotiated) or demand for certain public services may change suddenly. Certain programs may prove incapable of reaching their objectives and must therefore be reviewed. The government may change its priorities during the year (especially if an election has brought a new government to power). Finally, exceptional circumstances may arise at any moment (economic crisis, natural disaster, security issue). Cash-management systems must allow managers to ensure that the funds required to operate programs are available and to propose changes if an intervention is required. It is therefore necessary to constantly analyse the use of financial resources in programs and, more broadly, in departments—and to keep in mind that all expenditures must have been authorized beforehand by Parliament. Some unforeseen needs may require new budgetary appropriations (such requests are normally made through Supplementary Estimates).

Unforeseen events may therefore have important consequences for departments' operating budgets. To attenuate the effect of these consequences, managers must set up risk-management strategies. Risk may be defined as being the level of uncertainty that objectives will be reached: "Technically speaking, a risk is the expression of the likelihood and impact of an event with the potential to affect the achievement of an organization's objectives."[5] The goal of risk management is to estimate the likelihood that an unforeseen event will arise and to assess the impacts on a department's financial resources or one of its programs if such an event were to take place. Cash management must therefore integrate mechanisms that will make it possible to identify the risk factors for the department.

Payment of Obligations

Once the budgetary appropriations are adopted and allocated, managers may use them to finance (pay for) activities for which they are responsible (pay their employees, pay for purchases of goods and services, pay out grants, and so on). For greater control over the legality and integrity of financial transactions, the payment process involves two steps: expenditure initiation and payment. The legislation (Financial Administration Acts) clearly states that these two tasks must be performed independently of each other. Expenditure initiation consists of providing information that a financial transaction will eventually take place. This is an accounting commitment that confirms that the appropriations to be used for this expenditure are no longer available for another expenditure. The initiation occurs when the transaction is planned but before a formal payment agreement (such as a contract, a purchase order, or a hiring) is established with a supplier or individual. It must be verified to ensure that the funds committed are available and that the manager who approved the expenditure initiation has obtained the authority to do so (this authorization must be made in writing; ultimately, it is under the responsibility of the accounting officer). Both the statement of intent and verification of the commitment originate within the department, but must be generated by different people. Only once a commitment is made and verified can a request be made for payment of a cost incurred. A payment authorization is transmitted to the office of the Receiver General (or its provincial or territorial counterpart), which issues and sends the payment (generally a cheque) to the payee

Figure 8.1 The federal administration's coding system

Government-wide coding block					
Department / agency	Financial reporting account (FRA)	Authority	Program	Object	Transaction type
3 characters	5 characters	4 characters	5 characters	4 characters	1 character
XXX	XXXXX	XXXX	XXXXX	XXXX	X

Source: Receiver General (Canada), Chart of Accounts for 2017 to 2018, accessed 25 October 2017, https://www.tpsgc-pwgsc.gc.ca/recgen/pceaf-gwcoa/1718/2-eng. html#id2.2.
Contains information licensed under the Open Government Licence – Canada.

(employee, supplier, beneficiary of government assistance, and so on). The Receiver General must thus be seen as the government's cashier.

Because it executes all financial transactions made from the government's Consolidated Fund, the Office of the Receiver General can be considered one of the government's central agencies. The Receiver General's decision-making powers, however, are not as extensive as are those of other central agencies (the Treasury Board administrative branch or the department of the first minister, for example). The Office of the Receiver General should be viewed as more a subordinate than a decision maker in financial management policies. Nevertheless, it is an important agency and is placed directly under the authority of a minister (usually the minister of finance[6]).

The Receiver General has two mandates. First, it must conduct all monetary transactions on behalf of the government, including execution of instructions for payment by departments and public agencies and receipt of government revenues (from taxes, the sale of goods and services, loans, and so on). Second, it is responsible for keeping the government's accounting records, which are used to prepare the Public Accounts that the government must submit to Parliament each year. All financial transactions must be entered in various books of accounts. Together, these books constitute the government's chart of accounts. The entries are very detailed and are coded in a system that is used to classify all operations. Figure 8.1 presents the coding structure used by the federal government.

These codes identify six main categories of information:

Table 8.2 Categories and subcategories of objects of expenditure in the federal government's chart of accounts

Category 0—Services include the following standard objects

    01. Personnel

    02. Transportation and communications

    03. Information

    04. Professional and special services

    05. Rentals

    06. Repair and maintenance

Category 1—Goods, land, buildings, and works include the following standard objects

    07. Utilities, materials, and supplies

    08. Acquisition of land, buildings, and works

    09. Acquisition of machinery and equipment

Category 2—Transfer payments include the following standard object

    10. Transfer payments

Category 3—Other expenditures include the following standard objects

    11. Public debt charges

    12. Other subsidies and payments

Source: See source, Figure 8.1.

- Department/agency: The department or agency that authorized the transaction, from among the 170 departments and agencies of the federal government identified by a code (the list of departments and agencies comes from the schedules of the Financial Administration Act)
- Financial reporting account (FRA): The nature of the financial transaction (whether asset, debt, expenditure, or revenue)
- Authority: The parliamentary authorization obtained (identification of the budgetary appropriation or statutory expenditure)
- Program: The sector as determined by the general orientations and strategic results defined by the government (economic, social, international, and so on)
- Object: Description of the transaction to be recorded
- Transaction type: type of operation (internal or external transaction)

Table 8.3 Division of transfer payments in the federal government's chart of accounts

2. Transfer payments (standard object 10)
20 Transfer payments to persons
21 Transfer payments to industry
22 Transfer payments to provinces and territories
23 Transfer payments to or on behalf of international organizations and foreign countries
24 Transfer payments to organizations, including Crown corporations and non-profit organizations
26 Transfer payments to municipalities and local organizations
28 Reallocation of transfer payments

Source: See source, Figure 8.1.

The object category is the most detailed category, as it classifies all expenditures, revenues, and assets and liabilities with several hundred codes. For instance, Table 8.2 presents the four main categories and twelve subcategories use for transactions related to expenditures. Then come the divisions and subdivisions for each of the twelve subcategories. As an example, Table 8.3 presents the codes employed to record transfer payments (category 2 in Table 8.2) while Table 8.4 shows the codes used for transfer payments paid to individuals (code 20 in Table 8.3). The four-digit code in Table 8.4 is therefore used as the object code in the federal government's chart of accounts. The object code "2035" in Table 8.4, for instance, reports expenditures related to "Assistance to immigrants and refugees," which is described as "payments to immigrants and refugees to facilitate their settlement in Canada."

Awarding Contracts

Governments manage considerable volumes of financial transactions. The federal government has estimated that the total cash flow handled by the Office of the Receiver General amounts to more than $2.3 trillion per year[7]—more than the Canadian GDP (almost $2 trillion in 2014). Because of the large amounts of money involved, governments wield significant economic and purchasing power. On the one hand, they can

Table 8.4 Subdivision of transfer payments to individuals in the federal government's chart of accounts

20 Transfer payments to persons

200 Transfer payments to persons

    2001 Old Age Security payments

201 Payments for pensions

    2011 Pensions World Wars I and II

    2012 War veterans' allowances

    2013 Pensions to former government employees not entitled under current superannuation acts

    2014 Payments to former civilians and uniformed personnel

    2019 Other payments for pensions

202 Transfer payments to promote employment

    2022 Assistance to persons to encourage employment

    2023 Payments relating to improvement and promotion of employability of individuals

    2029 Other transfer payments to persons for promotion of employment

203 Other transfer payments to persons

    2032 Payments to Aboriginal people

    2035 Assistance to immigrants and refugees

    2041 Transfer payments to persons for research and development (including scholarships)

    2049 Other non-recoverable payments to persons

    2051 Recoverable payments to persons

    2055 Contingency recoverable payments to persons

    2057 Child tax benefit

    2060 Goods and Services Tax (GST)

Source: See source, Figure 8.1.

obtain goods and services at advantageous prices through volume discounts. On the other hand, they actively participate in the economic life of the country by financing important investment projects. Savings may be even greater if purchasing decisions are coordinated or centralized. For this reason, most Canadian governments entrust responsibility for managing purchases above a certain size to one department. The large volume of transactions also forces governments to be very transparent. Today, it would not be acceptable for public purchasing policies to unduly favour certain suppliers, to the detriment of economic efficiency. This has not always been the case. And even today, government directives have not completely eliminated favouritism, though it is now considered illegal or at least unethical. The "sponsorship scandal" is an example of the misuse of public funds that occurred in Canada. The scandal concerned the discovery of fraudulent use of public funds in 2003. The Office of the Auditor General deemed that all of the administrative rules regarding the awarding of sponsorship contracts had been broken.[8]

Public purchases are therefore subjected to supplementary rules that aim to standardize procedures and to solicit the largest possible number of bids. These rules are usually formulated by the Treasury Board Secretariat. It should be noted that public purchases are also subject to international rules. The North American Free Trade Agreement (NAFTA) forbids Canadian governments from limiting American and Mexican firms' access to public contracts above a certain value.[9] Canada is also a signatory to the World Trade Organization's Agreement on Government Procurement, which follows principles similar to those in NAFTA.[10]

One of the main mechanisms in government purchases is the call for tenders. Every public purchase valued above a certain threshold must go through a public bidding process. The goal of this process is to choose a supplier that is able to provide the government with goods or services at the best price possible. The process begins when the government calls for bids for a specific project. The call for tenders presents a detailed description of the services to be rendered and the criteria that must be met. Any qualified supplier may then present a fully confidential bid. At the end of the tendering period, all submissions are analysed. The supplier that has submitted the lowest-cost submission that respects all the criteria in the call for tenders, especially the quality criteria, is chosen.

Another procurement mechanism that has been gaining popularity in recent years is public-private partnerships (PPPs). These contracts consist of mandating one or several private companies (usually forming consortiums) to supply a good in exchange for performance-based remuneration. PPPs are used only in some cases, when the government is planning procurement of major assets, such as construction of a bridge, hospital, or prison. PPPs may also cover facility management: maintenance of a bridge, provision of health care services, administration of a prison. The use of PPPs allows governments to shift some of the financial risks associated with undertaking major projects. The private partner is paid only once the services are rendered, at a price set beforehand in the contract. In exchange, the firm obtains all the benefits that economies of costs may entail. Canadian governments became interested in PPPs relatively late compared to other countries (such as the United Kingdom, New Zealand, and France). Today, however, all governments use this form of procurement. In some cases, public bodies have been created to support PPP projects (e.g., PPP Canada, Société québécoise des infrastructures, Infrastructure Ontario, and Partnership BC). The use of PPPs has been criticized in a number of countries where the mechanism has been established.[11] In Canada, many question the real economic effectiveness and the transparency of this management mode.[12]

The rules and procedures established by Canadian governments to frame public purchases are intended to prevent financial misappropriation (illicit use of funds, favouritism, abuse of power, and so on). However, certain recent scandals have exposed the limitations of the current measures.[13] In recent years, a number of Canadian governments have tried to increase the efficiency and integrity of their procurement programs by establishing supplementary control and transparency mechanisms. For instance, the federal government created the position of procurement ombudsman, an independent administrative officer, in 2006.[14] The statute authorizes the ombudsman to (1) conduct investigations following submission of a complaint alleging an inappropriate practice; (2) provide a dispute-resolution mechanism when disputes rise during execution of a contract; and (3) conduct analyses and formulate recommendations to the government regarding its procurement practices.[15] It should be noted that the ombudsman's investigatory power does not include bringing lawsuits. The government of Quebec instituted a stricter mechanism for certification of suppliers: the Integrity in Public Contracts Act, adopted in 2012, requires all firms that wish to obtain a contract from the government to have "authorization to contract." This authorization is granted after an in-depth examination of the firm's activities on financial markets, within its industry, and with the tax authorities. Quebec's example has been followed by the federal and Ontario governments.

KEYWORDS

Allotment of appropriations • *Accounting officers* • *Chief financial officer* • *Cash management* • *Financial commitments* • *Receiver General* • *Public markets and calls for tender* • *Public-private partnerships*

TO FIND OUT MORE

Reading suggestions

Cohn, Daniel. "The New Public Autonomy? Public-Private Partnerships in a Multi-level, Multi-accountable, Political Environment: The Case of British Columbia, Canada." *Policy and Society* 27, no. 1 (2008): 29–42.

Graham, Andrew. *Canadian Public-Sector Financial Management*. 2nd ed. Kingston: School of Public Policy, Queen's University, 2014.

Smith, Alex. *The Accountability of Accounting Officers before Parliamentary Committees*. Ottawa: Parliament of Canada, 2008.

Database

Procurement data (Canada): https://buyandsell.gc.ca/procurement-data/ (provides a list and a search engine on past and actives tenders as well as awarded contracts)

Websites

Receiver General for Canada: https://www.tpsgc-pwgsc.gc.ca/recgen/txt/ apropos-about-eng.html

Public Services and Procurement (Canada): http://www.tpsgc-pwgsc.gc.ca/ comm/index-eng.html

The Canadian Public Procurement Council: http://www.cppc-ccmp. ca/?page_id=35&lang=fr&lang=en

World Trade Organization, *Government Procurement*: https://www.wto.org/ english/tratop_e/gproc_e/gproc_e.htm

Commission d'enquête sur l'octroi et la gestion des contrats publics dans l'industrie de la construction (Quebec): https://www.ceic.gouv.qc.ca/ la-commission/mandat.html (available in French only)

9 Optimization of Budgetary Resources

Both decision makers in central agencies and program managers in departments and public agencies perform important functions related to allocation and management of the government's financial resources. However, power is not shared equally between these two institutional groups. The central agencies have the authority to direct and oversee the activities of departments and other public bodies (an authority that is clearly stated in the statutes on financial management of governments). They are therefore responsible for determining how allocations and powers are assigned to program managers. The thrust of current budgetary processes in Canada is to make managers more accountable for their management activities (and the results achieved) in their departments. However, central agencies, and particularly the Treasury Board administrative branch, keep tight control over determination of budgetary orientations, financial management mechanisms, and accountability. Centralization of decision making allows for greater coordination and more cohesion in the management of public funds, but it limits managers' margin of manoeuvre because it does not necessarily grant them all the flexibility required to make their own decisions in light of the particular features of their programs. The challenge for the government thus consists of finding a fair balance between the decision-making power of central agencies and the delegation of decision-making power to lower levels of the public administration.

The purpose of a *financial management system* is to find the fair balance between centralization and decentralization of budgetary responsibilities. Financial management systems define the rules and decision-making procedures for each participant in the budgetary process and define accountability mechanisms. Their primary objective is to ensure that the government's budgetary resources are used optimally. Optimal management (or optimization) aims for efficient management of financial resources—that is, achieving the best results possible at the lowest cost.

Establishing an appropriate financial management system is a core budgetary concern of most governments in industrialized countries today. It is not a new concern. In the 1960s, many countries were interested in the question, as it was becoming more and more obvious that the state's financial resources were not unlimited. A number of financial management models were designed to respond to this new constraint. It was not easy to implement these models, however, as they involved considerable changes to traditional public-management methods. In addition, the reforms implemented did not provide the anticipated results.[1] In Canada, several provincial governments decided to observe attempts made elsewhere before engaging in their own reform process. The federal government assumed leadership in this area, with the provinces of Ontario and Quebec following to a certain extent.[2]

To date, none of the models proposed to reform financial management systems has produced satisfactory results. Despite this failure, the reforms have considerably influenced the budgetary process both in Canada and abroad. They have changed ways of doing things as well as public opinion. Today, it is no longer conceivable to design budget plans without taking into account the core concern of optimization of financial resources. To better understand the nature of these changes, we will take a closer look at the causes, characteristics, and results of the major reforms instituted in Canada, mainly by the federal government.

Past Reforms

From the beginning of Confederation to the late 1950s, budget management fell within a traditional conception of bureaucracy. Managers and their employees worked in a rigidly hierarchical organization, and their main tasks were to institute policies and follow directions based on operational control. The management principles were based on a *structural* financial management system. The goal of this system was to verify that all required authorizations had been obtained. Expenditures were listed and classified for each administrative unit, or structure, then aggregated by department and public agency. Each transaction was recorded on the basis of a classification that distinguished the various categories of goods and services acquired (salaries, rents, printing, telephone, and so on). Structural management systems stressed the relationship between costs and resources used. Although this model made it possible to closely track financial transactions, it lost points for efficiency and relevance because there were too many controls and they were too centralized. In the early 1960s, it was estimated that the federal government's Treasury Board had to examine more than sixteen thousand requests for expenditure authorizations per year (and only six ministers sat on the Treasury Board).[3] This kind of workload for the central agencies inevitably led to too much red tape and made program managers less accountable.

In 1962 the Royal Commission on Government Organization (known as the Glassco Commission, after its chair), instituted by the federal government to examine the operations of the civil service, recommended an in-depth reform of the financial management system. In the commissioners' view, the priority was to "let the managers manage." Rules that were too rigid did not allow managers to adapt their programs to new economic and social realities. Furthermore, strong hierarchical controls hobbled the upper echelons of the administration, to the point that they were unable to perform their budget-planning and -orientation tasks. The Glassco Commission's recommendations conveyed an increasingly widespread awareness in Canada, and elsewhere, of the limitations inherent to the traditional bureaucratic model from which structural financial management had emerged. A new model began to take shape, based on two general principles: economic rationality and seeing organizations as systems. Under economic rationality, public choices were examined in relation to both their costs and their benefits. Decisions should thus reflect the best cost-benefit ratios. Principles based on systemic management of organizations took into account the interdependence of organizational units: budgetary decisions had to be coordinated with a view to reaching common objectives. New financial management goals were proposed so that managers in the public administration could stress objectives to achieve and put budgetary controls into perspective.

The financial management model that was studied and critiqued the most during the 1960s and 1970s, in Canada and a number of other countries, was the planning, programming, and budgeting system (PPBS). This new model stressed reaching objectives, planning, and evaluation. It involved identifying the needs and goals of each program on the basis of past results and current demand (planning), formulating means of action (programming), and allocating financial resources (budgeting). As a system, it required that program managers have greater decision-making power. The federal government and several provinces (particularly Quebec and Ontario) adopted measures to implement principles of rationalization of budgetary choices. The results, however, were regarded as disappointing—due more to the feasibility than the merits of the approach. PPBS required too much decentralization of the decision-making process, which was incompatible with the desire to centralize financial control in order to limit budget growth.

In his 1976 report, the Auditor General of Canada stated his concern that "the Government has lost, or is close to losing, effective control of the public purse."[4] The financial situation of the government was deteriorating rapidly, while growth in public-sector debt seemed to have become uncontrollable. In response to the Auditor General's report, the federal government instituted the Royal Commission on Financial Management and Accountability (the Lambert Commission) to define how to provide sound financial management and ensure optimization of resources in the administration. In their final report, the commissioners also recommended decentralization of financial decision-making centres.[5]

To mediate the limitations of rationalization of budgetary choices, the *management by objectives system* was proposed. Like PPBS, this system stressed planning and the formulation and achievement of objectives. The main difference between the two systems had to do with resource allocation. Under management by objectives, allocations had to be determined jointly by the central agencies and the departments and agencies, and not solely by the latter. The underlying principles of management by objectives guided the reforms instituted by the federal government during the 1980s, including the establishment of budgetary envelopes.[6] Departments and public agencies were grouped into a few broad sectors of public intervention (there would be seven sectors in the federal public service) and would have to disburse budget amounts that were set by the Treasury Council. The ministers assigned to each sector (or envelope) had to distribute the funds among their departments and agencies.

The budgetary envelopes system forced departments to work together and collaborate with central agencies to determine budgetary allocations. If new funds were needed to create a program, they would have to be drawn from the sector budget. The system thus obliged managers to establish priorities in light of objectives and according to available resources. It also provided the government with a way to slow cost increases: the amount in the envelopes could be reduced, forcing departments to identify for themselves how to make savings. Like the preceding reforms, the one based on budgetary envelopes—and, more broadly, the management by objectives system—was difficult to apply. The detailed analyses of programs required by this management procedure proved complex to execute, and departments were encouraged to defend the relevance of their own programs rather than to promote sector-wide objectives.[7]

Following the ineffective reforms based on the principles of rationalization of budgetary choices and management by objectives, governments began to look more closely at the solutions offered by proponents of *new public management* (NPM).[8] According to the principles of NPM, public administrations had to abandon the traditional bureaucratic model (which involves hierarchy and controls) and adopt management methods used in the private sector, based on performance, cost savings, and customer satisfaction. Management was to focus no longer on objectives, but on results. As it did in other countries, NPM became very popular in Canada, not only in the federal administration but also in the provinces.[9] The principles of NPM ended up shaping the most extensive financial management reform conducted to date: the program review initiated in 1994, and subsequent reforms based on results-based management.

The 1994 Review of Federal Government Programs

One of the main causes of growth in public expenditures is the weak propensity of public administrations to recognize which programs are no longer relevant. In fact, it is easier to maintain existing programs (say "yes" to everything) than to decide to reduce or even eliminate some.[10] Over a number of years, however, governments have recognized the importance of periodically reviewing their programs. As far back as 1979, the Lambert Commission report recommended that the government establish a process of program evaluation in order to better allocate resources. After that, governments tried to reduce public expenditures by adopting a number of administrative reforms, but these were unsuccessful. The 1994 reform marked a significant change from previous attempts. Not only were departments asked to make budget cuts, but they were provided with very specific directions for identifying which programs were no longer relevant.

The 1994 reform instituted a broad program review. This exercise was led directly by a minister specially appointed for the purpose and covered all federal government programs. At the time it was tabled, the government considered this reform to be an occasional exercise. Vast resources were devoted to it, and the expectation was that the effects of decisions made following the reform would last several years.

The program review forced all departments to analyse each of their programs and determine their relevance. To continue to exist, each program had to meet six criteria, each of which was posed in the form of a question:

- Does the program serve the public interest?
- Is there a legitimate and necessary role for the public sector in this area?
- Is the role of the central government justified or should the program be rethought for the provincial level?
- Should the government execute the program in partnership with the private or voluntary sector?
- How could the program be restructured to make it more effective?
- Is the program affordable in relation to the government's fiscal parameters?

What was new about this exercise was not only the concern with the programs' effectiveness, but a substantial redefinition of the state's role. In the context of the review, public intervention was justified only if no other social sector could offer the services. From this point on, the state had a residual role, and many Crown corporations were privatized. The new conception of the Canadian state also redefined federal-provincial relations. The federal government now intended to decentralize the formulation and management of the provincial programs that it funded (in full or in part). This change explained, in part, the reduction in transfer payments to the provinces in 1996 and 1997 and the subsequent reforms of federal transfer programs. Notably, none of the six "tests" offered the opportunity to assign new responsibilities to the state. The review applied only to existing programs.

The aim of the program review was to rethink the role of the Canadian federal government in a context of budgetary restraint. In terms of the viability of the public purse, the exercise can be deemed a success. The government was faced with a considerable deficit in the mid-1990s, and the program review enabled it to save almost $30 billion over three years. The federal deficit, which stood at $42 billion in 1994, was gone by 1997. After that, the federal government was able to clear budget surpluses every year until the economic crisis of 2008. The program review was so successful that the government decided to use the six criteria (in modified form) to assess its programs on a regular basis.[11]

Although the program review helped to restore fiscal health by targeting a reduction in expenditures,[12] this mechanism did not allow for a reallocation of resources among programs. Such a reallocation was to become central to the government's concerns in the 2000s, when the question arose of how to use the budget surpluses. The government envisioned this reallocation as being made through a *results-management* system. Even today, this is the financial management system that prevails in the federal administration, and it is increasingly being used in provincial administrations. Four provinces (New Brunswick, Quebec, Saskatchewan, and Alberta) have adopted laws forcing the government to institute the system and to account for it publicly.

Results-Based Management

The results-based management model is another financial management mechanism that applies the principles of NPM. Results-based management was not developed in isolation from preceding management systems, but conveyed a desire to integrate performance and accountability measurements from the decision-making processes already in place. One of the main objectives of results-based management is to place citizens' concerns at the core of budgetary policies. Services funded by the public purse therefore have to respond to a need in the population. To reach this goal, each government program must have a specific "attainable," "observable," and "measurable" objective. Results-based management requires, as a consequence, that performance indicators be designed to measure the results obtained. These indicators serve to account for the activities of departments and public agencies and to identify aspects of programs that must be improved. Results-based management is a continuous activity performed throughout the budget cycle. The chart in Figure 9.1, taken from a 2004–2005 report published by the Office of the Auditor General of British Columbia, offers a good illustration of the main management and accountability mechanisms associated with the principles established by results-based management.

The Canadian federal government also uses principles of results-based management to encourage greater coordination among programs and administrative units. This desire to coordinate public activities has led the federal government to institute a *government-wide framework* for management that is designed to present the general objectives that it intends to achieve. The framework used by the federal government since 2010 is presented in Figure 9.2. This framework presents 16

Figure 9.1 The Government of British Columbia's management cycle based on results

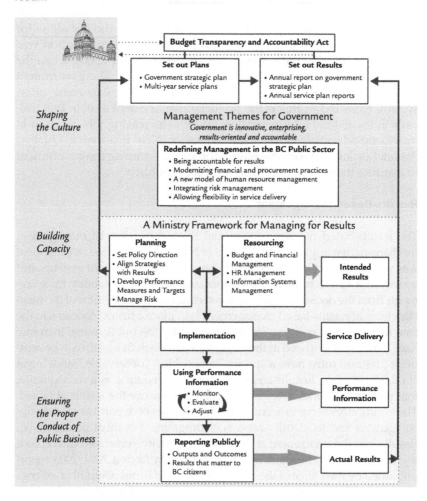

Source: Office of the Auditor General (British Columbia), *Building Momentum for Results-Based Management: A Study about Managing for Results in British Columbia* (Victoria: Office of the Auditor General of British Columbia, 2005), 14.

Figure 9.2 Government-wide framework of the federal government

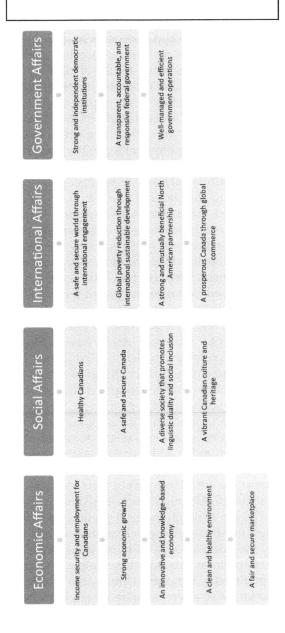

Spending Areas (4)

Government of Canada Outcome Areas (16)

Economic Affairs

- Income security and employment for Canadians
- Strong economic growth
- An innovative and knowledge-based economy
- A clean and healthy environment
- A fair and secure marketplace

Social Affairs

- Healthy Canadians
- A safe and secure Canada
- A diverse society that promotes linguistic duality and social inclusion
- A vibrant Canadian culture and heritage

International Affairs

- A safe and secure world through international engagement
- Global poverty reduction through international sustainable development
- A strong and mutually beneficial North American partnership
- A prosperous Canada through global commerce

Government Affairs

- Strong and independent democratic institutions
- A transparent, accountable, and responsive federal government
- Well-managed and efficient government operations

Source: Treasury Board Secretariat (Canada), *Whole-of-Government Framework*, accessed 28 November 2017, http://www.tbs-sct.gc.ca/ppg-cpr/frame-cadre-eng.aspx.

expected results, grouped into four general sectors: economic, social, international, and governmental affairs. All of the government's initiatives must comply with the government-wide framework. For instance, all departments must formulate a *program alignment architecture* (PAA) that lists all of their programs and groups them into several ministerial strategic results. The main goal for this architecture is to demonstrate the relevance and the expected results of all of these programs and to eliminate redundancies. For example, Tables 9.1 and 9.2 present the PAA for Department of the Environment programs. As we can see, all of the department's activities contribute to the government-wide framework's economic affairs sector (and to a single expected result: to contribute to a clean, healthy environment). The department administers nine programs, thirty subprograms, and five sub-subprograms, aligned with three departmental strategic results.

Aside from anchoring the programs to the government's general objectives, results-based management also requires the formulation and presentation of performance measurements and indicators. Table 9.3 presents the performance indicators chosen by the department, the targets, and the results obtained for one of the department's programs (Weather and Environmental Services for Canadians).[13]

Today, the results-based management system seems to have become the budgetary standard in Canada. Most Canadian provinces are following the federal example and have adopted the principles of this model of financial management.[14] However, results-based management has been slow to provide convincing evidence of budgetary effectiveness. For example, the Parliamentary Budget Officer observed that the continuous review of federal government programs did not lead to reallocation of resources from under-performing programs to better-performing ones.[15] Although this management model has certain advantages (one of which being that it triggers an effort to reflect on results to be achieved at the scales of the organization and the government apparatus), it also has some major weaknesses. For instance, the system is complex to manage. Managers must devote a large part of their resources to justifying their programs' activities. Although results-based management tends to decentralize the decision-making process, it requires more accountability. Program managers must produce numerous analyses and performance reports to justify their decisions. In addition, it has proved difficult to identify satisfactory performance indicators. Unlike in the private sector, which may use profitability indicators to judge the success of its activities, the public sector offers a very broad range of products and services

Table 9.1 Alignment of spending with the whole-of-government framework, Department of Environment and Climate Change

Strategic outcomes	Programs	Spending area	Government of Canada activity	2016–17 actual spending
SO 1:Canada's natural environment is conserved and restored for present and future generations	1.1 Biodiversity – wildlife and habitat	Economic Affairs	A clean and healthy environment	153,035,992
	1.2 Water resources			70,732,520
	1.3 Sustainable ecosystems			98,446,872
	1.4 Compliance promotion and enforcement – wildlife			17,511,301
SO 2:Canadians are equipped to make informed decisions to changing weather, water, and climate conditions	2.1 Weather and environmental services for Canadians			180,123,302
	2.2 Weather and environmental services for targeted users			15,643,525
SO 3:Threats to Canadians and their environment from pollution are minimized	3.1 Substances and waste management			87,801,448
	3.2 Climate change and clean air			149,504,223
	3.3 Compliance promotion and enforcement – pollution			40,339,332

Source: Environment and Climate Change (Canada), *Departmental Results Report 2016 to 2017* (Ottawa: Her Majesty the Queen in Right of Canada, 2017), 38.

Table 9.2 Strategic Outcomes and Program Alignment Architecture (PAA), Department of Environment and Climate Change

---

1. Strategic Outcome: Canada's natural environment is conserved and restored for present and future generations

---

1.1 Program: Biodiversity—Wildlife and Habitat

1.1.1 Subprogram: Biodiversity Policy and Priorities

1.1.2 Subprogram: Species at Risk

1.1.3 Subprogram: Migratory Birds

1.1.4 Subprogram: Habitat Conservation Partnerships

1.1.5 Subprogram: Protected Areas

1.2 Program: Water Resources

1.2.1 Subprogram: Water Quality and Aquatic Ecosystems Health

1.2.2 Subprogram: Water Resource Management and Use

1.2.3 Subprogram: Hydrometric Services

1.3 Program: Sustainable Ecosystems

1.3.1 Subprogram: Sustainability Reporting and Indicators

1.3.2 Subprogram: Ecosystem and Environmental Assessments and Monitoring

1.3.3 Subprogram: Community Engagement

1.3.3.1 Sub-Subprogram: EcoAction Community Funding

1.3.3.2 Sub-Subprogram: Environmental Damages Fund

1.3.3.3 Sub-Subprogram: Environmental Youth Employment

1.3.4 Subprogram: Great Lakes

1.3.5 Subprogram: St. Lawrence

1.3.6 Subprogram: Lake Simcoe/Southeastern Georgian Bay

1.3.7 Subprogram: Lake Winnipeg

1.3.8 Subprogram: Ecosystems Partnerships

1.4 Program: Compliance Promotion and Enforcement—Wildlife

2. Strategic Outcome: Canadians are equipped to make informed decisions on changing weather, water, and climate conditions

2.1 Program: Weather and Environmental Services for Canadians

2.1.1 Subprogram: Weather and Environmental Observations, Forecasts, and Warnings

2.1.2 Subprogram: Health-related Meteorological Information

2.1.3 Subprogram: Climate Information, Predictions, and Tools

---

(*Continued*)

Table 9.2 (Continued)

2.2 Program: Weather and Environmental Services for Targeted Users

    2.2.1 Subprogram: Meteorological Services in Support of Air Navigation

    2.2.2 Subprogram: Meteorological and Ice Services in Support of Marine Navigation

    2.2.3 Subprogram: Meteorological Services in Support of Military Operations

3. Strategic Outcome: Threats to Canadians and their environment from pollution are minimized

    3.1 Program: Substances and Waste Management

        3.1.1 Subprogram: Substances Management

        3.1.2 Subprogram: Effluent Management

        3.1.3 Subprogram: Marine Pollution

        3.1.4 Subprogram: Environmental Emergencies

        3.1.5 Subprogram: Contaminated Sites

    3.2 Program: Climate Change and Clean Air

        3.2.1 Subprogram: Climate Change and Clean Air Regulatory Program

            3.2.1.1 Sub-Subprogram: Industrial Sector Emissions

            3.2.1.2 Sub-Subprogram: Transportation Sector Emissions

        3.2.2 Subprogram: International Climate Change and Clean Air Partnerships

        3.2.3 Subprogram: Environmental Technology

    3.3 Program: Compliance Promotion and Enforcement—Pollution

Source: Environment and Climate Change (Canada), *Departmental Plan 2017 to 2018 Report* (Ottawa: Her Majesty the Queen in Right of Canada, 2017), 35–36.

to the population, the effects of which are difficult to measure over the short and long terms. The Department of the Environment performance indicators presented in Table 9.3 give a good illustration of this difficulty. The indicators chosen do not seem to cover all of the program's activities (they concern only weather alerts), and the targets chosen are not justified (why target 30 per cent of the population, for example, rather than a different proportion).

Like all previous systems, results-based management offers its own challenges. However, as some have noted, "No government has (yet) turned away from this approach, although there are many challenges to be overcome before it becomes institutionally and culturally accepted by managers and other government officials."[16] The question of resource optimization thus remains a core budgetary concern of governments.

Table 9.3 Performance indicators, Weather and Environmental Services for Canadians program, Department of Environment and Climate Change

Expected results	Performance indicator	Target	Results achieved
Canadians use Environment and Climate Change Canada's weather and environmental services	Public component of the Weather Warning Index (a weighted index of weather warning timeliness and accuracy) The indicator is a three-year moving average, calculated based on the timeliness and accuracy of five warning types: severe thunderstorm, rainfall, freezing rain, wind, and snowfall.	7.9	8.1 in 2014 to 2016
	Percentage of the population of a warned area who report having seen or heard a recent weather warning and who took actions in response.	30%	45% in 2015–16. Results are based on a telephone survey administered in 2015–16. The survey will be administered every two years to Canadians who live in areas where there is a weather warning.

Source: Environment and Climate Change (Canada), *Departmental Results Report 2016 to 2017*, 19.

FEATURE BOX: HAS RESULTS-BASED MANAGEMENT TRANSFORMED THE BUDGETARY PROCESS?

In 2012, the province of Alberta adopted a law establishing a framework for results-based management. This statute forced the government to review all public programs and implement recommendations resulting from this examination over the following five years. The review had to determine the relevance, effectiveness, and achievement of results of each of the 540 programs for which government departments and public agencies are responsible.

The Albertan initiative was similar to those undertaken recently in other Canadian jurisdictions (including New Brunswick and Quebec): several provincial governments instituted mechanisms for reviewing their programs inspired by results-based management. In most cases, the exercise was conducted using an analysis grid that presented a series of questions to guide the assessment process, such as: What is the goal of the program? Is it necessary? Are its results specific, attainable, and measurable? Is it possible to improve it?

However, the Albertan review process stands out from the other Canadian initiatives in two respects. First, review committees composed of members of the legislative assembly and external experts have been created to supervise the civil servants' work: the intention is to involve the population (through its representatives) and civil society in the decision-making process. Second, eleven "lines of business" were created to encourage a "horizontal" examination of programs—that is, to study their complementarity or lack thereof (e.g., "municipalities and regional development," "early-child development," and "health").

The exercise seems to have garnered some interesting results. Although it is still not known whether budgetary savings have been generated, the government's annual reports indicate that a number of programs were reviewed so that various services could be integrated. For example, individuals with handicaps can now find information about all the programs and services intended for them through a single portal (a measure involving 23 programs and 120 services), and new measures are gradually being instituted to reduce the use of the courts (notably in the field of family law).

It is open to debate, however, whether such a review process truly transforms the budgetary process. What is its legacy? Will it encourage governments and their managers to review the current budgetary process? Specifically, will governments seek to change the management framework to place more emphasis on horizontal management and to include external representatives in the decision-making process? There is not yet any sign of a true transformation of institutions and the budgetary process in Canada.

Source: Ministry of Finance (Alberta), *Results-Based Budgeting*, http://www.finance.alberta.ca/business/budget/results-based-budgeting/index.html (accessed 27 October 2017, link no longer valid).

KEYWORDS

Financial management systems • *Resource optimization* • *Planning, programming, and budgeting system (PPBS)* • *Budgetary envelopes* • *Program reviews* • *New public management* • *Results-based management* • *Centralization/decentralization*

TO FIND OUT MORE

Reading suggestions

Peters, B. Guy. "What Works? The Antiphons of Administrative Reform." In *Taking Stock: Assessing Public Sector Reforms*, ed. B.G. Peters and D.J. Savoie, 78–107. Montreal: McGill-Queen's University Press, 1998.
Treasury Board Secretariat (Canada). *Preparing and Using Results-Based Management and Accountability Frameworks*. Ottawa: Her Majesty the Queen in Right of Canada, 2005.
Treasury Board Secretariat (Canada). *Supporting Effective Evaluations: A Guide to Developing Performance Measurement Strategies*. Ottawa: Her Majesty the Queen in Right of Canada, 2010.

Periodicals

OECD Journal on Budgeting
Public Performance and Management Review

Statutes

Public Administration Act, CQLR c. A-6.01 (Quebec)
Growth and Financial Security Act, SS 2008, c. G-8.1 (Saskatchewan)
Results-based Budgeting Act, SA 2012, c. R-17.5 (Alberta)

PART 5

Budgetary Control

10 Internal Auditing and Evaluation Mechanisms

Assessment of budgetary policies is the last stage in the budgetary cycle. This task is important, as it involves examining whether the initial budgetary policy has been followed. The analysis involves two general facets that are independent of, but complementary to, each other: auditing and evaluation. The first is aimed at verifying whether funds have been used in compliance with authorizations granted. The second attempts to determine whether use of funds has given the expected results. Not only do audits and evaluations make it possible to pass judgment on past activities, but they are also used to prepare ensuing budgets. Knowing the strengths and weaknesses of current programs and management systems gives budgetary decision makers (central agencies and program managers) extra information for evaluating the quality and relevance of their activities and making changes if necessary. Audits and evaluations thus form the link between current and ensuing budgetary cycles. In this chapter, I examine more closely the role and functions of the federal mechanisms, to illustrate the main features of the internal audit and evaluation process in Canada. Once again, the situation is quite similar in the provinces and territories, although the scope of these mechanisms is not as extensive in the smaller provinces and in the territories.

Office of the Comptroller General

The Office of the Comptroller General is the body responsible for implementing internal evaluation operations (or internal audits) of the federal government. Each province and territory also has its own comptroller general. The position of Comptroller General is one of the oldest in the Canadian public administration. It was created in 1931 in the federal administration as the government was beginning to be increasingly concerned with the compliance of its financial transactions. The parliamentary procedure established back in 1867 was very clear on this point: the commitment of all expenditures and the collection of all revenues must be approved beforehand by Parliament. During the early period of Confederation, however, most expenditures were made without any real control over their legality and compliance, and a number of transactions were conducted without prior parliamentary authorization. The position of Comptroller General was established to correct this situation.[1]

The position has undergone a number of transformations since it was created.[2] It was abolished in 1969, when the responsibilities for auditing and evaluation were delegated to departmental managers in the context of major financial administrative reforms. It was re-established in 1978, however, as an independent agent, and was then integrated into the Treasury Board Secretariat in 1993. The 2006 reforms maintained the hierarchical link between the Secretariat and the Comptroller General and delegated certain auditing responsibilities to departments and public agencies; the reforms also reaffirmed the principle of the Comptroller General's independence. This series of changes illustrates the ambiguous nature of the internal audit function in the public sector. Because the probity of financial management is so important, the government is entitled to establish strict control mechanisms for the public service as a whole. However, these mechanisms must also be flexible enough to adapt to the wide variety of publicly funded programs. In other words, the challenge of the central agencies consists, yet again, of finding the right balance between centralization and decentralization – in this case, between kinds of audit tasks.

The Financial Administration Act provides the legal framework for the federal government's internal audit procedure. The principles set out in this statute have been codified in the Treasury Board Secretariat's *Policy on Internal Audit* and *Directive on Internal Audit*. In other words, the Secretariat writes the rules framing the government's internal audits, and the Office of the Comptroller General is responsible for implementing these rules. A number of internal auditing rules were amended subsequent to the adoption of the Federal Accountability Act in 2006, modifying certain provisions of the Financial Administration Act.[3] The main change is the creation of the position of chief financial officer in each department and public agency. Although these officers assist deputy ministers (accounting officers), they report to the Comptroller General.

The Office of the Comptroller General has three areas of responsibility. First, it operationalizes the rules issued by the Treasury Board Secretariat. It therefore designs the tools (standards) that all departments and public agencies must use to conduct their own auditing and control of budgetary funds. For example, it determines the detailed content of financial reports that departments must submit, provides a clear interpretation of the accounting principles to follow in charging financial transactions to various expense and revenue categories, determines the authority required to authorize and make payments and to collect revenues, and establishes risk-management audit mechanisms. Second, it acts as an internal oversight agent for the government by verifying the audit activities conducted by departments and public agencies. It therefore conducts departmental inspections and ensures that all problematic situations revealed in these inspections are corrected. Third, it acts as a human resources consultant to the Treasury Board Secretariat, ensuring that the managers responsible for the audit and their employees have the necessary skills and training. In most cases, these civil servants are required to have professional qualifications in accounting.

As we can see, the responsibilities of the Office of the Comptroller General consist more of steering the internal audit operations that each department and public agency must conduct than of conducting these operations itself. The flip side of this delegation is that departments and public agencies must report on their audits to the Comptroller General. This accountability is currently expressed in the preparation of numerous reports, as required by a directive from the Office. Excerpts of the directive are presented in Figure 10.1.

All departments and agencies are also required to publish their audit results.[4] Although this directive was designed to create more openness and transparency with regard to departments' use of public funds, it is not clear that it is having the expected effects. Indeed, publication of audit results may cause problems for officeholders, who may be accused of incompetence if an audit concludes that public resources are not being managed properly—even if there has been no misappropriation as such. The debate occasioned by the internal audit of the Department of Human Resources Development in 2000 illustrates this

Figure 10.1 Internal audit reports required by the Office of the Comptroller
General of Canada

**Submitting Internal Audit Products to the Office
of the Comptroller General (OCG)
[excerpt]**

Under the Directive on Chief Audit Executives, Internal Audit Plans, and
Support to the Comptroller General, deputy heads are responsible for
ensuring that, on a timely basis, the Office of the Comptroller General is
provided with key products. Moreover, in support of enabling an OCG audit
intelligence capability, the following list of products should be submitted:

- Annual Risk-Based Audit Plans
- Internal Audit reports[a] and Engagement Report Submission Form
- Annual Overview Report
- Chief Audit Executive (CAE) Annual Report
- Departmental Audit Committee (DAC) Annual Report
- Management letters from Internal Audit
- Management letters resulting from the audits of the Office of the Auditor
  General
- Practice Inspection reports
- Agendas of departmental audit committee meetings
- Minutes / Records of Decision from departmental audit committee
  meetings

The OCG will analyze the products and provide feedback on the quality
and on the trends arising from cross-government analysis.
[...]
Final audit reports should be posted on departmental web site to enable
public access; these reports should be posted within 90 days after Deputy
Head approval.

[a] Includes follow-up audits, and reviews. All reports sent to the OCG should
be complete, un-severed.

Source: Office of the Comptroller Genera (Canada), *Submitting Internal Audit Products
to the Office of the Comptroller General*, accessed on 30 November 2017, https://www.
canada.ca/en/treasury-board-secretariat.html.

point. At the time, the department decided to publish the results of an internal audit of its activities, although it was under no obligation to do so. The audit uncovered some missing documentation in the allocation of certain grants. Although the value of the department's grants totalled almost $1 billion, the audit involved a limited number of grant-receiving projects, with a total value of $30 million.[5] The audit revealed that 37 grants out of the 459 audited had incomplete paperwork and had therefore not complied with all of the control rules. However, this was not the conclusion reported in the media; rather, the reports inaccurately stated that the government had wasted $1 billion. The conclusions of an internal audit may therefore be interpreted differently (or misinterpreted) by different actors. Public-sector decision makers need rigorous audit reports to be able to improve their management methods. However, such rigour may be of no use if the internal audit exercise is addressed more to an external public than to governmental managers.[6]

Program Assessment

In parallel with the internal program audit, the Treasury Board Secretariat also conducts the federal government's evaluation activities. Formal evaluation mechanisms began to be instituted in the 1970s. The interest in evaluation at that time was explained by the implementation of new financial management systems that advocated the formulation and achievement of objectives for all programs (notably in the context of the planning, programming, and budgeting system). Evaluation therefore became an essential component of the program-management process.[7]

During the 1980s and 1990s, government departments were asked to develop and implement their own evaluation procedures. The Treasury Board Secretariat issued various directives and policies to prescribe certain principles. Many felt, however, that the evaluation activities that took place were unsatisfactory.[8] In addition, increased interest in the principles proposed by new public management led governments to reconsider the place of program evaluation in the budgetary process. In 2001, several reforms were instituted to better support and frame the program-evaluation function. The Centre of Excellence for Evaluation was created within the Treasury Board Secretariat to provide "advice and guidance in the conduct, use and advancement of evaluation practices" for the federal administration as a whole.[9] Each department also had to appoint an evaluation leader

Figure 10.2 The federal government's resource-optimization process

Value for Money	
Demonstration of Relevance	Demonstration of Performance

	Demonstration of Relevance	Demonstration of Performance
Core Issues	Demonstrated Need and Responsiveness	Achievement of Expected Outcomes (Effectiveness)
	Alignment with Government Priorities	Demonstration of Efficiency and Economy
	Alignment with Federal Roles and Responsibilities	

Source: Treasury Board Secretariat (Canada), *Assessing Program Resource Utilization When Evaluating Federal Programs* (Ottawa: Her Majesty the Queen in Right of Canada, 2013), 4.

and an independent evaluation committee. In 2006, the government amended the Financial Administration Act to make evaluation of programs obligatory every five years (on average, 20 per cent of each department's activities have to be evaluated per year). In 2009, the government required all departments to make public their program-evaluation reports and established the principle of independence of evaluation functions within departments. Through these changes, it sought to constitute a "reliable base of evaluation evidence" to strengthen the management of public programs.[10]

Figure 10.2 presents the main elements that should guide the program-evaluation function. The clear objective is resource optimization, as two main aspects are targeted: programs' relevance and performance must be demonstrated. All programs are subjected to five "tests" or "fundamental questions." These questions and the corollary sub-questions are presented in Table 10.1. Figure 10.3 shows an example of an evaluation report, which was conducted by the Department of Innovation, Science and Economic Development on its Computers for Schools program. Over the past five years, this program has delivered almost 370,000 refurbished computers to schools, libraries, not-for-profit organizations, Aboriginal communities, and some individuals. Computers are refurbished by students and recent graduates through an internship program. About three hundred interns are employed annually.[11]

With the reforms adopted in 2009, more and more program evaluations have been required in the federal administration. As Table 10.2 shows, the number of employees assigned to the task grew by 25 per cent between 2007 and 2011 (more recent data are not available).

Table 10.1 Fundamental questions to take into account in evaluations

	Issue 1: Continued need for program	Assessment of the extent to which the program continues to address a demonstrable need and is responsive to the needs of Canadians
Relevance	Issue 2: Alignment with government priorities	Assessment of the linkages between program objectives and (i) federal government priorities and (ii) departmental strategic outcomes
	Issue 3: Alignment with federal roles and responsibilities	Assessment of the role and responsibilities of the federal government in delivering the program
Performance (effectiveness, efficiency, and economy)	Issue 4: Achievement of expected outcomes	Assessment of progress toward expected outcomes (including immediate, intermediate, and ultimate outcomes) with reference to performance targets and program reach, program design, including the linkage and contribution of outputs to outcomes
	Issue 5: Demonstration of efficiency and economy	Assessment of resource utilization in relation to the production of outputs and progress toward expected outcomes

Source: Treasury Board Secretariat (Canada), *Supporting Effective Evaluations: A Guide to Developing Performance Measurement Strategies* (Ottawa: Her Majesty the Queen in Right of Canada, 2010).

Moreover, costs associated with professional services—that is, with use of external evaluation consultants—have dropped (by 20 per cent, according to the data in Table 10.2), which seems to indicate that the federal administration is expanding its expertise in this area. Evaluation results are used more and more by departments to plan and account for their activities. The data compiled by the Centre of Excellence for Evaluation with regard to use of evaluation results, reproduced in list form in Figure 10.3, indicate that a high proportion of departments use them

Figure 10.3 Evaluation of the Computers for Schools Program

Evaluation of Computers for Schools
[excerpt]

4.1 Relevance

- There is a continued need to provide refurbished computers to students and other Canadians. CFS provides an environmentally responsible means for governments and businesses to dispose of surplus computers. Additionally, providing youth with internships gives them opportunities to develop the skills necessary to enter the workforce.
- CFS aligns with federal responsibilities to foster access to technology, maximize the use of crown assets and contribute to sustainable development through the appropriate disposal of IT equipment. The CFS program does not duplicate or overlap any other government program.
- The objectives of the program are consistent with federal government priorities related to developing stronger digital skills among Canadians, providing work experience to youth and reducing the government's environmental footprint.

4.2 Performance

- CFS has distributed nearly 370,000 refurbished computers to beneficiaries over the past five years, with the majority delivered to schools. In addition to providing technology to schools and assisting not-for-profit organizations, the recent program expansion gives access to computer technology to Canadians who could not otherwise afford it.
- With respect to work experience, CFS enhances the employability of youth by providing hands-on experience in the IT field and assists in the development of both ICT and soft skills.
- About 300 interns were employed annually in CFS workshops across Canada, exceeding annual published targets. The program has contributed to learning opportunities for youth. There is an opportunity for the program to recruit additional female participants.
- The network of partners surrounding CFS brings with it substantial in-kind and cash donations. These donations enable the program to operate and succeed.
- The program reduces the environmental footprint of government and businesses through reuse and recycling of their computer equipment.
- The program demonstrates economy and efficiency and continues to meet delivery targets despite a reduction in resources over the assessment period. However, the program continues to mine data

---

(*Continued*)

Figure 10.3 (Continued)

---

manually, resulting in data quality issues and some challenges with program reporting.

4.3 Recommendation

The findings of the evaluation led to the following recommendation:

1. The CFS program should consider modernizing its data collection, capture and storage with a view to ensuring adequate performance information is available.
2. The CFS program should continue to explore the diversity of its interns and consider what more could be done to attract female candidates.

Source: Innovation, Science and Economic Development (Canada), *Computers for School: Final Evaluation Report* (Ottawa: Her Majesty the Queen in Right of Canada, 2017), 22–23.
Reproduced with the permission of the Minister of Industry [2017].

Table 10.2 Resources devoted to program evaluation, federal government, 2007–2011

	2007	2008	2009	2010	2011
Employees[a]	409	418	474	459	500
Salary[b]	28.4	32.3	37.1	38.2	39.0
Professional Services[b]	17.9	20.5	19.1	17.6	14.3

Source: Treasury Board Secretariat (Canada), *2012 Annual Report on the Health of the Evaluation Function* (Ottawa: Her Majesty the Queen in Right of Canada, 2014).
[a] Full-time equivalents.
[b] Millions of dollars.

to prepare the principal reports that they must submit to the Treasury Board and to Parliament.

From its inception until the 2009 reform, the federal government's evaluation function was treated as essentially an internal process. The main "clients" for evaluations were the managers, and the objective was to encourage continuous improvement of program management. The modifications made to the evaluation policy in 2009 somewhat changed the goal of the exercise. Because all evaluation results are now published, the public has also become a "client." The question is whether this change will eventually further politicize the evaluation function in Canada.

Figure 10.4 Use of evaluation results for production of other reports

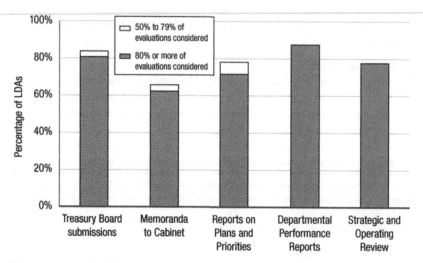

Note: as reported by 35 large departments and agencies (LDAs). Data for 2011.
Source: Treasury Board Secretariat (Canada), *2012 Annual Report on the Health of the Evaluation Function* (Ottawa: Her Majesty the Queen in Right of Canada, 2014).

Departmental Mechanisms

The federal government's recently adopted policies and directives demonstrate a desire to decentralize execution of the audit and control functions. The central agencies are more in a steering position: they issue the general rules that the departments must follow (a role played by the Treasury Board and its secretariat) and offer technical support (Office of the Comptroller General and Centre of Excellence for Evaluation). Implementation of this decentralization is accompanied by a new oversight framework, also decentralized, under the responsibility of external committees that are mandated to ensure that the activities conducted by program managers remain both neutral and independent of all undue influences.

All federal departments must now integrate audit and evaluation functions into the highest levels of their organization. The deputy head (the deputy minister) of each department is responsible for these functions and must account for all of his or her department's activities to the Treasury Board and to Parliament. To assist in the execution of this mandate, the deputy head is obliged to establish independent audit and evaluation units in his or her department. These units are led by senior civil servants, a chief audit executive and a departmental head of evaluation, who must ensure that the activities conducted under their responsibility (audit and evaluation, respectively) are complete, independent, objective, and neutral. Their main tasks are to set up and supervise the audit or evaluation tasks of the department, advise the deputy head, and see to the quality and probity of analyses entrusted to them by the central agencies. For this reason, they have access to all of the department's resources.

All departments are also required to establish committees of independent experts, the departmental audit committee and the departmental evaluation committee, to ensure that the integrity of activities is respected. The departmental audit committee is composed of three people, at least two of whom come from outside the federal administration, are chosen jointly by the Comptroller General and the deputy head, and are appointed for a period of four years, renewable once. This committee must submit an annual report to the deputy head, who presents his or her own assessment of the department's evaluation activities and makes recommendations. The reports of the departmental audit committee are public. The departmental evaluation committee is formed from the department's senior civil servants, including the deputy minister, the deputy head, and the departmental head of evaluation. The main functions of this committee are to approve the department's evaluation activities, ensure that all requirements of the policy for evaluating the government are respected in the framework of each of the evaluations, and respond to the recommendations made in the context of the evaluations.

KEYWORDS

Comptroller General • *Internal audit* • *Program evaluation* • *Departmental committees*

TO FIND OUT MORE

Reading suggestions

Good, David A. *The Politics of Public Management: The HRDC Audit of Grants and Contributions.* Toronto: Toronto University Press, 2005.
Jarvis, Mark D. "The Adoption of the Accounting Officer System in Canada: Changing Relationships?" *Canadian Public Administration* 52, no. 4 (2009): 525–47.

Lindquist, Evert. "How Ottawa Assesses Department/Agency Performance: Treasury Board's Management Accountability Framework." In *How Ottawa Spends, 2009–2010: Economic Upheaval and Political Dysfunction*, ed. A.M. Maslove, 47–88. Montreal/Kingston: McGill-Queen's University Press, 2009.

Periodicals

Canadian Journal of Program Evaluation

Websites

Office of the Comptroller General (Treasury Board Secretariat, Canada): https://www.canada.ca/en/treasury-board-secretariat/corporate/organization.html
Centre of Excellence for Evaluation (Treasury Board Secretariat, Canada): https://www.canada.ca/en/treasury-board-secretariat/services/audit-evaluation/centre-excellence-evaluation.html
Canadian Evaluation Society: https://evaluationcanada.ca
Public Sector Accounting Board: http://www.frascanada.ca/public-sector-accounting-board/index.aspx

11 External Budgetary Audit and Evaluation Mechanisms

The Canadian parliamentary system takes accountability very seriously. Indeed, one of the main responsibilities of parliamentarians is to oversee the government's actions and to ask it to justify them, if necessary. The accountability function led to the establishment of one of the oldest Canadian parliamentary institutions, the Office of the Auditor General (the equivalent of supreme audit institutions found in other countries[1]). It also produced one of the most interesting—even radical[2]—innovations of recent decades: the creation of an independent parliamentary budget office. Although the mandate of these two institutions is somewhat similar (supporting parliamentarians' accountability oversight), each intervenes at a different stage in the budget cycle. The Auditor General is responsible for analysing the government's financial results, whereas the parliamentary budget office deals with budget forecasts and estimates. The work of the Auditor General is thus done at the end of the budget cycle, once the budgetary policies have been executed; the work of the Parliamentary Budget Officer is done much earlier, usually at the beginning of the cycle, after the budget estimates are presented but before the budgetary policies are adopted.

The Auditor General

The function of Auditor General exists in all Canadian legislative assemblies (the position is called "provincial auditor" in Nova Scotia). The Office of the Auditor General of Canada was established in 1877, with the adoption of the Public Accounting Act, and the provincial auditor positions were established in roughly the same era (in 1867 in Quebec; a little later in other provinces). The creation of the Office of the Auditor General formalized the practice of conducting audits of financial transactions, already underway in the administration, and connecting the audits to the executive branch. Today, the activities of the Auditor General of Canada are governed by the Auditor General Act and the corresponding provincial statutes.[3]

For most of the twentieth century, tasks carried out by auditors general (federal and provincial) consisted solely of examining the probity of the government's financial operations. This meant verifying that expenditures were justified and complied with parliamentary authorizations, and that the Public Accounts presented accurate information. With the proliferation of governmental activities and the increasing size of budgets, it was proposed that the mandate of auditors general be broadened; many questioned the real significance of conducting strictly accounting-related audits of the government's financial activities. In 1976, the Auditor General of Canada painted a gloomy picture of the situation, declaring in his annual report that Parliament was no longer effectively controlling the public purse. In reaction, the federal government created the Royal Commission on Financial Management and Accountability (chaired by Justice Lambert). The commission recommended that the Auditor General's mandate be expanded to allow for "value for money" audits. The statute was amended to incorporate this change in 1977. Since then, in addition to oversight of financial operations, the Auditor General has been mandated to issue an opinion measuring management of public programs against the criteria of performance, savings, and efficiency (section 7.1 of the Auditor General Act).

The Canadian statute has been amended several times to broaden the Auditor General's mandate. The Auditor General may now conduct inquiries into and examinations of all subjects that he or she deems important, submit to Parliament more than one report per year, and study the activities of Crown corporations and recipients of public funds. The most important change has been the creation of the Environmental Commissioner position in 1995. Placed under the direct authority of the Auditor General, the Environmental Commissioner presents to Parliament analyses and recommendations regarding the federal government's environmental-protection and sustainable-development policies. Except for the position of Environmental Commissioner, provincial auditors general have responsibilities similar to those of the federal Auditor General: verifications (or audits) of financial statements and verifications of resource optimization (performance audits). The Auditor General of Canada is also the auditor for each of the three territorial legislative assemblies and reports directly to them.

Figure 11.1 Expenditures of the Office of the Auditor General of Canada, 2017–2018 (planned spending)

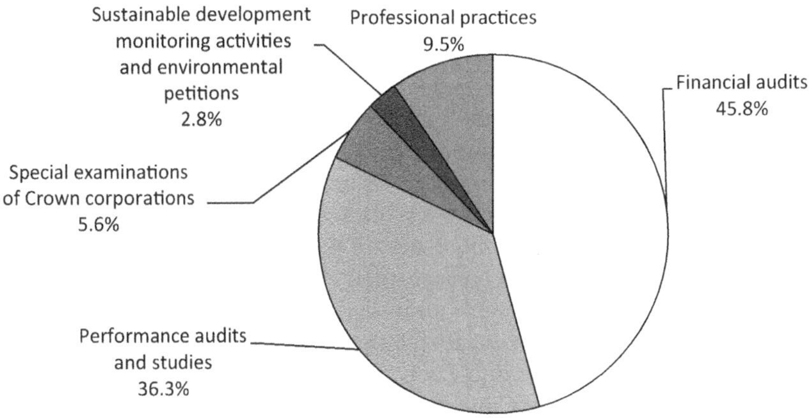

Source: Office of the Auditor General (Canada), *Departmental Plan, 2017–2018* (Ottawa: Her Majesty the Queen in Right of Canada, 2017).

The Auditor General is an agent of Parliament. He or she works for members of the legislature and must account for his or her activities only to parliamentarians. The Auditor General's main legislative interlocutor is the Public Accounts Committee, which is responsible for receiving and examining the government's Public Accounts, the Auditor General's reports, and the activities of the Office of the Auditor General. The Auditor General has great autonomy from the executive branch, as his or her appointment requires the assent of the House. The mandate usually lasts between eight and ten years and is non-renewable. The duration of this mandate enables the Auditor General to act without being subjected to undue external influence.[4] The Auditor General sets his or her own operating budgets, which are submitted to Parliament for approval;[5] hires his or her employees directly (respecting the usual staffing regulations of the federal administration); and determines the vast majority of activities that he or she will conduct. The Auditor General also has almost total access to the government's documents.

The Auditor General directs the Office of the Auditor General, which is a large agency. For instance, the Office of the Auditor General of Canada employs almost six hundred civil servants, about two-thirds of whom are assigned to auditing. The Office's annual budget is almost $100 million, a level that has remained relatively stable in recent years. As Figure 11.1 shows, the budget is shared almost equally between activities related to certification and compliance of financial statements (financial audits) and those related to performance analysis (performance audits and studies), and includes several other, less-important expenditure items.

In all Canadian legislatures, the audit documents submitted to the House fall into two categories. Financial statement audits, which examine the compliance of the government's financial operations, are presented when the government's Public Accounts are tabled. These audits contain the Auditor General's opinion regarding the probity of the financial statements, with reservation (i.e., presenting the Auditor General's concerns) or without reservation. In the last sixteen years, the Auditor General of Canada has accepted all Public Accounts tabled by the Canadian government without reservation. The Auditor General of Canada also audits the financial statements of other entities (including territorial administrations and Crown corporations). In total, the Office of the Auditor General of Canada conducts almost one hundred audits of financial statements each year.

Performance audits deal with questions linked to the quality of management of financial resources. The results of these audits are presented in the Auditor General's annual reports submitted to Parliament. In them, the Auditor General makes observations about several specific programs or sectors (sectors may be under the responsibility of more than one department or agency). In general, between twenty-five and thirty programs are examined each year by the Auditor General of Canada (a smaller number are examined by provincial auditors general). Table 11.1 shows the programs that were examined during the 2016–2017 and 2017–2018 fiscal years. The Office of the Auditor General chooses which programs or activities will be audited based on the importance of the issues associated with these programs or activities; requests made by parliamentarians and, more broadly, issues arising from the public interest (although the Office is under no obligation to respond to these requests); and the elevated risks that deficient management might represent in certain areas.

Performance audits require a long evaluation process; federal audits may take up to eighteen months. This process is composed of the following main steps:[6]

1. Establish audit objectives and criteria for the assessment of performance
2. Gather the evidence necessary to assess performance against the criteria

3. Report both positive and negative findings
4. Draw conclusions based on the objectives of the audit
5. Make recommendations for improvement when there are significant differences between criteria and assessed performance

Through these audits, the Auditor General tries to ensure that government programs are managed economically and efficiently and that the government has the means to measure their effectiveness. The

Table 11.1 Programs and activities audited by the Office of the Auditor General of Canada, 2016 and 2017

May 2016	November 2016	May 2017	November 2017
• Venture Capital Action Plan • Detecting and preventing fraud in the citizenship program • The governor in council appointment process in administrative tribunals • Drug benefits—Veterans Affairs Canada • Canadian Army Reserve—National Defence	• The Beyond the Border Action Plan • Income tax objections—Canada Revenue Agency • Preparing Indigenous Offenders for Release—Correctional Service Canada • Oversight of passenger vehicle safety—Transport Canada • Canadian Armed Forces recruitment and retention—National Defence • First Nations' specific claims—Indigenous and Northern Affairs Canada • Operating and maintenance support for military equipment—National Defence	• Managing the risk of fraud • Customs duties • Preventing corruption in Immigration and Border Services • Mental health support for members—Royal Canadian Mounted Police • Temporary Foreign Worker Program—Employment and Social Development • Civil aviation infrastructure in the North—Transport Canada • Fossil fuel subsidies	• Phoenix pay problems • Call centres—Canada Revenue Agency • Settlement services for Syrian refugees—Immigration, Refugees and Citizenship Canada • Oral health programs for First Nations and Inuit—Health Canada • Preparing women offenders for release—Correctional Service Canada • Royal Military College of Canada—National Defence

Source: Office of the Auditor General of Canada, *Reports to Parliament*, http://www.oag-bvg.gc.ca/internet/English/parl_lp_e_856.html (accessed 30 November 2017).

Office's analyses do not deal with the basis for public programs—
that is, the government's decision whether and how to take action.
However, certain external observers feel that the Office's analyses, rather than being neutral, promote the principles of new public
management.[7]

Although the Office is entirely independent of the government, the
two work closely together. This collaboration takes place not only at the
information-gathering stage but also during the formulation of recommendations. In fact, the Office shares its conclusions with the government before it submits them to the legislative assembly. The government
may therefore present its responses to the Auditor General's recommendations at the same time as the Office publishes its reports. Most of the
time, these responses indicate that the government accepts the Office's
conclusions and recommendations and that corrective measures have
already been or will soon be instituted. Not everyone approves of this
collaboration between the Office of the Auditor General and the government. Some feel that it allows the Auditor General to stay above the
partisan debates that take place in Parliament,[8] whereas others see it
as conveying too strong an interdependence between the central agencies (mainly the Treasury Board Secretariat at the federal level) and the
Office. In fact, it is notable that an audit-based culture and results-based
management are increasingly shared by the Office of the Auditor General and the government's central agencies;[9] it is a culture in which the
professional accounting organizations whose norms are increasingly
used by Canadian public administrations also participate.[10] It should
be noted that parliamentarians are relatively absent from debates over
the orientations of the Office.

The relationship between the Auditor General and Parliament is also
subject to debate. Over the years, the Office's expertise and credibility have developed to the point that the Auditor General has become
an essential actor in the parliamentary budgetary process. Some feel
that it is more accurate to say that the Auditor General is related to,
rather than at the service of, parliamentarians.[11] Others feel, however,
that parliamentarians are effective, though not necessarily in the way
presumed. Through the Public Accounts Committee, which publicly
examines its reports, the Office of the Auditor General has an important
public (and media) forum within which to discuss and explain in depth
the analysis of its conclusions.[12]

Finally, it is worth emphasizing the excellent relationship that the
Auditor General has with the public and the media. The Auditor

General's reports are highly anticipated and widely covered in the press. Their content receives abundant commentary in the public square and is used by opposition parties to make things difficult for the government.

The Parliamentary Budget Officer

Unlike the position of Auditor General, that of Parliamentary Budget Officer was created recently. The federal government adopted the statute establishing the position in 2006, and appointed its first holder in 2008.[13] Among the provinces, Ontario is the only one to have created its own position of parliamentary budget officer, the Financial Accountability Officer, in 2013. Its first holder was chosen in spring 2015.[14] Because the position of Financial Accountability Officer was established only recently, and because its powers are similar to those of the federal Parliamentary Budget Officer, I will focus on the latter.

The mandate of the Parliamentary Budget Officer is to oversee the reliability of the government's budgetary forecasts. This oversight is performed ahead of the budgetary cycle, and not after, as is the case for the Auditor General. The Parliamentary Budget Officer has very broad powers. He or she provides Parliament with "analysis, including analysis of macroeconomic and fiscal policy, for the purposes of raising the quality of parliamentary debate and promoting greater budget transparency and accountability" (Parliament of Canada Act, art. 79.01). The Parliamentary Budget Officer is also mandated to estimate the costs of any bills tabled in Parliament and to examine other issues related to the financial situation and to the government's budget estimates, if a parliamentarian or a parliamentary committee so requests. In 2011, a more formal process of requests for information was established when the Standing Committee on Public Finances of the House of Commons adopted a motion asking the Officer to present his or her financial and economic projections to the committee twice a year (in spring and fall).

Compared to the Auditor General of Canada, the Parliamentary Budget Officer has limited resources. The annual budget is about $3 million and the office includes a team of a dozen economists and financial analysts. The Officer's discretionary power with regard to management of his or her activities was also initially more limited, as the position was placed under the authority of the Parliamentary Librarian and thus had to report to this person and not directly to parliamentarians. Furthermore, the Parliamentary Budget Officer was appointed by the government, without consultations with the other parties in the House, for a renewable five-year mandate. As a number of observers have noted, this mode of appointment infringes on the Officer's freedom of action, as he or she might hesitate to criticize the government if he or she wishes the mandate to be extended. The Parliamentary Budget Officer gained more independence in 2017: the mandate was extended to seven years (renewable up to fourteen years in office in total); the Officer is now directly accountable to the presidents of the House and the Senate; and he or she is appointed with the consent of all parties and groups recognized in Parliament.

Despite the constraints during the initial years of tenure, the first Parliamentary Budget Officer was prolific, as he managed to produce an average of twenty reports per year on different subjects.[15] Some of these reports are now part of a regular cycle of publications. Each year, the Parliamentary Budget Officer publishes a report on the government's financial viability that presents the country's economic and financial prospects over the very long term (seventy-five-year projections). Every quarter, the Officer produces an expenditure monitor – a study that indicates if and to what extent the budgetary appropriations made by Parliament have been used. This document is accompanied by a consultable database that presents the information by department and agency, and by appropriation category. A second database was created more recently to make it possible to perform budget simulations by analysing different fiscal policy scenarios, including measuring effects that changes in tax rates or tax appropriations might have on federal government revenues. Each year, some parliamentarians ask to receive estimates on costs that might be engendered by changes to fiscal policies (e.g., modified tax rates or tax credits). This tool makes it possible to respond, in part, to these requests.[16]

The early years of the Parliamentary Budget Officer were fairly tumultuous. Despite limited resources and difficulty accessing some information[17] (the government was very reluctant to provide certain data requested[18]), the Officer's analyses had an undeniable impact – on more than one occasion providing a well-founded demonstration of the inaccuracy of the government's estimates.[19] Like the Auditor General's, the Parliamentary Budget Officer's reports are anticipated and critiqued. As Table 11.2 shows, of all the senior civil servants who report to Parliament, the Auditor General and the Parliamentary Budget Officer receive the most media coverage. This situation illustrates two issues inherent to the parliamentary accountability process. First, budgetary questions are complex, and their analysis requires a degree of expertise that not all

Table 11.2 Canadian print media coverage of parliamentary officers, 2012

Agents of Parliament	Office holder	Mentions in articles
Auditor General	Michael Ferguson	2,130
Parliamentary Budget Officer	Kevin Page	1,862
Chief Electoral Officer	Marc Mayrand	582
Privacy Commissioner	Jennifer Stoddart	553
Conflict of Interest and Ethics Commissioner	Mary Dawson	441
Commissioner of Official Languages	Graham Fraser	375
Information Commissioner	Suzanne Legault	254
Public Sector Integrity Commissioner	Mario Dion	137
Commissioner of Lobbying	Karen Shepherd	106

Source: Geneviève Tellier, "Le directeur parlementaire du budget," 44.
Note: Research was conducted using the Factiva database and the names of the office-holders as keywords. The results presented in this table are not exhaustive, as some articles may deal with agents of Parliament without mentioning their names. However, this information seems sufficiently complete to provide comparisons among the office-holders. The research covered the period from 1 January to 31 December 2012. (It should be noted that I found no references to the Parliamentary Librarian—neither William Young nor his successor, Sonia L'Heureux.)

parliamentarians possess. It is therefore necessary that specialized agencies help them process the materials submitted to them. Second, recommendations by experts, whether the Auditor General or the Parliamentary Budget Officer, will inevitably embarrass the government and be used by the opposition parties for partisan purposes. Although it is a fundamental principle of parliamentarianism that governments be accountable to elected representatives of the population, expert recommendations will inevitably be used by opposition parties for partisan purposes.

The partisan use of the Parliamentary Budget Officer's studies stands as a warning to governments to be prudent when they institute external monitoring mechanisms. The Canadian government, for example, has been criticized several times for creating a structure that has few resources with which to fulfil its broad mandate.[20] This situation is not unique to Canada; attempts to limit budgetary oversight have been observed in countries such as Hungary and

Table 11.3 OECD countries with a parliamentary budget agency, 2000, 2007, and 2017

2000	2007	2017	Staff
1. Italy	1. Italy	1. Italy	26–50 people
2. Japan	2. Japan	2. Japan	10–25 people
3. Mexico	3. Mexico	3. Mexico	26–50 people
4. Netherlands	4. Netherlands	4. Netherlands	> 50 people
5. Poland	5. Poland	5. Poland	< 10 people
6. Sweden	6. Sweden	6. Sweden	26–50 people
7. United States	7. United States	7. United States	> 50 people
	8. South Korea	8. South Korea	> 50 people
	9. United Kingdom	9. United Kingdom	10–25 people
	10. Canada	10. Canada	10–25 people
	11. Hungary	11. Hungary	< 10 people
	12. Israel	12. Israel	26–50 people
	13. Portugal	13. Portugal	< 10 people
		14. Australia	26–50 people
		15. Austria	< 10 people
		16. Greece	< 10 people
		17. Serbia	< 10 people

Source: Organisation for Economic Co-operation and Development, *International Budget Practices and Procedures Database*, https://search.oecd.org/governance/budgeting/internationalbudgetpracticesandproceduresdatabase.htm (accessed 24 March 2017).

Venezuela. It is worth mentioning that the establishment of oversight agencies for budgetary estimates is a relatively recent phenomenon around the world. Although some of these bodies have existed for some decades (including the US Congressional Budget Office, created in 1974, considered the gold standard in this regard[21]), the vast majority have been established in the last ten years. Table 11.3 presents the list of OECD member countries that have created such an agency.

That these oversight institutions are quite new reflects a marked trend towards providing parliamentarians with more resources and power to debate budgetary and financial issues. This phenomenon is not unique to Canada: there seems to be an increasingly widespread desire to strengthen the work of parliamentarians.

Budgetary Debates in the Public Square

In Canada, neither on the federal scene nor in the provinces and territories is there an independent agency responsible for oversight of public budgets. However, a number of non-governmental research institutes examine governments' budgetary initiatives. These organizations are funded mainly by the private sector or by not-for-profit organizations (such as unions and pressure groups) and, to a lesser extent, by the financial contributions of individuals. Some of them are hosted by Canadian universities (e.g., the Mowat Centre at the University of Toronto) or frequently receive contributions from academic researchers (such as the Institute for Research on Public Policy and the C.D. Howe Institute). Their main objective is to provide alternatives to the government's budgetary proposals. Together, these organizations present a wide range of opinions, and their proposals come from both the left (including the Canadian Centre for Policy Alternatives, the Broadbent Institute, and the Institut de recherche et d'information socio-économiques) and the right (the Fraser Institute, the Montreal Economic Institute, the Atlantic Institute for Market Studies, and the Canada West Foundation). Some organizations have a national vocation, but not all, and many national organizations have provincial sections.

Such groups have made a relatively recent appearance in Canada. The first ones were created in the 1970s, with a few exceptions.[22] The presence of research institutes in Canada has been strongly influenced by the American experience. Although the Canadian institutes do not have financial resources and expertise at the levels observed in the United States, their influence seems to have grown in recent years.

Although Canadian research institutes do not participate directly in the formulation of governments' budgetary policies, their analyses are now part of the public debate, and therefore, ultimately, of governments' choices. Their reports are covered in the media and critiqued in the public square. Furthermore, governments seem more and more inclined to listen to them and to ask them to help develop innovative policies. A good number of these organizations now participate actively in prebudget consultations (those conducted by both departments of finance and legislative assemblies), thus taking advantage of a supplementary public forum.

FEATURE BOX: WHO OVERSEES THE AUDITOR GENERAL OF CANADA?

As the Auditor General's role is to oversee the government's activities, it seems legitimate to wonder who oversees the activities of the Office of the Auditor General. The parliamentary rules provide certain accountability mechanisms. Each year, the Auditor General must appear before the Public Accounts Committee of the House and answer questions from parliamentarians with regard to his or her activities. The Auditor General also submits to Parliament reports presenting a summary of activities and the management strategies that he or she intends to develop in coming years. The government appoints an external auditor that audits the Office of the Auditor General's financial statements every year; these financial statements and the opinion of the external auditor are also submitted to Parliament and may be examined by parliamentarians.

In addition, the Office of the Auditor General of Canada has established its own accountability mechanisms. Some of these mechanisms are internal—performed by the Office itself. One unit of the Office (the Practice Review Team) is responsible for performance evaluations of the audits conducted by the Auditor General. The results of these internal evaluations are published every year. The Office is also submitted to external controls. The External Audit Committee, formed of three members, two of whom are independent of the Office, formulate opinions on the Office's internal control mechanisms. Other external committees express opinions and provide recommendations. The Independent Advisory Committee on Government Accounting and Auditing Standards, for instance, advises the Auditor General on questions related to professional accounting standards.

The Office also recently innovated by submitting to an external audit performed by peers—that is, other auditors. The first audit took place in 1999 under the responsibility of a group of Canadian experts from private-sector accounting firms. In 2003, the Office asked a group of foreign legislative auditors to audit its activities. This group was formed of auditors from the audit offices of France, the Netherlands, and Norway and from the National Audit Office of the United Kingdom (observers from the US General Accounting Office were also present). Canada was among the first countries to submit to such an external peer audit (the others were in Estonia in 1999, the Czech Republic in 2000, and Poland and the Slovak Republic in 2011[1]). A second external peer audit took place in 2009 (by a group of auditors from Australia, the Netherlands, Denmark, Sweden, and Norway). A third peer audit is planned before the end of the current Auditor General of Canada's mandate.

[1] International Organization of Supreme Audit Institutions, special issue on peer review, *International Journal of Government Auditing* 38, no. 4 (2011): 5.

KEYWORDS

Office of the Auditor General of Canada • *External audit* • *Standing Committee on Public Accounts* • *Audits of financial statements* • *Performance audits* • *Parliamentary Budget Officer* • *Media*

TO FIND OUT MORE

Reading suggestions

Canadian Public Administration 47, no. 2 (2004). Special issue on the role and influence of auditors general in Canadian government, ed. A. Tupper.
Stapenhurst, Rick, Riccardo Pelizzo, David M. Olson, and Lisa Von Trapp, eds. *Legislative Oversight and Budgeting*. Washington, DC: World Bank, 2008.
Taft, Jordan. "From Change to Stability: Investigating Canada's Office of the Auditor General." *Canadian Public Administration* 59, no. 3 (2016): 467–85.

Database

Research Tools (Office of the Parliamentary Budget Officer): http://www. pbo-dpb.gc.ca/en/data_tools

Websites

Office of the Parliamentary Budget Officer: http://www.pbo-dpb.gc.ca/en/
Financial Accountability Office of Ontario: http://fao-on.org/en/
Congressional Budget Office (United States): https://www.cbo.gov/
Office of the Auditor General of Canada: http://www.oag-bvg.gc.ca/internet/
    English/admin_e_41.html
Office of the Auditor General (Newfoundland and Labrador): http://www.
    ag.gov.nl.ca/ag/
Office of the Auditor General (Prince Edward Island): http://www.assembly.
    pe.ca/index.php3?number=1012317
Office of the Auditor General (Nova Scotia): http://www.oag-ns.ca/
Auditor General of New Brunswick: http://www2.gnb.ca/content/gnb/en/
    contacts/dept_renderer.163.html
Auditor General of Quebec: http://www.vgq.gouv.qc.ca/default-EN.aspx
Office of the Auditor General of Ontario: http://www.auditor.on.ca/
Office of the Auditor General (Manitoba): http://www.oag.mb.ca/
Office of the Provincial Auditor of Saskatchewan: https://auditor.sk.ca/
Auditor General of Alberta: http://www.oag.ab.ca/
Office of the Auditor General of British Columbia: http://www.bcauditor.com/

Conclusion

Analysis of the budgetary cycle opens the door to a better understanding of the state of public finance and, more broadly, the mechanisms governing state activities. Budgetary decisions are the result of choices made by many actors—sometimes but not always acting in concert—who want to take initiative but face certain constraints (economic, financial, political, managerial, and others). To quote Wildavsky once again, a budget is not simply "a document, containing words and figures, which proposes expenditure for certain items and purposes." It is "a web of social as well as legal relationships in which commitments are made by all parties: politicians, public servants, interest groups, and citizens."[1]

Looking at the Canadian budgetary process, we may try to discern a "Canadian model." The rules and institutions in the Canadian system have been strongly influenced by the British system. Distribution of responsibilities and authority between the executive branch and the legislative branch (with the executive branch holding broader budgetary decision-making powers and Parliament having the predominant role in accountability) and a flexible legal framework are characteristics that have been directly borrowed from the Anglo-Saxon model. This model has been adapted, but not substantially transformed, in Canada.

However, what is specifically Canadian is the federal system. Canada is composed of many distinct public administrations with important budgetary powers. Although the provinces and territories played a secondary role within the Canadian federation at its inception, this is certainly not the case today. Combined, their budgets are larger than that of the federal government, and their budgetary responsibilities are exercised in a number of major sectors (health, education, and social services in particular). Canadian federalism is not characterized by strong collaboration among the provinces and territories or between the provinces, the territories, and the federal government. Although discussions take place, each remains generally free to make its own choices (within the boundaries set by the Constitution) and none has to be accountable to the others. Although such division of responsibilities is less propitious for the implementation of shared policies, it makes it easier to adapt budgetary initiatives to regional specificities and to adopt innovative policies. A number of budgetary reforms may arise in a few provinces and/or territories and then spread to others (as was the case for balanced-budget laws).

It is therefore possible to refer to a Canadian model. What does this mean? Canada currently is a model student when it comes to budgetary restraint. It began to clean up its public finance in the late 1990s, and it recovered quite well from the 2008 financial crisis. However, there are a number of indications that this performance is not really the result of more rigorous financial management. On the one hand, although the federal government's financial situation has improved considerably, this is not the case for most Canadian provinces and territories (and also municipalities). Many are struggling to balance their budgets, and for those that manage to do so it is at the cost of drastic service reductions. It is not yet clear whether these reductions can be maintained indefinitely. On the other hand, the recent administrative reforms instituted by the federal government do not seem to have led to an effective reallocation of resources, even though audit and internal evaluation activities have increased. The program review launched in 1994 (and the annual strategic departmental reviews that followed) and the adoption of results-based management should be seen as exercises that have made it possible to substantially reduce public budgets (and deficits) rather than to reform program management. The improvement of the federal government's (and certain provinces') public finance was made possible by strong political leadership, which was exerted in the context of institutions that grant broad responsibilities to the executive branch and assisted by a highly favourable economic context. The effectiveness of the reforms to financial management systems, however, is yet to be shown.

The financial health of governments is not the only factor worth considering when one assesses the quality of the budgetary process. Issues linked to openness and transparency of budgetary decisions are also important. Canadian parliamentarians, like those in many other countries, have not been primary players: although their support for budgetary policy is crucial for the government, they do not participate actively in the decision-making process. Many are therefore demanding that Canadian lawmakers be granted more power. In the Canadian system, certain reforms are underway to attempt to strengthen parliamentarians' role in two areas. First, supplementary accountability mechanisms have been established. The most visible reform is the one that led to establishment of the position of Parliamentary Budget Officer. This senior parliamentary civil servant provides extra expertise to lawmakers in their examination of and commentary on the budgetary initiatives presented by the government. Second, new procedures have been established to increase parliamentarians' representation mechanism. Prebudget consultations allow lawmakers to solicit public opinion and use suggestions received to formulate recommendations on the content of the next budget. Although both of these mechanisms are still imperfect, they may nevertheless help parliamentarians and, indirectly, the general public to have a better comprehension of budgetary issues.

Notes

Introduction

1 Organisation for Economic Co-operation and Development, *Government at a Glance 2013* (Paris: OECD, 2013), chap. 1.
2 And not only in Canada. For a detailed analysis of this phenomenon in Western countries, see Carl Dahlström, B. Guy Peters, and Jon Pierre, eds, *Steering from the Centre: Strengthening Political Control in Western Democracies* (Toronto: University of Toronto Press, 2011).
3 For examples of sociological and political analyses of budgetary questions, see Marc Leroy, *Taxation, the State and Society: The Fiscal Sociology of Interventionist Democracy* (Brussels: Peter Lang, 2011); Issac William Martin, *The Permanent Tax Revolt: How the Property Tax Transformed American Politics* (Stanford: Stanford University Press, 2008); Gerald J. Miller, *Government Budgeting and Financial Management in Practice: Logics to Make Sense of Ambiguity* (Boca Raton: CRC Press, 2012).
4 Aaron B. Wildavsky, *The Politics of the Budgetary Process*, 4th ed. (Boston: Little, Brown, 1984). Donald J. Savoie and David A. Good are the main Canadian proponents of this tradition.
5 Charles O. Jones, *An Introduction to the Study of Public Policy* (Monterey: Brooks/Cole, 1984).
6 See, e.g., Michael Howlett, M. Ramesh, and Anthony Perl, *Studying Public Policy, Policy Cycles and Policy Subsystems*, 3rd ed. (Don Mills: Oxford University Press, 2009).
7 Peter Deleon, "The Stages Approach to the Policy Process: What Has It Done? Where Is It Going?" in *Theories of the Policy Process*, ed. P.A. Sabatier (Boulder: Westview, 1999).

8 For instance, the Stability and Growth Pact of the European Union lays out a set of budgetary rules that countries' members must follow, such as national public deficit and debt limits (which cannot be above, respectively, 3 per cent and 60 per cent of gross domestic product).

9 See, for example, Bruno Théret, *Protection sociale et fédéralisme: L'Europe dans le miroir de l'Amérique du Nord* (Montreal: Presses de l'Université de Montréal, 2002).

1 The Size and Composition of Canadian Public-Sector Budgets

1 In contrast, some countries saw a marked expansion of their public sector, including South Korea (by 13.0 percentage points), Finland (7.5), and Japan (6.6). For most other OECD countries, expenditures fluctuated by under three percentage points. See Organisation for Economic Co-operation and Development, *Economic Outlook, Analysis and Forecasts*, http://www.oecd.org/eco/outlook/ (accessed 5 July 2017).

2 Richard A. Musgrave, *The Theory of Public Finance: A Study in Public Economy* (New York: McGraw-Hill, 1959). Other means of classification were proposed in the wake of Musgrave's work. Bird, for example, identifies five roles played by the state: consumer, producer, employer, redistributor, and reallocator. Leroy offers the following five functions: financial, economic, social, ecological and territorial, and political. See Richard M. Bird, *The Growth of Government Spending in Canada* (Toronto: Canadian Tax Foundation, 1970); Leroy, *Taxation, the State and Society*.

3 More formally, we could define the welfare state as being the group of public programs related to social solidarity functions. See François-Xavier Merrien, *L'État-providence* (Paris: Presses universitaires de France, 1997).

4 Statistics Canada is currently reviewing its classifications of expenditures and revenues in order to standardize its data to fit with the norms issued by the United Nations. Currently, the data available do not give detailed information on the budgets of Canadian public administrations after 2008 or compare Canadian disaggregated data with those presented by the OECD. This information should be available in coming years. Unless otherwise indicated, the Canadian annual budgetary data cover the financial year from 1 April to 31 March for the federal government and the provincial and territorial governments, and from 1 January to 31 December for local governments.

5 For a detailed analysis of the circumstances that led to the implementation and evolution of the Canadian welfare state, see Keith Banting and John Myles, eds, *Inequality and the Fading of Redistributive Politics* (Vancouver:

UBC Press, 2013); Alvin Finkel, *Social Policy and Practice in Canada* (Waterloo: Wilfrid Laurier University Press, 2006); James J. Rice and Michael J. Prince, *Changing Politics of Canadian Social Policy* (Toronto: University of Toronto Press, 2013). For an excellent study on the history of taxation in Canada, read Shirley Tillotson, *Give and Take: The Citizen-Taxpayer and the Rise of Canadian Democracy* (Vancouver: UBC Press, 2017). For an examination of the evolution of the modern state in other countries, see Peter H. Lindert, *Growing Public: Social Spending and Economic Growth since the Eighteenth Century* (Cambridge: Cambridge University Press, 2004); Vito Tanzi and Ludger Schuknecht, *Public Spending in the 20th Century: A Global Perspective* (Cambridge: Cambridge University Press, 2000).

6 Gosta Esping-Andersen, *The Three Worlds of Welfare Capitalism* (Princeton: Princeton University Press, 1990).

7 These are non-financial assets. There are also financial assets, composed mainly of investments (such as bank deposits, securities). Assets may be tangible (material goods) or intangible (services—for example, intellectual property rights). There are also liabilities, which are contractual obligations such as debt and accounts payable.

8 Capital consumption expenditure is measured by estimating the depreciation in the value of goods and services caused by their use. This depreciation takes account of the total lifespan of the good or service in question and the loss of its value due to its use during a specific period. For example, one might estimate that a vehicle has a lifespan of four years associated with a depreciation of 50 per cent of its initial value in the first year, 30 per cent in the second year, and 10 per cent in the last two years.

9 This category includes health care institutions (hospitals, community organizations, health councils) and universities.

10 Most local administrations are municipalities. This category includes school boards (responsible for day-to-day management of elementary and high schools) and Aboriginal local governments.

11 For an analysis of the evolution of infrastructure expenditures in Canada, see Éric Champagne and Olivier Choinière, "Le financement des infrastructures municipales et les défis du fédéralisme fiscal canadien," *Gestion et management public* 4, no. 3 (2016): 25–36.

12 Jason Jacques, *Federal Tax Expenditures: Use, Reporting and Review* (Ottawa: Library of Parliament, 2011).

13 Organisation for Economic Co-operation and Development, *Recent Tax Policy Trends and Reforms in OECD Countries* (Paris: OECD, 2010). The study examined tax expenditures in Canada, France, Germany, Japan, Korea, the

Netherlands, Spain, Sweden, the United Kingdom, and the United States. For a similar analysis, see Luc Godbout, *L'intervention gouvernementale par la politique fiscal: Le rôle des dépenses fiscales: Étude comparée, Canada, États-Unis, France* (Paris: Économica, 2006).

14 A number of public programs produce goods or services that economists call "public goods"—goods or services that, once produced, may be used by all without any restriction. This is the case, for instance, for national defence; when a territory is protected by the armed forces, all of its inhabitants benefit from this protection, whether they want it or not. In the view of certain economists, the state should confine itself to producing these "public goods" and leave the production of other goods and services to the private sector.

15 On this subject, see Issac William Martin, Ajay K. Mehrotra, and Monica Prasad, eds, *The New Fiscal Sociology: Taxation in Comparative and Historical Perspective* (Cambridge: Cambridge University Press, 2009).

16 The federal government gave an independent agency the mandate to set the contribution rates in 2008. For a number of years, the Employment Insurance fund had recorded large surpluses, a situation denounced by many who saw this as a disguised extra tax assumed by workers and firms. To correct the situation, the government decided that contribution rates should be set as a function of the needs of the program only. Although new rates were supposed to come into effect in 2011, the reform was suspended several times, due notably to the financial crisis in 2008, which ate up the surplus in the fund.

17 Brett Stuckey and Adriane Yong, *A Primer on Federal Social Security Contribution* (Ottawa: Parliament of Canada, 2011).

18 These contributions represent 12.3 per cent of total provincial revenues in Nova Scotia and 11.3 per cent in Ontario, compared to 6.0 per cent in Newfoundland and Labrador, 6.3 per cent in Manitoba, and 6.8 per cent in Quebec (2008 data).

19 For more information on this subject, see Philipp Genschel, "Globalization, Tax Competition, and the Welfare State," *Politics & Society* 30, no. 2 (June 2002): 245–75; Duane Swank and Sven Steinmo, "The New Political Economy of Taxation in Advanced Capitalist Democracies," *American Journal of Political Science* 46, no. 3 (July 2002): 642–55.

20 Data from 2014, Statistics Canada, *Table 12-10-0011-01 - International merchandise trade for all countries and bu Principal Trading Partners, monthly (x 1,000,000)*, CANSIM database, http://www5.statcan.gc.ca/cansim/a26?lang=eng&id=2280069 (accessed 27 May 2015).

21 Organisation for Economic Co-operation and Development, *Recent Tax Policy Trends and Reforms in OECD Countries* (Paris: OECD, 2004).

22 The HST is collected by the federal government on behalf of the provinces. In Quebec, it is the opposite: the provincial government collects the GST on behalf of the federal government.

23 Each province is free to set its taxation rate and define its tax base (what is and is not taxed). The provinces and the federal government have very similar tax bases. However, the rates differ: the GST is currently set at 5 per cent of the sale price, whereas the provincial VATs are between 8 and 10 per cent. There are no sales taxes in Alberta and the Canadian territories. British Columbia, Saskatchewan, and Manitoba have all decided not to reform their sales tax into a VAT. Although in a number of countries the VAT rate differs according to the nature of the good or service purchased (the rates are higher for "non-essential" products), this principle does not apply in Canada except for products exempted from the GST, HST, or QST (deemed to be "essential" products).

24 On this subject, see the speech given by the governor of the Bank of Canada on 3 November 2014, "The Legacy of the Financial Crisis: What We Know and What We Don't," https://www.bankofcanada.ca/wp-content/uploads/2014/11/remarks-031114.pdf.

2 Canadian Federalism

1 Statistics Canada, *Estimates of Population by Census Metropolitan Area*, CANSIM database, https://www150.statcan.gc.ca/t1/tbl1/en/tv.action?pid=1710007801 (accessed 9 November 2017, link no longer valid).

2 Data compiled for the period 2007–2017. Statistics Canada, *Population estimates on July 1st, by age and sex*, CANSIM database, https://www150.statcan.gc.ca/t1/tbl1/en/tv.action?pid=1710000501&request_locale=en (accessed 9 November 2017).

3 As Alain Noël notes, Canadian federalism aims to recognize the rights of national minorities. On this point, it is similar to the Swiss and Belgian federal systems but distinct from other forms of federalism designed more to create a counterweight to the federal government (the United States, Germany, and Australia, for example). See Noël, "Fédéralisme d'ouverture et pouvoir de dépenser au Canada," *Revista d'Estudis Autonòmics i Federals* 7 (October 2008): 10–36.

4 In 1996, the federal government changed the name of the program to Employment Insurance.

5 The provinces were favourable to the federal government's initiative to institute a national pension program, with the exception of Quebec. In

1966, the Canada Pension Plan and the Régime de rentes du Québec were established. In 1967, the federal government adopted the Guaranteed Income Supplement to help the poorest elderly.

6 In fact, the Canadian Constitution grants exclusive authority to collect revenues on lotteries to the federal government, which ceded its right to the provinces.

7 It is worth noting that the federal government collects income tax and various other taxes on behalf of the majority of provinces. However, the provinces set their respective taxation rates.

8 These data include local public administrations. See Ronald L. Watts, *Comparing Federal Systems*, 3rd ed. (Montreal: McGill-Queen's University Press, 2008).

9 Unlike in the US Senate, the provinces and territories do not all have the same number of senators.

10 For the territories, the instrument used is Territorial Formula Financing.

11 "Parliament and the government of Canada are committed to the principle of making equalization payments to ensure that provincial governments have sufficient revenues to provide reasonably comparable levels of public services at reasonably comparable levels of taxation" (article 26[2] of the Constitution Act, 1982). This constitutional amendment is a formal recognition of the Canadian equalization system instituted in 1957.

12 It should be noted that in recent years, the federal government has met with the provinces and territories more to inform them of its intentions than to come to a negotiated agreement. The last agreement negotiated was the Social Union Framework Agreement concluded in 1999 with a three-year term (without Quebec's consent, however).

13 Determination of the national standard has been the subject of frequent discussions and modifications since equalization was established. Since 2007, the standard has been determined as a function of average rates applied in all ten provinces for thirty-three separate sources of revenue. Before 2007, the national standard was determined excluding the richest and poorest provinces from the calculations. It should also be noted that processing of the revenues from natural resources is different from that from other sources (the formula uses real revenues and not theoretical revenues). For more detailed explanations, see Édison Roy-César, *Canada's Equalization Formula* (Ottawa: Parliament of Canada, 2008); Daniel Béland et al., *Fiscal Federalism and Equalization Policy in Canada: Political and Economic Dimensions* (Toronto: University of Toronto Press, 2017).

14 The CHT and CST replaced the Canada Health and Social Transfer in 2004. In fact, programs related to conditional transfer payments have undergone

a number of changes since they were created. For a detailed analysis, see James Gauthier, *The Canada Social Transfer: Past, Present and Future Considerations* (Ottawa: Parliament of Canada, 2012).

15 Between 1994 and 2015 five provinces incurred penalties for not respecting certain conditions of the Canada Health Act: Newfoundland and Labrador (for a total of $383,779), Nova Scotia ($378,937), Manitoba ($2,355,201), Alberta ($3,585,000), and British Columbia ($3,613,675) (Health Canada, *Canada Health Act: Annual Report 2015–2016* [Ottawa: Her Majesty the Queen in Right of Canada, 2016]).

16 In Canada, the expression "fiscal imbalance" refers to all financial relations among various levels of government. On this subject, see the report by the government of Quebec's Commission on Fiscal Imbalance, *A New Division of Canada's Financial Resources: Final Report* (Quebec City: Government of Quebec, 2002). For an examination of the concept of fiscal federalism in various federations, see George Anderson, *Fiscal Federalism: A Comparative Introduction* (Don Mills: Oxford University Press, 2010).

17 For a more detailed analysis of the constitutional rules targeting municipalities, see Michael Dewing, William R. Young, and Erin Tolley, *Municipalities, the Constitution, and the Canadian Federal System* (Ottawa: Parliament of Canada, 2006).

18 During the constitutional negotiations in 1987 (Meech Lake Accord) and 1992 (Charlottetown Accord), it had been agreed to include in the Constitution a clause providing withdrawal with full financial compensation. With the failure of these negotiations, the likelihood that such a provision will be enshrined in the Constitution has become very low. For a detailed account of the debates on the federal spending power, see Karine Richer, *The Federal Spending Power* (Ottawa: Parliament of Canada, 2007); Mollie Dunsmuir, *The Spending Power: Scope and Limitations* (Ottawa: Parliament of Canada, 1991).

19 Department of Finance (Canada), *Fiscal Reference Tables* (Ottawa: Government of Canada, 2017).

20 Commission on Fiscal Imbalance, *Final Report*, 56.

21 Quebec's position was articulated within the 2002 Commission on Fiscal Imbalance. See the commission's website, http://www.groupes.finances. gouv.qc.ca/desequilibrefiscal/index_ang.htm, for more information.

22 For a more complete description, see Andrew Sancton and Robert Young, eds, *Foundations of Governance: Municipal Governments in Canada's Provinces* (Toronto: IPAC/IAPC and University of Toronto Press, 2009).

23 Lydia Miljan and Zachary Spicer, *De-Amalgamation in Canada: Breaking Up Is Hard to Do* (Vancouver: Fraser Institute, 2015); Lydia Miljan and Zachary

Spicer, *Municipal Amalgamation in Ontario* (Vancouver: Fraser Institute, 2015).

3 Canadian Budget-Making Authorities

1 The political systems of the territories have some specific features. For instance, Nunavut and Northwest Territories each use a "consensus style of government." For more information on this, see the government of Nunavut website, https://www.gov.nu.ca/node/924.

2 Parliament is the name of the institution that exercises the federal government's legislative power. The provinces and territories use other names (Legislative Assembly, House of Assembly, and National Assembly). I use the terms "Parliament," "legislative assembly," "legislature," and "the House" interchangeably.

3 A first minister may appoint an unelected minister. Convention requires, however, that this minister run for election as quickly as possible. If the minister is defeated, he or she must resign the ministerial position.

4 See Luc Bernier, Keith Brownsey, and Michael Howlett, eds, *Executive Styles in Canada: Cabinet Structures and Leadership Practices in Canadian Government* (Toronto: University of Toronto Press/Institute of Public Administration of Canada, 2005); Graham White, *Cabinets and First Ministers* (Vancouver: UBC Press, 2005).

5 For a more detailed analysis of each of these functions, see C.E.S. Franks, *The Parliament of Canada* (Toronto: University of Toronto Press, 1987).

6 In the Canadian parliamentary system, all members of Parliament, whether they are ministers or not, may table bills. Bills tabled by government are distinguished from those presented by members of Parliament by their number. In the House of Commons, government bills are numbered from C-1 to C-200 (and from S-1 to S-200 if the bill is presented to the Senate first – which is possible, but not common), and other bills bear numbers starting at C-201 (S-201 in the Senate). Bill numbers are assigned by chronological order of presentation in the House.

7 The names of the analogous committees in the provinces and territories may be different.

8 The objective of organic laws is to specify the constitutional rules. For this reason, they have precedence over "ordinary" laws. For a detailed description of the different legal frames related to the budgetary process, see Organisation for Economic Co-operation and Development, "The Legal

Framework for Budget Systems: An International Comparison," special issue, *OECD Journal on Budgeting* 4, no. 3 (2004).

9 Each provincial and territorial government has its own statute for management of public finance. See the list of statutes at the end of this chapter.

10 Nor does the federal government collect corporate income tax for the Ontario and Alberta governments. Revenu Québec, the Ministry of Finance of Ontario, and the Department of Treasury Board and Finance of Alberta collect taxes under their responsibility.

11 This figure includes military personnel of about 90,000. Data on employment presented in this section are for 2011 (Statistics Canada, *Table 10-10-0025-01 - Archived - Public sector employment, wages and salaries, seasonally unadjusted and adjusted*, CANSIM database, https://www150. statcan.gc.ca/t1/tbl1/en/tv.action?pid=1010002501 [accessed 29 July 2015]).

12 Formerly the Department of Public Works and Government Services.

13 Bernier, Brownsey, and Howlett, *Executive Styles in Canada*.

14 This theme has been documented thoroughly by Donald Savoie, *Governing from the Centre: The Concentration of Power in Canadian Politics* (Toronto: University of Toronto Press, 1999); Savoie, *Power: Where Is It?* (Montreal/ Kingston: McGill-Queen's University Press, 2010).

15 Wildavsky, *Politics of the Budgetary Process*.

4 Setting the Agenda for Budget Actions

1 For a detailed analysis of provincial structures, see Bernier, Brownsey, and Howlett, *Executive Styles in Canada*.

2 An example of a presentation to the federal Treasury Board is found on the Secretariat's website: https://www.canada.ca/en/treasury-board-secretariat/services/treasury-board-submissions/guidance/treasury-board-submission-template-form.html.

3 Strategic reviews are gaining popularity in the provinces, but are not performed everywhere. Quebec has recently established a similar mechanism, in response to the recommendations formulated by the Commission on Permanent Program Review (Commission de révision permanente des programmes). More information on the commission is available on the government's website: https://www.tresor.gouv.qc.ca/ministre-et-secretariat/revision-des-programmes/.

4 Cited in Savoie, *Governing from the Centre*, 166.

5 Wildavsky, *Politics of the Budgetary Process*. Most empirical analyses confirm Wildavsky's thesis.

6 Some propose that zero-based budgeting be used. However, the complexity of activities in the public sector makes this method impractical at the governmental scale.

7 Cabinet meetings are confidential. This makes it possible to have frank discussions away from the attention of the media and the general public.

8 David A. Good, *The Politics of Public Money*, 2nd ed. (Toronto: University of Toronto Press, 2014).

9 For a more detailed description and an analysis of these new mechanisms, see Geneviève Tellier, "La participation citoyenne au processus d'élaboration des budgets: Une analyse des mécanismes instaurés par les gouvernements fédéral et provinciaux canadiens," *Téléscope* 17, no. 1 (Winter 2011): 95–115.

5 Formulation of the Fiscal Framework

1 The Commission of Inquiry into the Sponsorship Program and Advertising Activities, chaired by the Honourable Justice John H. Gomery, was charged with investigating government expenditures deemed inappropriate by the Auditor General of Canada.

2 Testimony of Paul Martin, *Public Hearings*, vol. 73, Commission of Inquiry into the Sponsorship Program and Advertising Activities, 10 February 2005.

3 Another considerable factor is the first minister's support of the minister of finance. This support is not automatic, but when it exists it provides the minister of finance with a degree of authority beyond that of other Cabinet members. For a more detailed analysis, see Savoie, *Governing From the Centre*, 156–92; J.P. Lewis, "The Relationship between Premiers and Treasurers," in *The Guardian: Perspectives on the Ministry of Finance of Ontario*, ed. P. Dutil (Toronto: University of Toronto Press, 2011).

4 But the Canada Border Services Agency collects customs duties. It should also be noted that most provinces have concluded an agreement with the federal government for the Canada Revenue Agency to collect their income and sales taxes on their behalf.

5 However, the law was amended to abolish the Ontario Economic Forecast Council in 2015.

6 The average gap between the projected balance and the actual balance was $10 billion per year between 1994 and 2003.

7 One study notes that the budgetary forecasts are of better quality in certain provinces and territories than in others, a situation that the authors of the study attribute in large part to the presence or absence of rules governing the presentation of coherent, high-quality budgetary information. See Colin Busby and William B.P. Robson, *Canada's 2012 Fiscal Accountability Rankings* (Toronto: C.D. Howe Institute, 2013). On this subject, see also Geneviève Tellier, "Balanced-Budget Legislation: The Rationale, Consequences and Lessons the Federal Government Can Draw from the Experiences of Canadian Provinces," in *How Ottawa Spends, 2015–2016: The Liberal Rise and the Tory Demise*, ed. C. Stoney and B.G. Doern (Montreal/Kingston: McGill-Queen's University Press, 2016).

8 The electoral defeat of the federal Conservative Party in 1993 is usually attributed to its reform of the sales tax. On this point, see Geoffrey Hale, *The Politics of Taxation in Canada* (Peterborough: Broadview, 2002), and Good, *The Politics of Public Money*.

9 The distinction is often made between tax evasion, which is illegal, and tax avoidance, which is not. For a detailed examination of the efforts deployed by the Canada Revenue Agency to combat tax avoidance, see Standing Committee on Finance (Canada), *The Canada Revenue Agency, Tax Avoidance and Tax Evasion: Recommended Actions* (Ottawa: House of Commons, 2016). On taxpayer behaviour, see Pierre P. Tremblay and Guy Lachapelle, *Le contribuable héros ou malfaiteur?* (Sainte-Foy: Presses de l'Université Laval, 1996).

10 The federal government's 1997 budget plan reaffirmed the government's support for these general principles (Department of Finance [Canada], *Building the Future for Canadians: Budget 1997*, 18 February [Ottawa: Her Majesty the Queen in Right of Canada, 1997], annex 5).

11 Alberta was until recently an exception: it had a 10 per cent flat tax between 1999 and 2014. A few days after its historic victory in 2015, the Alberta New Democratic Party (centre-left) announced the establishment of multiple tax rates (which took effect in 2015).

12 For a more detailed discussion of the advantages and disadvantages of public deficits, see J.P. Lewis, "The Case for Balanced Budgets," in *Approaching Public Administration: Core Debates and Emerging Issues*, eds R.P. Leone and F.L.K. Ohemeng (Toronto: Emond Montgomery, 2011); Geneviève Tellier, "Why Public Deficits Are Not (Always) Bad," in Leone and Ohmeng, *Approaching Public Administration*.

13 In her memoirs, the former minister of finance of Saskatchewan described how the ratings agencies' evaluations were a key element in the province's

budget reforms in the early 1990s. See Janice Mackinnon, *Minding the Public Purse: The Fiscal Crisis, Political Trade-Offs, and Canada's Future* (Montreal/London: McGill-Queen's University Press, 2003).

14 Department of Finance (Canada), *Debt Management Report, 2015–2016* (Ottawa: Her Majesty the Queen in Right of Canada, 2016), 51.

15 Key rates are very-short-term interest rates used by the Canadian banks to lend funds for very short terms (one day). These rates normally influence the interest rates set by banks for loans and deposits by individuals and firms.

16 The Canadian banking system is composed of six major chartered banks (the charter regulates their activities, as stated in the Bank Act), which hold about 90 per cent of the country's banking assets. The Bank of Canada has always had close relations with the chartered banks.

17 Initially, the target was an inflation "range" of between 1 and 3 per cent. This target was later brought to the median point of the range.

18 For a presentation of the federal government's directions in this field, see Markus Sharaput, "Harper Government Industrial Strategy and Industrial Policy in the Economic Crisis," in *How Ottawa Spends 2010–2011: Recession, Realignment, and the New Deficit Era*, ed. B.G. Doern and C. Stoney (Montreal/Kingston: McGill-Queen's University Press, 2010).

19 It should be mentioned that the government was a minority government, and rejection of such a plan would probably have caused it to fall.

6 Parliamentary Rules

1 The Crown had to obtain the consent of its peers. See Donald J. Savoie, *Court Government and the Collapse of Accountability in Canada and the United Kingdom* (Toronto: University of Toronto Press, 2008).

2 Constitution Act, 1867, preamble.

3 The territories have established some structures that reflect their own traditions (such as consensus government).

4 And several budgetary principles existed before Confederation. For a description of the period preceding Confederation, see Norman Ward, *The Public Purse: A Study in Canadian Democracy* (Toronto: University of Toronto Press, 1962), chap. 2.

5 In the fall of 2017 the Canadian government, under the leadership of the Liberal Party, indicated that a number of parliamentary reforms were underway, including "improv[ing] reporting to Parliament," "strengthen[ing] Parliamentary committees so that they can better scrutinize legislation," and "exercis[ing] due diligence regarding costing analysis

prepared by departments for all proposed legislation and programs." For
an update on the status of these reforms, see https://www.canada.ca/en/
privy-council/campaigns/mandate-tracker-results-canadians.html.

6 European Union, *Strengthening Economic Governance in the European Union:
Report of the Task Force to the European Council* (Brussels: European Union,
2010); Organisation for Economic Co-operation and Development, "OECD
Best Practices for Budget Transparency," *OECD Journal on Budgeting* 1, no.
3 (2002), 7–14; Ian Lienert, *Role of the Legislature in Budget Processes*, 2010/04
(Washington, DC: International Monetary Fund, 2010).

7 André Bernard, *Politique et gestion des finances publiques: Québec et Canada*
(Québec: Presse de l'Université du Québec, 1992); Audrey O'Brien and
Marc Bosc, *House of Commons Procedure and Practice* (Ottawa: House of
Commons, 2009).

8 When Parliament is not in session and the government is facing
extraordinary circumstances, certain temporary budget measures may
be adopted without the prior consent of Parliament (through the use of
"special warrants"). But the government must ensure that it obtains the
authorization of parliamentarians once the House is back in session.

9 C.E.S. Franks, *Some Comments on the Estimates Process*, submission to the
Standing Committee on Government Operations and Estimates, 37th
Parliament, 2nd Session (2003).

10 The expression "finance bill" is rarely used in Canada. Rather, reference
is made to various categories of bills, such as appropriation (or supply),
ways and means motions, and loan bills.

11 Formally, the Canadian Parliament votes on supply bills that, once
adopted, become appropriation acts. "Appropriation bills" can be used
as a generic term to identify bills introduced by government asking
permission to use public funds.

12 The examinations are conducted by standing committees of the House
of Commons and the Senate. They are called "standing" because they
exist for the duration of the parliament. There are currently twenty-six
such committees in the House of Commons and seventeen in the Senate.
Usually, the standing committees include about ten MPs representing all
recognized parties in the House or between five and fifteen senators (the
composition of the committees reflects the distribution of seats in each
of the chambers). Some are joint committees—that is, composed of both
MPs and senators. However, these committees do not deal with budgetary
questions (except under rare circumstances).

13 Library of Parliament (Canada), *The Parliament We Want* (Ottawa: Her
Majesty the Queen in Right of Canada, 2003); Standing Committee on

Government Operations and Estimates (Canada), *Meaningful Scrutiny: Practical Improvements to the Estimates Process*, 37th Parliament, 2nd Session (Ottawa: Parliament of Canada, 2003); Standing Committee on Government Operations and Estimates (Canada), *Strengthening Parliamentary Scrutiny of Estimates and Supply*, 41st Parliament, 1st session (Ottawa: Parliament of Canada, 2012); Standing Committee on Procedure and House Affairs (Canada), *The Business of Supply: Completing the Circle of Control*, 36th Parliament, 1st Session (Ottawa: Parliament of Canada, 1998). It is interesting to read the public expression of discontent by an MP who was a member of the governing party regarding his own party's attitude: B. Rathgeber, *Irresponsible Government* (Toronto: Dundurn, 2014).

14 Parliamentary Budget Officer, *Comparing the Federal Fiscal Sustainability Analyses of PBO and Finance Canada* (Ottawa: Library of Parliament, 2013).

15 Department of Finance (Canada), *Economic and Fiscal Implications of Canada's Aging Population* (Ottawa: Her Majesty the Queen in Right of Canada, 2012).

16 Standing Committee on Government Operations and Estimates (Canada), *Strengthening Parliamentary Scrutiny*; Standing Committee on Government Operations and Estimates (Canada), *Meaningful Scrutiny*; Standing Committee on Procedure and House Affairs (Canada), *The Business of Supply*.

17 See chapter 1.

18 This is one of the main recommendations made by a House of Commons committee in 2012 and, more recently, by the Auditor General of Canada in 2015. See Standing Committee on Government Operations and Estimates (Canada), *Strengthening Parliamentary Scrutiny*; Office of the Auditor General (Canada), *2015 Spring Reports of the Auditor General of Canada. Report 3 – Tax-Based Expenditures* (Ottawa: Her Majesty the Queen in Right of Canada, 2015), 6.

19 Joachim Wehner, *Legislatures and the Budget Process. The Myth of Fiscal Control* (New York: Palgrave Macmillan, 2010); see especially chap. 3.

20 The index is 17 for Ireland, 21 for Australia and the United Kingdom, and 26 for New Zealand.

21 The scores are: 56 for Denmark, 61 for Norway, and 65 for Sweden.

7 The Parliamentary Calendar

1 As mentioned above, the provinces and territories do not have a Senate.

2 The procedure is more specific in British Columbia: the minister of finance must publish a prebudget report by 15 September, and the

recommendations flowing from the consultations must be presented to the legislature by 15 November.

3 In fact, the federal government could simply not present budget speeches, because it could function very well without adopting a financial act. Indeed, the great majority of income taxes, other taxes, and other tax measures do not have to be approved each year by parliamentarians, as these measures have an indefinite lifespan. The government therefore does not need MPs' assent to obtain funds. The procedure is different in the British Parliament, in which all tax measures are valid for only one year. The British government must therefore table a financial act every year. See O'Brien and Bosc, *Procedure and Practice*, note 400.

4 Written versions of speeches are available on the websites of the respective legislatures and ministers of finance. The text of federal budget speeches is available at https://lop.parl.ca/sites/ParlInfo/default/en_CA/Parliament/procedure/budgets.

5 More precisely, the presentation of a ways and means motion is followed by two votes. First, the House must approve the ways and means motion. This motion presents the new tax rates and the conditions for their implementation. Lawmakers may neither debate nor amend the motion. Second, the House votes on the basis of the measure by adopting the bill or bills associated with the ways and means motion. This bill must comply with the limits presented in the motion. Whereas ways and means motions are presented and adopted soon after the presentation of a notice of ways and means motion, ways and means bills may be tabled in the House much later in the parliamentary session.

6 A government has been defeated following a budget vote in Parliament twice: the Liberal government in 1974 and the Progressive Conservative government in 1979. In both cases, they were minority governments in the House.

7 A fifth category could be added: "omnibus" or "umbrella" bills, composed of several initiatives, each of which would usually be presented in a separate bill, but that the government considers appropriate to present and discuss jointly. Omnibus bills may combine initiatives of different natures (spending, revenue, borrowing).

8 The Parliamentary Budget Officer recommended that this situation be corrected:

"Parliamentarians may wish to consider establishing a process of review for existing tax expenditures similar to that provided for all other public expenditures. As well, legislators may wish to provide guidance to the Government regarding the types of reports and information that would support any such review process. This could include:

- Evaluation reports prepared to a similar standard as program evaluations.
- Integrated presentation of tax expenditures in the Estimates documents." (Jacques, *Federal Tax Expenditures*, 6)

9 Recently, the federal government used a single bill (an omnibus bill) instead of the four or five usually tabled. This way of doing things was denounced by the opposition parties, which felt that they did not have enough time or resources to examine the bill.

10 This was long referred to as the "Blue Book" because of the colour of its title page.

11 There are exceptions to this rule. The Canadian Parliament, for example, authorizes the Official Opposition to request that the appropriations of two departments be studied in plenary committee (that is, with all MPs). In some provinces, all appropriations are examined in plenary committee.

12 They may not, however, reduce interim appropriations.

13 Formerly known as the Reports on Plans and Priorities (RPPs) and the Departmental Performance Reports (DPRs), respectively. The provincial legislative assemblies receive similar reports.

14 Standing Committee on Government Operations and Estimates (Canada), *Meaningful Scrutiny*, 1. For a similar conclusion, see John A. Chenier, Michael Dewing, and Jack Stillborn, "Does Parliament Care? Parliament Committees and the Estimates," in *How Ottawa Spends, 2005–2006: Managing the Minority*, ed. B.G. Doern (Montreal/Kingston: McGill-Queen's University Press, 2005).

15 This is also true for ministers. On this subject, see David A. Good, "Parliament and Public Money: Players and Police," *Canadian Parliamentary Review* 28, no. 1 (Spring 2005): 17–21.

16 A number of parliamentary committees have made such recommendations. See, for example, Standing Committee on Procedure and House Affairs (Canada), *The Business of Supply*; Standing Committee on Government Operations and Estimates (Canada), *Strengthening Parliamentary Scrutiny*.

17 In some provinces, the Public Accounts must be presented earlier, in summer.

18 Chairing of committees by opposition MPs is also found in the Canadian provinces. In the Canadian Parliament, the House regulation was also amended several years ago to have four more standing committees chaired by opposition MPs. One of these committees is the Standing Committee on Government Operations and Estimates, which frequently rules on budgetary questions (the other committees are on status of women, access

to information, protection of personal information and ethics, and scrutiny of regulations).

19 According to McGee, only Uganda has adopted a system similar to Canada's (David G. McGee, *The Budget Process: A Parliamentary Imperative* [London: Commonwealth Parliamentary Association with Pluto Press, 2007]).

20 Ontario was the first jurisdiction to institute prebudget consultation parliamentary mechanisms, in 1987, followed by the federal government in 1994 and British Columbia in 2000.

21 The detailed results of this study are presented and discussed in Geneviève Tellier, "Improving the Relevance of Parliamentary Institutions: An Examination of Legislative Pre-Budget Consultations in British Columbia," *Journal of Legislative Studies* 21, no. 2 (April 2015), 192–212; Tellier, "Pre-Budget Consultations in British Columbia: The Participants' Perspective," *Canadian Parliamentary Review* 35, no. 1 (Spring 2012), 29–35; Tellier, "L'usage des consultations prébudgétaires au Canada: Étude du cas de la Colombie-Britannique," in *Les réformes des finances publiques: Enjeux politiques et gestionnaires*, ed. M. Djouldem, G. Tellier, and C. de Visscher (Paris: Bruylant, 2014).

8 The Budgetary Management System

1 The title "deputy minister" is not used in certain public bodies, but there is a senior civil servant with the same responsibilities.

2 The responsibilities of accounting officer were given to federal deputy ministers following the recommendations formulated during the Gomery Commission. Elsewhere in Canada, these responsibilities are assumed by lower-ranking public servants, and consequently it is the minister, not the deputy minister, who is ultimately answerable to Parliament for the accounting activities of his or her department.

3 For a detailed analysis of the function of deputy minister in Canada (for the federal and provincial governments), see Jacques Bourgault and Christopher Dunn, eds, *Deputy Ministers in Canada* (Toronto: University of Toronto Press, 2014).

4 Treasury Board Secretariat (Canada), *Directive on Delegation of Spending and Financial Authorities* (Ottawa: Her Majesty the Queen in Right of Canada, n.d.); Treasury Board Secretariat (Canada), *A Manager's Guide to Operating Budgets* (Ottawa: Her Majesty the Queen in Right of Canada, n.d.).

5 Treasury Board Secretariat (Canada), *Guide to Integrated Risk Management: A Recommended Approach for Developing a Corporate Risk Profile* (Ottawa: Her

Majesty the Queen in Right of Canada, 2016). This definition is used by most governments in Canada.

6 For the federal government it is the Department of Public Services; in Ontario, the Ministry of Government and Consumer Services; in Quebec, responsibility for procurements is assumed directly by the Secrétariat du Conseil du Trésor.

7 Share Services Canada, *Report on Plans and Priorities 2015–2016* (Ottawa: Her Majesty the Queen in Right of Canada, 2015).

8 Office of the Auditor General (Canada), *2003 November Report of the Auditor General of Canada* (Ottawa: Her Majesty the Queen in Right of Canada, 2003).

9 These values are $25,200 for acquisition of goods, $80,400 for services, and $10.4 million for construction work. There are a few exceptions. For more information, see chapter 10 of the North American Free Trade Agreement, "Government Procurement," https://www.nafta-sec-alena.org/Home/Texts-of-the-Agreement/North-American-Free-Trade-Agreement.

10 For more information, see "WTO and Government Procurement," https://www.wto.org/english/tratop_e/gproc_e/gproc_e.htm.

11 See, for example, the cases presented by Graeme A. Hodge and Carsten Greve, *The Challenge of Public-Private Partnerships: Learning from International Experience* (Cheltenham: Edward Elgar, 2005).

12 In particular, there are questions about whether the private sector is truly assuming the risks of public-private partnerships. On this subject, see the analyses presented by Christian Rouillard and Pierre-André Hudon, "Le partenariat public-privé: Un instrument d'action publique au cœur de la reconfiguration de l'État québécois," *Économie et solidarités* 38, no. 2 (2007): 7–26; Daniel Cohn, "The New Public Autonomy? Public-Private Partnerships in a Multi-Level, Multi-Accountable, Political Environment: The Case of British Columbia, Canada," *Policy and Society* 27, no. 1 (September 2008): 29–42; Matti Siemiatycki and Naeem Farooqi, "Value for Money and Risk in Public–Private Partnerships," *Journal of the American Planning Association* 78, no. 3 (July 2012): 286–99.

13 For example, the sponsorship scandal at the federal level (see above) and also the events brought to light by the Quebec commission of inquiry into the awarding and management of public contracts in that province's construction industry (the Charbonneau Commission). The Quebec commission's mandate was to examine the existence of stratagems and, where appropriate, to paint a picture of those that might involve activities of possible collusion and corruption in the awarding and management of public contracts in the construction industry, including, in particular,

agencies, government corporations, and municipalities, and involving possible links with political party financing (Décret 1119–2011, adopted 9 November 2011 by the government of Quebec).

14 The ombudsman is under the aegis of the Department of Public Services and Procurement. The position was created as one of the many measures adopted by the federal government under the Accountability Act, enacted in response to the recommendations of the Gomery Commission, which investigated the sponsorship scandal.

15 For more information on the activities of the procurement ombudsman, see Office of the Procurement Ombudsman (Canada), *Annual Report 2016–2017* (Ottawa: Her Majesty the Queen in Right of Canada, 2017).

9 Optimization of Budgetary Resources

1 For a review of the literature on this subject, see Carole Pretorius and Nico Pretorius, *Review of Public Financial Management Reform Literature* (London: Department for International Development, 2008). For an empirical case study (looking at eight provincial and national juridictions), see Valérie Martin and Marie-Héléne Jobin, "La gestion axée sur les résultats: Comparaison des cadres de gestion de huit juridictions," *Canadian Public Administration/Administration publique du Canada* 47, no. 3 (September 2004): 304–31.

2 A good summary of reforms in Ontario can be found in Caroline Dufour, "Coping with Complexity: Innovation and Resistance in Crafting the Expenditure Budget, 1962–1985," in *The Guardian: Perspectives on the Ministry of Finance of Ontario*, ed. P. Dutil (Toronto: University of Toronto Press, 2011). For an analysis of the case of Quebec, see Lucie Rouillard, "La modernisation du processus budgétaire: Évolution ou révolution?" in *Le processus budgétaire au Québec*, ed. G. Lachapelle, L. Bernier, and P.P. Tremblay (Sainte-Foy: Presses de l'Université du Québec, 1999); Raymond Garneau, "La budgétisation par programme: Rationalité budgétaire contre rationalité politique," in *Le processus budgétaire au Québec*, ed. Lachapelle, Bernier, and Tremblay.

3 Royal Commission on Government Organization (Canada), *Report 2: Financial Management* (Ottawa: Queen's Printer, 1962), 102.

4 Auditor General of Canada (Canada), *Report of the Auditor General of Canada to the House of Commons for the Fiscal Year Ended March 31, 1976* (Ottawa: Minister of Supply and Services Canada, 1976).

5 Royal Commission on Financial Management & Accountability (Canada), *Final Report* (Ottawa: Minister of Supply and Services Canada, 1979).

6 The budgetary envelope system was the main element in the reform of the financial management system initiated when the *policy and expenditure management* system was implemented in 1979.

7 The failure of the budgetary envelope system may also be attributed to a lack of budgetary rigour by the government of the time. For instance, although the amounts in the envelopes were decreased, reserves were increased at the same time in order to fund new initiatives. These reserves were used by the minister of finance.

8 Another resource-optimization mechanism was developed, but it did not raise much interest in Canada. Zero-based budgeting was intended to correct the faults in marginalist decision-making processes by suggesting that all program budgets be examined in depth and only the best-performing programs (in terms of costs, benefits, relevance, and so on) be retained.

9 Evert Lindquist, "How Ottawa Reviews Spending: Moving beyond Adhocracy?" in *How Ottawa Spends, 2006/2007: In from the Cold: The Tory Rise and the Liberal Demise*, ed. B.G. Doern (Montreal/Kingston: McGill-Queen's University Press, 2006); Doug McArthur, "Policy Analysis in Provincial Governments in Canada: From PPBS to Network Management," in *Policy Studies in Canada: The State of the Art*, ed. L. Dobuzinskis, M. Howlett, and D. Laycock (Toronto: IPAC/University of Toronto Press, 2007).

10 On this point, see Aaron B. Wildavsky, "Controlling Public Expenditures: The Theory of Expenditure Limitation," *OECD Journal on Budgeting* 2, no. 4 (2003): 27–47; Allen Schick, "The Role of Fiscal Rules in Budgeting," *OECD Journal on Budgeting* 3, no. 3 (2003): 7–34.

11 Treasury Board Secretariat (Canada), *Preparing and Using Results-Based Management and Accountability Frameworks* (Ottawa: Her Majesty the Queen in Right of Canada, 2005).

12 The program review was not the only factor in eliminating the deficit. In the view of many, this result should be credited to strong leadership by then-prime minister Jean Chrétien and his minister of finance, Paul Martin, as well as a favourable economic and political situation (see Allan M. Maslove and Kevin D. Moore, "From Red Books to Blue Books: Repairing Ottawa's Fiscal House," in *How Ottawa Spends, 1997–1998. Seeing Red: A Liberal Report Card*, ed. G. Swimmer [Ottawa: Carleton University Press, 1997]). For a more critical analysis of the success of the program review, see Joanne Kelly, "The Pursuit of an Elusive Ideal: Spending Review and Reallocation under the Chrétien Government," in *How Ottawa Spends,*

2003–2004: Regime Change and Policy Shift, ed. B.G. Doern (Don Mills: Oxford University Press, 2003).

13 There are too many programs, subprograms, and sub-subprograms to be presented here. The complete list of performance indicators can be found in the department's *Departmental Results Report 2016 to 2017*.

14 Benoît Rigaud and Paul-Émile Arsenaul, "Budget Governance in Canada: Comparing Practices within a Federation," *OECD Journal on Budgeting* 13, no. 1 (2013): 9–30.

15 Parliamentary Budget Officer (Canada), *Updated Analysis of Performance Budgeting during Recent Fiscal Consolidation* (Ottawa: Parliament of Canada, 2015).

16 Jens Kromann Kristensen, Walter S. Groszyk, and Bernd Bühler, "Outcome-Focused Management and Budgeting," *OECD Journal on Budgeting* 1, no. 4 (2002): 7–34.

10 Internal Auditing and Evaluation Mechanisms

1 Ward, *The Public Purse*, 168.

2 For a detailed account of several reforms, see Steve Jacob, "Trente ans d'évaluation de programme au Canada: L'institutionnalisation interne en quête de qualité," *Revue française d'administration publique* 119, no. 3 (2006).

3 This legislative change concerns the federal government only.

4 This obligation does not exist in every province.

5 It is not unusual for audits to proceed by sampling instead of an exhaustive – and expensive – examination of all of a program's financial transactions.

6 For a complete analysis of this case by a person who was closely involved, see David A. Good, *The Politics of Public Management: The HRDC Audit of Grants and Contributions* (Toronto: University of Toronto Press, 2005).

7 There are few studies documenting the evaluation functions at the provincial and territorial scale. One may presume, however, that the evaluation functions appeared later in the provinces and territories, with the popularity of new public management theories in the provinces. On this subject see McArthur, "Policy Analysis in Provincial Governments."

8 The Office of the Auditor General conducted six audits between 1978 and 2009, all observing "the poor quality and insufficient impact of evaluations" (*2013 Spring Reports of the Auditor General of Canada. Chapter 1 – Status Report on Evaluating the Effectiveness of Programs* [Ottawa: Her Majesty the Queen in Right of Canada, 2013]), 9.

9 Centre of Excellence for Evaluation, "About the Centre of Excellence for Evaluation," https://www.canada.ca/en/treasury-board-secretariat/services/audit-evaluation/centre-excellence-evaluation/about-centre-excellence-evaluation.html (accessed 10 July 2015).

10 Treasury Board Secretariat (Canada), *Assessing Program Resource Utilization When Evaluating Federal Programs* (Ottawa: Her Majesty the Queen in Right of Canada, 2013).

11 Industry Canada, *Evaluation of the Canada Small Business Financing Program: Final* (Ottawa: Her Majesty the Queen in Right of Canada, 2014), 1.

11 External Budgetary Audit and Evaluation Mechanisms

1 Parliamentary accountability mechanisms may vary widely from one country to another. They can, however, be grouped into two general categories: those under the responsibility of external agencies invested with legal power (such as the Cour des comptes in France and Belgium) and those directly under the responsibility of the legislature (such as the General Accounting Office in the United States and the National Audit Office in the United Kingdom). The Canadian mechanisms clearly follow the British tradition of the National Audit Office. For a comparative analysis of various systems, see Rick Stapenhurst and Louis M. Imbeau, eds, *Contemporary Developments in Parliamentary Oversight in Francophone Countries* (Ottawa: Canadian Audit and Accountability Foundation, n.d.); and Louis M. Imbeau and Rick Stapenhurst, *Le contrôle parlementaire des finances publiques dans les pays de la Francophonie* (Québec: Presses de l'Université Laval, 2019).

2 Gary Levy, "A Parliamentary Budget Officer for Canada," *Canadian Parliamentary Review* 31, no. 2 (Summer 2008): 39–44.

3 For a description of the similarities and differences among the auditor general positions in Canada, see Jonathan Malloy, "An Auditor's Best Friend? Standing Committees on Public Accounts," *Canadian Public Administration* 47, no. 2 (Summer 2004): 165–83; Jean Crête et al., "Que vérifient les vérificateurs provinciaux?" in *Les surveillants de l'État démocratique*, ed. J. Crête (Sainte-Foy: Presses de l'Université Laval, 2014). These two studies show that there are more similarities than differences; the differences involve mainly the resources granted to the auditors general, which are usually proportionate to the size of the province. The Office of the Auditor General of Canada is by far the largest such agency in the country, in terms of both budget and human resources.

4 This mandate is renewable and of shorter duration in some provinces.

5 Recently, the government intruded into the Auditor General's budget—asking that the Auditor General also contribute to the public administration's cost-reduction efforts—an action that the Auditor General has denounced on several occasions.

6 This is how the Office of the Auditor General describes the procedure. See Office of the Auditor General of Canada, "What We Do," http://www. oag-bvg.gc.ca/internet/English/au_fs_e_371.html.

7 Denis Saint-Martin, "Managerialist Advocate or 'Control Freak'? The Janus-Faced Office of the Auditor General," *Canadian Public Administration* 47, no. 2 (Summer 2004): 121–40.

8 Comments by senior civil servants, including some from the Office of the Auditor General of Canada, on this subject can be found in Good, *The Politics of Public Money*, especially chapter 5.

9 See, notably, works by Sharon L. Sutherland, including *The Office of the Auditor General of Canada: Government in Exile?* (Kingston: School of Public Policy Studies, 2002); see also Saint-Martin, "Managerialist Advocate or 'Control Freak'"?

10 For a more in-depth analysis of the place and influence of accounting standards in the public sector, see M. Djouldem, "Les nouvelles normes comptables de l'État: Des instruments pour la performance et la transparence de l'action publique?" in *Les réformes des finances publiques*, ed. M. Djouldem, G. Tellier, and C. de Visscher (Paris: Bruylant, 2014), 111–57.

11 David C. Docherty, *Legislatures* (Vancouver: UBC Press, 2005), 133.

12 Malloy, "An Auditor's Best Friend?"

13 The position of Parliamentary Budget Officer was created by the Federal Accountability Act (adopted in 2006), which amends the Parliament of Canada Act. It was subsequently amended by the Budget Implementation Act, 2017, No. 1.

14 To date, no other province has indicated its desire to establish such a position, although the subject is raised during election campaigns. The government of Quebec seems more inclined to delegate the tasks that would fall to a parliamentary budget officer to the province's Auditor General.

15 For a detailed description of the reports presented by the Parliamentary Budget Officer during the first five years of his mandate, see Geneviève Tellier, "Le directeur parlementaire du budget: Le nouveau chien de garde financier du gouvernement fédéral canadien?" in *Les surveillants de l'État démocratique*, ed. J. Crête (Sainte-Foy: Presses de l'Université Laval, 2014). On the independence of the Parliamentary Budget Officer during his first years in office, see Brooke Jeffrey, "The Parliamentary Budget Officer Two

Years Later: A Progress Report," *Canadian Parliamentary Review* 33, no. 4 (Winter 2010): 37–45.

16 The URLs for these websites are provided at the end of this chapter.

17 Another likely source of tension was the openly confrontational relationship between the first holder of the position and the Harper government; see Ian Lee and Philip Cross, "The Parliamentary Budget Officer: The First Five Years," in *How Ottawa Spends, 2014–2015: The Harper Government – Good to Go?*, ed. B.G. Doern and C. Stoney (Montreal/Kingston: McGill-Queen's University Press, 2014), 40–52. The new Officer (appointed in 2013) nevertheless had to deal with similar constraints (Parliamentary Budget Officer [Canada], *2013–14 Report on Activities of the Parliamentary Budget Office* [Ottawa: Parliament of Canada, 2014]).

18 One case even went to court.

19 This was notably the case for the estimated cost of acquiring fighter planes and for accrued expenses of correctional institutions following the adoption of stricter criminal laws.

20 Notably, the Harper government tried to limit the Officer's margin of manoeuvre by reducing his operating budget by 30 per cent (although it had to backtrack on this decision due to the measure's unpopularity), by forcing him to examine certain aspects of budgetary policy (all private bills are supposed to be evaluated by the Officer; this directive has not been fully complied with because the Officer does not have the budget necessary to do so), and by limiting his access to certain sources of information.

21 The Congressional Budget Office has considerable resources: it employs almost 250 people and publishes an average of 2,000 studies and analyses each year.

22 The Canadian Tax Foundation was founded in 1946 and the Conference Board of Canada in 1954. For a more detailed description, see Donald J. Savoie, *Breaking the Bargain: Public Servants, Ministers, and Parliament* (Toronto: University of Toronto Press, 2003), chap. 6; Savoie, *Power: Where Is It?*, chap. 8.

Conclusion

1 Wildavsky, *Politics of the Budgetary Process*, 1, 5.

Bibliography

Anderson, George. *Fiscal Federalism: A Comparative Introduction*. Don Mills: Oxford University Press, 2010.

Atkinson, Michael M., Daniel Béland, Gregory P. Marchildon, Kathleen Mcnutt, Peter W.B. Phillips, and Ken Rasmussen. *Governance and Public Policy in Canada: A View from the Provinces*. North York: University of Toronto Press, 2013.

Auditor General of Canada. *Report of the Auditor General of Canada to the House of Commons for the Fiscal Year Ended March 31, 1976*. Ottawa: Minister of Supply and Services Canada, 1976.

Banting, Keith, and John Myles, eds. *Inequality and the Fading of Redistributive Politics*. Vancouver: UBC Press, 2013.

Béland, Daniel, André Lecours, Gregory P. Marchildon, Haizhen Mou, and M. Rose Olfert. *Fiscal Federalism and Equalization Policy in Canada: Political and Economic Dimensions*. Toronto: University of Toronto Press, 2017.

Bernard, André. *Politique et gestion des finances publiques: Québec et Canada*. Québec: Presse de l'Université du Québec, 1992.

Bernier, Luc, Keith Brownsey, and Michael Howlett, eds. *Executive Styles in Canada: Cabinet Structures and Leadership Practices in Canadian Government*. Toronto: University of Toronto Press/Institute of Public Administration of Canada, 2005.

Bird, Richard M. *The Growth of Government Spending in Canada*. Toronto: Canadian Tax Foundation, 1970.

Bourgault, Jacques, and Christopher Dunn, eds. *Deputy Ministers in Canada*. Toronto: University of Toronto Press, 2014.

Busby, Colin, and William B.P. Robson. *Canada's 2012 Fiscal Accountability Rankings*. Toronto: C.D. Howe Institute, 2013.

Champagne, Éric, and Olivier Choinière. "Le financement des infrastructures municipales et les défis du fédéralisme fiscal canadien." *Gestion et management public* 4, no. 3 (2016): 25–36.

Chenier, John A., Michael Dewing, and Jack Stillborn. "Does Parliament Care? Parliament Committees and the Estimates." In *How Ottawa Spends, 2005–2006: Managing the Minority,* edited by Bruce G. Doern, 200–21. Montreal/Kingston: McGill-Queen's University Press, 2005.

Cohn, Daniel. "The New Public Autonomy? Public-Private Partnerships in a Multi-level, Multi-accountable, Political Environment: The Case of British Columbia, Canada." *Policy and Society* 27, no. 1 (2008): 29–42.

Commission on Fiscal Imbalance. *A New Division of Canada's Financial Resources: Final Report.* Quebec City: Government of Quebec, 2002.

Crête, Jean, Nouhoun Diallo, Patricia Rasamimanana, and Fatma Timlelt. "Que vérifient les vérificateurs provinciaux?" In *Les surveillants de l'État démocratique,* edited by Jean Crête, 75–105. Sainte-Foy: Presses de l'Université Laval, 2014.

Dahlström, Carl, B. Guy Peters, and Jon Pierre, eds. *Steering from the Centre: Strengthening Political Control in Western Democracies.* Toronto: University of Toronto Press, 2011.

Deleon, Peter. "The Stages Approach to the Policy Process: What Has It Done? Where Is It Going?" In *Theories of the Policy Process,* edited by Paul A. Sabatier, 19–32. Boulder: Westview, 1999.

Department of Finance, Canada. *Building the Future for Canadians: Budget 1997.* 18 February. Ottawa: Her Majesty the Queen in Right of Canada, 1997.

—*Economic and Fiscal Implications of Canada's Aging Population.* Ottawa: Her Majesty the Queen in Right of Canada, 2012.

—*Debt Management Report, 2015–2016.* Ottawa: Her Majesty the Queen in Right of Canada, 2016.

—*Fiscal Reference Tables.* Ottawa: Government of Canada, 2017.

Dewing, Michael, William R. Young, and Erin Tolley. *Municipalities, the Constitution, and the Canadian Federal System.* Ottawa: Parliament of Canada, 2006.

Djouldem, Mohamed. "Les nouvelles normes comptables de l'État : des instruments pour la performance et la transparence de l'action publique?" In *Les réformes des finances publiques, enjeux politiques et gestionnaires,* edited by Mohamed Djouldem, Geneviève Tellier, and Christian de Visscher, 111–57. Paris: Bruylant, 2014.

Dobell, Peter, and Martin Ulrich. "Parliament's Performance in the Budget Process: A Case Study." *Policy Matters* 3, no. 5 (2002): 1–24.

Docherty, David C. *Legislatures.* Vancouver: UBC Press, 2005.

Dufour, Caroline. "Coping with Complexity: Innovation and Resistance in Crafting the Expenditure Budget, 1962–1985." In *The Guardian: Perspectives on the Ministry of Finance of Ontario,* edited by Patrice Dutil, 229–56. Toronto: University of Toronto Press, 2011.

Dunsmuir, Mollie. *The Spending Power: Scope and Limitations.* Ottawa: Parliament of Canada, 1991.

Esping-Andersen, Gosta. *The Three Worlds of Welfare Capitalism.* Princeton: Princeton University Press, 1990.

European Union. *Strengthening Economic Governance in the European Union: Report of the Task Force to the European Council.* Brussels: European Union, 2010.

Finkel, Alvin. *Social Policy and Practice in Canada.* Waterloo: Wilfrid Laurier University Press, 2006.

Franks, C.E.S. *The Parliament of Canada.* Toronto: University of Toronto Press, 1987.

Garneau, Raymond. "La budgétisation par programme: Rationalité budgétaire contre rationalité politique." In *Le processus budgétaire au Québec,* edited by Guy Lachapelle, Luc Bernier, and Pierre P. Tremblay, 33–41. Sainte-Foy: Presses de l'Université du Québec, 1999.

Gauthier, James. *The Canada Social Transfer: Past, Present and Future Considerations.* Ottawa: Parliament of Canada, 2012.

Genschel, Philipp. "Globalization, Tax Competition, and the Welfare State." *Politics & Society* 30, no. 2 (2002): 245–75.

Godbout, Luc. *L'intervention gouvernementale par la politique fiscale. Le rôle des dépenses fiscales: Étude comparée, Canada, États-Unis, France.* Paris: Économica, 2006.

Good, David A. "Parliament and Public Money: Players and Police." *Canadian Parliamentary Review* 28, no. 1 (2005): 17–21.

—*The Politics of Public Management: The HRDC Audit of Grants and Contributions.* Toronto: University of Toronto Press, 2005.

—*The Politics of Public Money.* 2nd ed. Toronto: University of Toronto Press, 2014.

Graham, Andrew. *Canadian Public-Sector Financial Management.* 2nd ed. Kingston: School of Public Policy, Queen's University, 2014.

Hale, Geoffrey. *The Politics of Taxation in Canada.* Peterborough: Broadview, 2002.

Health Canada, *Canada Health Act: Annual Report 2015–2016.* Ottawa: Her Majesty the Queen in Right of Canada, 2016.

Hodge, Graeme A., and Carsten Greve. *The Challenge of Public-Private Partnerships: Learning from International Experience.* Cheltenham: Edward Elgar, 2005.

Howlett, Michael, M. Ramesh, and Anthony Perl. *Studying Public Policy, Policy Cycles and Policy Subsystems.* 3rd ed. Don Mills: Oxford University Press, 2009.

Imbeau, Louis M., and Rick Stapenhurst. *Le contrôle parlementaire des finances publiques dans les pays de la Francophonie*. Sainte-Foy: Presses de l'Université Laval, 2019.

Industry Canada. *Evaluation of the Canada Small Business Financing Program: Final*. Ottawa: Her Majesty the Queen in Right of Canada, 2014.

Jacob, Steve. "Trente ans d'évaluation de programme au Canada: L'institutionnalisation interne en quête de qualité." *Revue française d'administration publique* 119, no. 3 (2006): 515–31.

Jacques, Jason. *Federal Tax Expenditures: Use, Reporting and Review*. Ottawa: Library of Parliament, 2011.

Jarvis, Mark D. "The Adoption of the Accounting Officer System in Canada: Changing Relationships?" *Canadian Public Administration* 52, no. 4 (2009): 525–47.

Jeffrey, Brooke. "The Parliamentary Budget Officer Two Years Later: A Progress Report." *Canadian Parliamentary Review* 33, no. 4 (2010): 37–45.

Jones, Charles O. *An Introduction to the Study of Public Policy*. Monterey: Brooks/Cole, 1984.

Kelly, Joanne. "The Pursuit of an Elusive Ideal: Spending Review and Reallocation under the Chrétien Government." In *How Ottawa Spends, 2003–2004: Regime Change and Policy Shift*, edited by Bruce G. Doern, 118–33. Don Mills: Oxford University Press, 2003.

Kristensen, Jens Kromann, Walter S. Groszyk, and Bernd Bühler. "Outcome-Focused Management and Budgeting." *OECD Journal on Budgeting* 1, no, 4 (2002): 7–34.

Lee, Ian, and Philip Cross. "The Parliamentary Budget Officer: The First Five Years." In *How Ottawa Spends, 2014–2015: The Harper Government – Good to Go?*, edited by Bruce G. Doern and Christopher Stoney, 40–52. Montreal/Kingston: McGill-Queen's University Press, 2014.

Leroy, Marc. *Taxation, the State and Society: The Fiscal Sociology of Interventionist Democracy*. Brussels: Peter Lang, 2011.

Levy, Gary. "A Parliamentary Budget Officer for Canada." *Canadian Parliamentary Review* 31, no. 2 (2008): 39–44.

Lewis, J.P. "The Case for Balanced Budgets." In *Approaching Public Administration: Core Debates and Emerging Issues*, edited by Roberto P. Leone and Frank L.K. Ohemeng, 211–21. Toronto: Emond Montgomery, 2011.

—"The Relationship between Premiers and Treasurers." In *The Guardian: Perspectives on the Ministry of Finance of Ontario*, edited by Patrice Dutil, 74–106. Toronto: University of Toronto Press, 2011.

Library of Parliament, Canada. *The Parliament We Want*. Ottawa: Her Majesty the Queen in Right of Canada, 2003.

Lienert, Ian. *Role of the Legislature in Budget Processes*. No. 2010/04. Washington, DC: International Monetary Fund, 2010.

Lindert, Peter H. *Growing Public: Social Spending and Economic Growth since the Eighteenth Century*. Cambridge: Cambridge University Press, 2004.

Lindquist, Evert. "How Ottawa Reviews Spending: Moving beyond Adhocracy?" In *How Ottawa Spends, 2006/2007: In From the Cold: The Tory Rise and the Liberal Demise*, edited by Bruce G. Doern, 185–207. Montreal/Kingston: McGill-Queen's University Press, 2006.

—"How Ottawa Assesses Department/Agency Performance: Treasury Board's Management Accountability Framework." In *How Ottawa Spends, 2009–2010: Economic Upheaval and Political Dysfunction*, edited by Allan M. Maslove, 47–88. Montreal/Kingston: McGill-Queen's University Press, 2009.

Mackinnon, Janice. *Minding the Public Purse: The Fiscal Crisis, Political Trade-Offs, and Canada's Future*. Montreal/London: McGill-Queen's University Press, 2003.

Malloy, Jonathan. "An Auditor's Best Friend? Standing Committees on Public Accounts." *Canadian Public Administration* 47, no. 2 (2004): 165–83.

Martin, Issac William. *The Permanent Tax Revolt: How the Property Tax Transformed American Politics*. Stanford: Stanford University Press, 2008.

Martin, Issac William, Ajay K. Mehrotra, and Monica Prasad, eds. *The New Fiscal Sociology: Taxation in Comparative and Historical Perspective*. Cambridge: Cambridge University Press, 2009.

Martin, Valérie, and Marie-Héléne Jobin. "La gestion axée sur les résultats: Comparaison des cadres de gestion de huit juridictions." *Canadian Public Administration/Administration publique du Canada* 47, no. 3 (2004): 304–31.

Maslove, Allan M., and Kevin D. Moore. "From Red Books to Blue Books: Repairing Ottawa's Fiscal House." In *How Ottawa Spends, 1997–1998. Seeing Red: A Liberal Report Card*, edited by Gene Swimmer, 23–49. Ottawa: Carleton University Press, 1997.

McArthur, Doug. "Policy Analysis in Provincial Governments in Canada: From PPBS to Network Management." In *Policy Studies in Canada: The State of the Art*, edited by Laurent Dobuzinskis, Michael Howlett, and David Laycock, 238–64. Toronto: IPAC/University of Toronto Press, 2007.

McGee, David G. *The Budget Process: A Parliamentary Imperative*. London: Commonwealth Parliamentary Association with Pluto Press, 2007.

Merrien, François-Xavier. *L'État-providence*. Paris: Presses universitaires de France, 1997.

Miljan, Lydia, and Zachary Spicer. *De-amalgamation in Canada: Breaking Up Is Hard to Do*. Vancouver: Fraser Institute, 2015.

—*Municipal Amalgamation in Ontario*. Vancouver: Fraser Institute, 2015.

Miller, Gerald J. *Government Budgeting and Financial Management in Practice: Logics to Make Sense of Ambiguity*. Boca Raton: CRC, 2012.

Morgan, Clara. *Gender Budgets: An Overview*. Ottawa: Parliament of Canada, 2007.

Munn-Rivard, Laura. *Gender-Sensitive Parliaments: 2. The Work of Legislators*. Ottawa: Parliament of Canada, 2013.

Musgrave, Richard A. *The Theory of Public Finance: A Study in Public Economy*. New York: McGraw-Hill, 1959.

Noël, Alain. "Fédéralisme d'ouverture et pouvoir de dépenser au Canada." *Revista d'Estudis Autonòmics i Federals* 7 (2008): 10–36.

O'Brien, Audrey, and Marc Bosc. *House of Commons Procedure and Practice*. Ottawa: House of Commons, 2009. http://www.ourcommons.ca/procedure-book-livre/Document.aspx?sbdid=7C730F1D-E10B-4DFC-863A-83E7E1A694 0E&sbpidx=1&Language=E&Mode=1.

Office of the Auditor General, Canada. *2003 November Report of the Auditor General of Canada*. Ottawa: Her Majesty the Queen in Right of Canada, 2003.

—*Parliamentary Committee Review of the Estimates Documents: 2003 March Report of the Auditor General of Canada*. Ottawa: Minister of Public Works and Government Services Canada, 2003.

—*2013 Spring Reports of the Auditor General of Canada: Chapter 1 – Status Report on Evaluating the Effectiveness of Programs*. Ottawa: Her Majesty the Queen in Right of Canada, 2013.

—*2015 Spring Reports of the Auditor General of Canada: Report 3 – Tax-Based Expenditures*. Ottawa: Her Majesty the Queen in Right of Canada, 2015.

Office of the Procurement Ombudsman, Canada. *Annual Report 2016–2017*. Ottawa: Her Majesty the Queen in Right of Canada, 2017.

Organisation for Economic Co-operation and Development. "OECD Best Practices for Budget Transparency." *OECD Journal on Budgeting* 1, no. 3 (2002): 7–14.

—"The Legal Framework for Budget Systems: An International Comparison." Special issue, *OECD Journal on Budgeting* 4, no. 3 (2004): 1–479.

—*Recent Tax Policy Trends and Reforms in OECD Countries*. Paris: OECD, 2004.

—*Recent Tax Policy Trends and Reforms in OECD Countries*. Paris: OECD, 2010.

—*Government at a Glance 2013*. Paris: OECD, 2013.

Parliamentary Budget Officer, Canada. *Comparing the Federal Fiscal Sustainability Analyses of PBO and Finance Canada.* Ottawa: Library of Parliament, 2013.

—*2013–14 Report on Activities of the Parliamentary Budget Office.* Ottawa: Parliament of Canada, 2014.

—*Updated Analysis of Performance Budgeting during Recent Fiscal Consolidation.* Ottawa: Parliament of Canada, 2015.

Peters, B. Guy. "What Works? The Antiphons of Administrative Reform." In *Taking Stock: Assessing Public Sector Reforms,* edited by B. Guy Peters and Donald J. Savoie, 78–107. Montreal: McGill-Queen's University Press, 1998.

Pretorius, Carole, and Nico Pretorius. *Review of Public Financial Management Reform Literature.* London: Department for International Development, 2008.

Rathgeber, Brent. *Irresponsible Government.* Toronto: Dundurn, 2014.

Rice, James J., and Michael J. Prince. *Changing Politics of Canadian Social Policy.* Toronto: University of Toronto Press, 2013.

Richer, Karine. *The Federal Spending Power.* Ottawa: Parliament of Canada, 2007.

Rigaud, Benoît, and Paul-Émile Arsenaul. "Budget Governance in Canada: Comparing Practices within a Federation." *OECD Journal on Budgeting* 13, no. 1 (2013): 9–30.

Rouillard, Christian, and Pierre-André Hudon. "Le partenariat public-privé: Un instrument d'action publique au cœur de la reconfiguration de l'État québécois." *Économie et solidarités* 38, no. 2 (2007): 7–26.

Rouillard, Lucie. "La modernisation du processus budgétaire: Évolution ou révolution?" In *Le processus budgétaire au Québec,* edited by Guy Lachapelle, Luc Bernier, and Pierre P. Tremblay, 43–58. Sainte-Foy: Presses de l'Université du Québec, 1999.

Roy-César, Édison. *Canada's Equalization Formula.* Ottawa: Parliament of Canada, 2008.

Royal Commission on Financial Management & Accountability, Canada. *Final Report.* Chaired by Allen Thomas Lambert. Ottawa: Minister of Supply and Services Canada, 1979.

Royal Commission on Government Organization, Canada. *Report 2: Financial Management.* Chaired by J. Grant Glassco. Ottawa: Queen's Printer, 1962.

Saint-Martin, Denis. "Managerialist Advocate or 'Control Freak'? The Janus-Faced Office of the Auditor General." *Canadian Public Administration* 47, no. 2 (2004): 121–40.

Sancton, Andrew, and Robert Young, eds. *Foundations of Governance: Municipal Governments in Canada's Provinces.* Toronto: IPAC/IAPC and University of Toronto Press, 2009.

Savoie, Donald J. *Governing from the Centre: The Concentration of Power in Canadian Politics*. Toronto: University of Toronto Press, 1999.

—*Breaking the Bargain: Public Servants, Ministers, and Parliament*. Toronto: University of Toronto Press, 2003.

—*Court Government and the Collapse of Accountability in Canada and the United Kingdom*. Toronto: University of Toronto Press, 2008.

—*Power: Where Is It?* Montreal/Kingston: McGill-Queen's University Press, 2010.

Schick, Allen. "The Role of Fiscal Rules in Budgeting." *OECD Journal on Budgeting* 3, no. 3 (2003): 7–34.

Sharaput, Markus. "Harper Government Industrial Strategy and Industrial Policy in the Economic Crisis." In *How Ottawa Spends, 2010–2011: Recession, Realignment, and the New Deficit Era*, edited by Bruce G. Doern and Christopher Stoney, 109–27. Montreal/Kingston: McGill-Queen's University Press, 2010.

Share Services Canada. *Report on Plans and Priorities 2015–2016*. Ottawa: Her Majesty the Queen in Right of Canada, 2015.

Siemiatycki, Matti, and Naeem Farooqi. "Value for Money and Risk in Public-Private Partnerships." *Journal of the American Planning Association* 78, no. 3 (2012): 286–99.

Smith, Alex. *The Accountability of Accounting Officers before Parliamentary Committees*. Ottawa: Parliament of Canada, 2008.

Standing Committee on Finance, Canada. *The Canada Revenue Agency, Tax Avoidance and Tax Evasion: Recommened Actions*. Ottawa: House of Commons, 2016.

Standing Committee on Government Operations and Estimates, Canada. *Meaningful Scrutiny: Practical Improvments to the Estimates Process*. 37th Parliament, 2nd Session, chaired by Reg Alcock. Ottawa: Parliament of Canada, 2003.

—*Strengthening Parliamentary Scrutiny of Estimates and Supply*. 41st Parliament, 1st session, chaired by Pat Martin. Ottawa: Parliament of Canada, 2012.

Standing Committee on Procedure and House Affairs, Canada. *The Business of Supply: Completing the Circle of Control*. 36th Parliament, 1st Session, chaired by Peter Adams. Ottawa: Parliament of Canada, 1998.

Stapenhurst, Rick, and Imbeau Louis M., eds. *Contemporary Developments in Parliamentary Oversight in Francophone Countries*. Ottawa: Canadian Audit and Accountability Foundation, n.d.

Stapenhurst, Rick, Riccardo Pelizzo, David M. Olson, and Lisa Von Trapp, eds. *Legislative Oversight and Budgeting*. Washington, DC: World Bank, 2008.

Stuckey, Brett, and Adriane Yong. *A Primer on Federal Social Security Contributions*. Ottawa: Parliament of Canada, 2011.

Sutherland, Sharon L. *The Office of the Auditor General of Canada: Government in Exile?* Kingston: School of Public Policy Studies, 2002.

Swank, Duane, and Sven Steinmo. "The New Political Economy of Taxation in Advanced Capitalist Democracies." *American Journal of Political Science* 46, no. 3 (2002): 642–55.

Taft, Jordan. "From Change to Stability: Investigating Canada's Office of the Auditor General." *Canadian Public Administration* 59, no. 3 (2016): 467–85.

Tanzi, Vito, and Ludger Schuknecht. *Public Spending in the 20th Century: A Global Perspective.* Cambridge: Cambridge University Press, 2000.

Tellier, Geneviève. *Les dépenses des gouvernements provinciaux: L'influence des partis politiques, des élections et de l'opinion publique sur la variation des budgets publics.* Sainte-Foy: Presses de l'Université Laval, 2005.

—"La participation citoyenne au processus d'élaboration des budgets: Une analyse des mécanismes instaurés par les gouvernements fédéral et provinciaux canadiens." *Téléscope* 17, no. 1 (2011): 95–115.

—"Why Public Deficits Are Not (Always) Bad." In *Approaching Public Administration: Core Debates and Emerging Issues,* edited by Roberto P. Leone and Frank L.K. Ohemeng, 222–32. Toronto: Emond Montgomery, 2011.

—"Pre-Budget Consultations in British Columbia: The Participants' Perspective." *Canadian Parliamentary Review* 35, no. 1 (2012): 29–35.

—"L'usage des consultations prébudgétaires au Canada: Étude du cas de la Colombie-Britannique." In *Les réformes des finances publiques: Enjeux politiques et gestionnaires,* edited by Mohamed Djouldem, Geneviève Tellier, and Christian de Visscher, 83–107. Paris: Bruylant, 2014.

—"Le directeur parlementaire du budget: Le nouveau chien de garde financier du gouvernement fédéral canadien?" In *Les surveillants de l'État démocratique,* edited by Jean Crête, 19–54. Sainte-Foy: Presses de l'Université Laval, 2014.

—"Improving the Relevance of Parliamentary Institutions: An Examination of Legislative Pre-budget Consultations in British Columbia." *Journal of Legislative Studies* 21, no. 2 (2015): 192–212.

—"Balanced-Budget Legislation: The Rationale, Consequences and Lessons the Federal Government Can Draw from the Experiences of Canadian Provinces." In *How Ottawa Spends, 2015–2016: The Liberal Rise and the Tory Demise,* edited by Christopher Stoney and Bruce G. Doern, 228–59. Montreal/Kingston: McGill-Queen's University Press, 2016.

Théret, Bruno. *Protection sociale et fédéralisme: L'Europe dans le miroir de l'Amérique du Nord.* Montreal: Presses de l'Université de Montréal, 2002.

Tillotson, Shirley. *Give and Take: The Citizen-Taxpayer and the Rise of Canadian Democracy.* Vancouver: UBC Press, 2017.

Treasury Board Secretariat, Canada. *Preparing and Using Results-Based Management and Accountability Frameworks*. Ottawa: Her Majesty the Queen in Right of Canada, 2005.

—*Supporting Effective Evaluations: A Guide to Developing Performance Measurement Strategies*. Ottawa: 2010.

—*Assessing Program Resource Utilization When Evaluating Federal Programs*. Ottawa: Her Majesty the Queen in Right of Canada, 2013.

—*Guide to Integrated Risk Management: A Recommended Approach for Developing a Corporate Risk Profile*. Ottawa: Her Majesty the Queen in Right of Canada, 2016.

—*2017–18 Estimates: Parts I and II. The Government Expenditure Plan and Main Estimates*. Ottawa: Her Majesty the Queen in Right of Canada, 2017.

—*Directive on Delegation of Spending and Financial Authorities*. Ottawa: Her Majesty the Queen in Right of Canada, n.d.

—*A Manager's Guide to Operating Budgets*. Ottawa: Her Majesty the Queen in Right of Canada, n.d.

Tremblay, Pierre P., and Guy Lachapelle. *Le contribuable héros ou malfaiteur?* Sainte-Foy: Presses de l'Université Laval, 1996.

Ward, Norman. *The Public Purse: A Study in Canadian Democracy*. Toronto: University of Toronto Press, 1962.

Watts, Ronald L. *Comparing Federal Systems*. 3rd ed. Montreal/Kingston: McGill-Queen's University Press, 2008.

Wehner, Joachim. *Legislatures and the Budget Process: The Myth of Fiscal Control*. New York: Palgrave Macmillan, 2010.

White, Graham. *Cabinets and First Ministers*. Vancouver: UBC Press, 2005.

Wildavsky, Aaron B. *The Politics of the Budgetary Process*. 4th ed. Boston: Little Brown, 1984.

—"Controlling Public Expenditures: The Theory of Expenditure Limitation." *OECD Journal on Budgeting* 2, no. 4 (2003): 27–47.

Wildavsky, Aaron, and Naomi Caiden. *The New Politics of the Budgetary Process*. 5th ed. New York: Pearson Longman, 2004.

Index

Printed and bound by CPI Group (UK) Ltd, Croydon, CR0 4YY

16/04/2025

14658337-0001